COMMITMENT
DIDIER
DROGBA

Didier Drogba's profits from the sale
of *Commitment* will be donated to
the Didier Drogba Foundation.

COMMITMENT
DIDIER
DROGBA

MY AUTOBIOGRAPHY

with Debbie Beckerman

HODDER

First published in Great Britain in 2015 by Hodder & Stoughton
An Hachette UK company

First published in paperback in 2016

1

A CIP catalogue record for this title is available from the British Library

Paperback ISBN: 978 1 473 62068 1
Ebook ISBN: 978 1 473 62071 1

Typeset in Cambria by Palimpsest Book Production Ltd, Falkirk, Stirlingshire

Printed and bound by CPI Group (UK) Ltd, Croydon, CR0 4YY

Hodder & Stoughton policy is to use papers that are natural,
renewable and recyclable products and made from wood grown
in sustainable forests. The logging and manufacturing processes
are expected to conform to the environmental regulations of
the country of origin.

Hodder & Stoughton Ltd
Carmelite House
50 Victoria Embankment
London EC4Y 0DZ

www.hodder.co.uk

This book is dedicated to all the fans of the different teams I've played for, and to my parents, wife and children – without you there is no me.

CONTENTS

ACKNOWLEDGEMENTS

S PECIAL thank you to all the managers I've worked with and who made me the player I am, but above all I want to thank all the persons who had an influence on me, the ones who inspired me to become the man I am. I can't name all of them or I would have to write another book! Thank you to all my team-mates – I have worked with so many talented individuals, and consider myself lucky to be able to count so many as friends. Thanks to my parents for the education they gave me, and thanks to my uncle Michel Goba – because of you I had a dream and made it a reality. Thanks to all my coaches from my time in Levallois Perret. Thanks to Marc Westerloppe and Alain Pascalou for challenging me all these first four years in the professional team. Thanks to Guy Lacombe who strongly believed in me. Thanks to José, the special one, and to Roman – I already told you but you changed my life and my family's lives, and I will always be grateful to you. Thank you Stephane Renaud, the man with special hands. To Caroline McAteer and all the team at Sports PR Company . . . merci. Thierno, Pierre and Mathias at XL Sport and Pape Diouf, thank you for all these successful years.

Thank you to David Luxton and Debbie Beckerman and to Roddy Bloomfield and all his team at Hodder & Stoughton.

PROLOGUE

AU REVOIR

I WANTED to play my last-ever game for Chelsea at Stamford Bridge. I also wanted people to know this in advance, so I made the announcement a few hours before our final game of the season. We would be presented with the Premier League trophy, and I could bow out in the way I wanted to. That meant more to me than many people realised. Those who know me well, however, understood how important this opportunity to say goodbye was to me.

All my life, I have been taken away from places and people I love, often with little warning, often through no desire of my own. This time – finally – it would be different. I was the one who had decided to leave; I was the one who had decided to say 'au revoir' – which literally means 'see you again' in French – and the parting felt very different.

Certain preparations were made behind my back in advance of kick-off. By the time I got to the stadium for our final game that Sunday morning the manager had spoken to John Terry and they had decided to give me the captain's armband for the day, which really moved me because there was no need for them to have done that. I was also the nominated penalty-taker, should there be one, ahead of our usual choices. One final plan had been concocted between José Mourinho and Sunderland's manager, Dick Advocaat, and all the players were in on it, but I didn't find out about that until it was too late, once I could nothing about it.

The game itself was a serious affair, not a goodbye parade or an exhibition game. After half an hour, an ongoing knee problem meant I had to be substituted. As I was about to come off, I suddenly found myself surrounded by the entire team, and the next thing I knew John Obi Mikel and Branislav Ivanović were trying to hoist me up and carry me off the pitch. I was laughing because it took me so much by surprise, but I was also really uncomfortable. Although I like trying to entertain people, I'm actually very shy, and unless I'm the one who has decided to take centre-stage, I don't like all the attention being on me. My team-mates knew that, of course, and although I protested at first, I soon realised there was no point in resisting. I also think that, because they know I'm a passionate, emotional man, what they were really trying to do was make me cry. Well, I didn't! The entire stadium clapped and cheered as I went off and I waved to everyone. This was a happy moment for me, not a sad one.

We won the game comfortably and then the fun really started. Firstly, there was the trophy presentation. I never take winning trophies for granted. In fact, I never take anything for granted. The life I have had makes sure of that. You can win something today and think that the year after it's going to be yours again. The next thing you know, you've gone to another club, or the team isn't the same, and you have to wait another five years – as was the case with Chelsea – before you manage to repeat that win. So I always think it's really important to enjoy each win, each trophy, as if it is your last – because it might be just that.

I'd brought a mini camcorder to record as much of the day as I could. My memories will always be in my heart and in my head, but I wanted to do it for others – for my family, for my children – so that they could always have those memories as well. Plus, I will see a lot of happy faces when I watch the footage.

There were so many moments of joy during the celebrations. The moment when the manager took the crown from the trophy and placed it on my head, as if he was crowning me king of Stamford Bridge; the moment when I went round the pitch with the cup itself to share it with all the fans, those fans without whom this club and we the players would be nothing; the moment when I made a farewell speech to the packed stadium.

That was a great – though emotionally difficult – moment for me because I was finally able to thank publicly some of the many special people who had helped me so much over the years. Firstly, I thanked Mr Abramovich for everything he has given to this club. His generosity has paid off because we have won everything there is to win. Then I thanked José Mourinho, who is truly the Special One for me because he gave me the chance to come to the club and then to come back to it. I also thanked, among all my ex-team-mates, Frank Lampard, another very special guy, because without all his assists, there would not have been so many goals or trophies. Frank was himself having his last day as a footballer in

England, but in typical, selfless fashion, he had thoughtfully sent me and others a text message that very morning, congratulating 'his brothers' on our league title.

Back in the dressing room, it was time for more celebration, more fun, more singing and dancing – and a lot of champagne. I don't think any player escaped being sprayed by me. At one stage, the owner (whom I did avoid spraying, I must admit) realised that I was the only one who hadn't received a single drop, so he made sure someone else had a bottle and came to get me. I was the last to leave the dressing room. I wanted to enjoy every last moment there, to savour the sight and smell of it, to consign the details once and for all to my mental hard drive, so that I would never ever forget what it was like, and never ever forget what an honour it had been to be a part of its history.

Surprisingly perhaps for some, there were no tears from me. In 2012, when I left for the first time, I had been very emotional. We had just won the Champions League. I'd had a very difficult season, but as a team we had built something really strong together that had enabled us to win this amazing, longed-for trophy. At the time, I hadn't really wanted to leave, so I was very sad. Plus, I thought I would never return to Chelsea. For me, that departure was final.

This time round, my departure felt very different. I knew I was coming back. It wasn't the end of the road for me and the club. A few days before, I had been given the club's word that I could come back as soon as my playing career was over. That's what they wanted, and that's what I wanted. I now knew what was going to happen next, which was a privilege.

José came up to me in the dressing room. Almost everyone

else had left. We understand each other so well; we have a unique connection. As we're both emotional men, there was no need for many words. He just gave me a big hug, a big smile, and left me with the words: 'Go. And come back.' Simple. Very simple.

1

WHERE IS HOME?

U NTIL the age of five, I lived a carefree existence. Our house was always full of laughter, full of people and full of life. We lived in Abidjan, the largest city in Ivory Coast, located on the southeast coast of the country. We were not well off, but we were never aware, as children, that we lacked for anything. However, my father, Albert, had come from a poor background, and he had had a difficult start in life, losing his own father, the breadwinner, when he was a young boy. Through his own drive to educate himself and to succeed, my father had managed to forge a good career as a bank employee, working in the main local bank, the BICICI, in the Abidjan business centre. This enabled him to support his mother financially. By the time I was born, on 11 March 1978, he had also built our family house through sheer hard work and determination.

Ever since the death of his own father, my father had become the head of the family. As such, he was expected to look after not only his mother, wife and young family, of whom I was the eldest, but also his two younger sisters and their families. In African culture it's traditional for the head of the family to take on this responsibility, so my two aunts lived in our house, along with their own husbands and children. As a result, I grew up surrounded by cousins, aunts and uncles, which was fantastic because it meant that no one could be selfish. It's ingrained in our culture – we share everything we have, whether it's food, belongings or our home. At meal times, for example, we never sat down without first thinking, 'Who isn't here, who hasn't eaten?' and we'd call out to them to make sure they came to share the meal. I therefore grew up in an atmosphere where it was normal to take care of others, especially those who were less fortunate than we were. That approach was instilled in me by my dad from my very earliest years, and it has been a huge influence in my life.

There was a big courtyard outside the house where we ate and the children played. Other houses opened out onto it, too, so there was a real sense of community. Everyone knew and respected their neighbours. That sharing and living within a huge extended family and community are what I remember most about the first five years of my life. I also remember vividly the annual visits by my uncle, Michel Goba, who was my dad's younger brother. Michel lived in France, and was a professional footballer. The fact that he lived in France gave him a sort of god-like status in my eyes, and my family's, too. He would arrive laden with presents, items from mysterious, far-flung countries that I would dream about and, most excitingly for me, shirts from famous football teams. On one occasion, I remember being incredibly happy when a little replica Argentina football shirt emerged from his luggage. He had managed to get hold of one after the 1982 World Cup in Spain, and I treasured it so much that I still have it to this day.

Michel would talk about his life in France, and tell stories about his football career. I was entranced, and although I couldn't understand much about his daily life, I could certainly understand what he said about football. Even when I was tiny, all I ever did was play football. I did have toys, but if truth be told, I really just wanted to kick a ball about. My uncle came with his wife, Frédérique, who was from Brittany, and I loved her visits. She and Michel hadn't yet had children of their own, and she would play with me for hours. I think she liked me, and the feeling was mutual. So during one visit, when I realised they were about to leave, I started begging to go back with them. In the end, my uncle suggested to my parents that I go and live with them. 'I'll treat him like my son,' he reassured them.

At that stage, my parents had two children, me and my sister, Danièle, who was just a baby. My mother, Clotilde, was finishing her studies and planning to work in the bank, just like my dad. They understood that sending me to live in France with Michel and Frédérique would give me a better chance of doing well in life. They knew how tough life in Ivory Coast was, even for those who, like them, had an education. So, like many African parents, the chance to send their child to Europe to live with a relative in order for him to receive a good start in life was one that they gladly seized, even though for them it would obviously be really painful to see me go. But they accepted the situation– and it's important for me to explain that it's a completely common and normal one in Africa – because they knew how much I would benefit. I would get a good education and would be brought up in the loving, stable home of my uncle and aunt.

I, too, was thrilled at the idea of going, or rather I was until it dawned on me, as we were setting off to drive to the airport a few weeks later, that actually, I really was leaving my mother behind, and I had no real idea where I was going nor when I would see her and my family again. The reality suddenly hit me, and I sat anxiously in the car, wishing the moment would never come when I had to say goodbye to her. That was a hard, hard journey.

As the first-born and a son, I was really close to my mother, who is the gentlest and sweetest person. Early on, she had nicknamed me 'Tito' after the Yugoslav leader whom she much admired. She treated me, in some ways, as her little comrade–in–arms. So for her to wave me off on my journey into the unknown was incredibly hard. As for me, I only remember sobbing as I finally left my parents behind, my mother holding Danièle in her arms. I boarded the plane to France alone, clutching my favourite comforter to keep me company. The flight took about six hours and I cried for almost the entire time. Occasionally, the air hostess assigned to keep an eye on me would ask me how I was, even though it was pretty obvious. The journey felt bewildering and endless, and although I did sleep a bit, I was relieved when we finally touched down in Bordeaux and I was reunited with my uncle and aunt.

When I look back at this whole episode, and however well everything turned out for me in the end, there is no doubt in my mind that it was an experience that affected me deeply. Being uprooted – however willingly – leaves its mark on a person. When that person is a five-year-old boy, who leaves behind everything he has ever known, his mother, his father, his family, his home, this cannot but shape him.

I was uprooted, but I never forgot those roots and have long felt a burning need to reclaim them. Furthermore, like many who are forced to seek a life elsewhere and start afresh, the subconscious sense that I had lost the permanence and stability of my life back home undoubtedly affected me, however loved I was by my uncle and aunt in France. Given the direction my life took in the ten years that followed, this early experience definitely contributed to making me who I am today, someone who has always felt a need to be loved and to belong, to put down roots and to create a stable family environment.

My first home with my new 'parents' was in Brest. My aunt and uncle lived in a good part of town, but to say it felt like a culture shock after Abidjan is an understatement. Everything was much, much greyer. And quieter! Plus, I was the only black kid in the class, so I stood out from day one. At least my mother tongue was French, so I didn't have to learn a whole new language, but everything else about my life was new. I had to make new friends, eat new foods and generally adapt fast to my new surroundings.

Within a year, my uncle, who had been playing for Brest, was transferred, and we moved to Angoulême. It's a pleasant provincial town about 120 kilometres northeast of Bordeaux, and is mainly known for its annual *Festival international de la bande dessinée*, a huge festival celebrating those illustrated, comic-style books that are so popular in France. The whole experience of being uprooted, of having to make a new start, make new friends, adapt to new circumstances began all over again.

Especially in those early years, I regularly spent playtimes with my class teachers because none of the other kids wanted to play with me. I was obviously such an outsider and was so different from them that there was a subconscious, not exactly racism because I don't believe that's what it was, more a sort of naïve exclusion, born out of ignorance. My colour set me apart from them, so they just weren't interested in befriending me. Some would even rub my skin to see if I really was that colour! They didn't know any better, so I don't blame them, but this situation happened time and again, every time I changed school. Gradually, after a few weeks, things would improve, and I would make friends, but I used to dread the start of each school year, when invariably I was yet again the new kid. Each time, I would have to stand up and introduce myself and I found that excruciating. Like all kids, all I wanted was to have friends, but it took a bit of time for that to happen, until the barriers were broken down. Then, just as I started to feel settled, I'd be off again.

My biggest problem was not so much making friends – I would always manage that in the end. My biggest problem was keeping them, because with depressing predictability, no sooner had I found some than I would have to move away. The knowledge that I would have to start all over again almost every year was very difficult for me.

In addition, I soon realised that, in many of the places we moved to, we were considered a curiosity. I noticed that when I walked down the street with my uncle, the curtains would be twitching – literally – as people watched us go past. Sometimes, the shutters would even close, or people would simply stare at us in the street, and as soon as we caught their eye, they would immediately look away. We were probably the talk of the neighbourhood. Now it makes me laugh but, at the time, it wasn't easy.

Soon after my arrival, Michel and Frédérique formally applied to become my legal guardians in France but the paper-work was extraordinarily complicated and the procedure extremely lengthy. So time ran out, and I was no longer allowed to remain in the country, which meant that, after a couple of years in France, I returned to my parents in Ivory Coast; or rather, I returned on holiday in the summer of 1985, aged seven, only to learn that I was staying for good – at least for the time being. It was fantastic finally to be back living with my parents and my family, and I was incredibly happy.

The fact was, when I had been in France, there were some moments when I had been really sad and lonely. I would survive on occasional (expensive) phone calls from my parents, but it was agony to hang up, especially after speaking to my mother, whom I ached to see again. I would walk slowly back to my room, lie on my bed and just cry, because I missed her so much.

By the time I returned to Ivory Coast, my father's job had taken him to the administrative capital, Yamoussoukro, a city that is about 100 kilometres inland and north of Abidjan. Whereas the population of Abidjan is about 4.5 million, that of the capital is barely 200,000. I was not interested in that, however. I was just so happy to be back home, playing with my brother and sisters, cousins and friends. In fact, that year I spent with my family remains the happiest part of my child-hood. My main memory of that time is of playing a lot – playing in the street, playing football, not having to wear any shoes, enjoying a carefree life once again. Sometimes, I'd play in football tournaments with my cousins, and I'd get injured – not badly, but injured all the same – and my dad would get really angry with me because I hadn't bothered to wear any shoes when I played. The fact that I didn't feel the need to protect my feet summed up how relaxed life there was. We would play football for hours on end, competing for trophies made out of cut-off plastic bottles that we had filled with sweets, pretending to be our idols. Mine was Maradona.

Strangely, or maybe because by then I had learned how to adapt fast to new situations, I have no memory of having any difficulty settling back into a family life with siblings that, in effect, I did not know. I just got straight back into the swing of it. As well as Danièle, I now had Nadia, who was two years younger than her, and then Joël, who was born in October of 1985, soon after I arrived.

The only element of my new life that was less fun was that my father now paid very close attention to my school results. He was quite strict and had expectations for me, especially regarding education. Consequently, he suffered no nonsense when it came to school grades that dipped below what he thought was acceptable. So if I came anywhere lower than fifth in class, I would be punished. In contrast, my mother was the nurturing one, and she would always be there to protect us. In retrospect, I believe that I got the best education from my parents because it contained an ideal mix – unconditional love and strong structure. Although I didn't live with them for very long, it was long enough for that approach to rub off on me. Furthermore, my upbringing instilled in me two essential values – respect for others and hard work.

After a year in Ivory Coast, I was told that my uncle and aunt had sorted out the paperwork enabling me to become their legal ward, so I would be going back to live with them in France. Unsurprisingly, I did not want to go. The first time had been tough, but I had been so young that I had not fully realised what I was leaving behind. This time, I knew what the implications were and I did not know when I would next see my family. In fact, I remember thinking that I might never see them again, and as much as I loved my uncle and aunt and as much as they loved me, it would never be the same as having my immediate family and my parents around me. I could feel the difference – even though I knew the difference was in my head, not in the way they treated me. It was none-theless a very difficult time for me. On a positive note, it helped that their two young children, Marlène and Kévin, were like siblings to me, and I helped to look after them and played with them a lot.

When I returned, it was to Dunkirk, right up in northern France. It was there that, in 1987, aged nine, I was able to get my first football licence and play in my first proper team. I felt very professional and proud because we were playing in the same strip as the senior team for which my uncle played.

My uncle played up-front. He was a striker and he taught me so much when I was growing up. When I look back on my life with him, I always picture the two of us in Dunkirk, going down to the beach on Sundays. He would show me all sorts of tricks. For example, he taught me how to use my body against a defender, and how to time a jump effectively. When I saw him jumping up for a ball, I used to think that he stayed in the air for ever, as if he was flying. I just wanted to copy him in every way, and it's no coincidence, I suppose, that I ended up playing in the same position as he did and being known, among other things, for my ability to deal with defenders as well as my ability in the air! I would go to his games and watch this powerful man playing in front of a stadium full of cheering fans, and this really fuelled my passion for the game and made me yearn to follow in his footsteps. In short, my uncle was my idol, and without him I would not be where I am today.

Abbeville, a small, northern town was our next stop, in 1989. I went straight into the first year of secondary school, which was tough at first – the change to senior school is always a big leap for kids, never mind if you arrive knowing no one, having transferred from a different town, and are a different colour from everyone else in your class. Still, I did manage to settle in reasonably well.

Unfortunately, within a year, we were off again. This time to Tourcoing, the hardest of all the places I ever went to, and the one that provides me with my worst memories. Tourcoing is a small town, part of the city of Lille. Friendships were not easy to make, and I was starting adolescence, which is often a difficult time. When I played football, even within the club I trained with, I was always hearing comments about the colour of my skin, and that was really painful. Feeling like the outsider, I was too easily led, largely because I was happy to go along with others, and wanted to 'fit in', to belong to a group, not because I wanted to do anything stupid. I had a few friends, but none that I really hung out with after school, unlike others who would regularly go off and get up to no good, nicking scooters, petty thieving, smoking, all the usual sorts of things that kids did when they were growing up around there.

Fortunately, I now realise, I used to avoid a lot of that, not on purpose, but because most days my schedule would be school, home, training, home, bed. I didn't really have the time to do crazy things, which was just as well, because I could quite easily have gone off the rails, as many boys did from there. I think my parents and my uncle and aunt were aware of the dangers, and the latter two in particular tried hard to protect me, because Tourcoing is a tough, working-class town where a lot of people don't feel they have any prospects in life.

Consequently, it was quite a lonely time for me, and to a large extent I lived in my own bubble, separated from the rest of what my peers were getting up to. In the end, though, this existence served me well. I now realise that my childhood, while tough in many ways, was a great learning experience because it taught me to adapt really fast to whatever situation I found myself in. New team, new country? No problem. I have always managed. I'm not saying it has always been fun or easy, but I learned from a young age how to deal with anything life gave me and just to get on with it. The bad thing about those years of constant change is that I developed an outer shell in order to cope, and by the time I reached adolescence, I had become introverted and extremely shy. All my feelings were hidden inside and, if anyone asked me a question, I would just mumble a one-word answer. Sometimes, even now, I can still be shy, and my shyness may be misinterpreted. In truth, I'm still not good at showing or saying what I'm thinking but I'm working on it.

Tourcoing lasted one year, but the year after, in Vannes, was no better. That was because by then, I was in full adolescent mode and my schoolwork really started to suffer badly. I was starting to rebel against my uncle and aunt, to disagree with some of their boundaries and rules. Through no fault of their own, it would hurt me when I heard my cousins Marlène and Kévin calling their parents '*Maman*' and '*Papa*' and I could not do the same. I couldn't concentrate in class any more, and although I was never one to mess around in class and be disrespectful to the teacher, I went from being a studious and hard-working pupil to one who struggled and didn't actually care.

In short, my head was not in a good place. That's not entirely surprising because by now my parents and brothers and sisters had actually left Ivory Coast and settled in the outskirts of Paris, so it's not as if they were still in a different country. I was really missing my mum and my family, and I think a part of me really yearned to be reunited with them.

My father had lost his job back home, because the economy was in a really bad way, so he had had no choice but to come to France in search of work. Initially, he had left my mother and siblings behind, which must have been so tough for everyone. He had slept on friends' sofas for weeks, if not months, found himself some work, and done what so many immigrants before and since have done – put up with immense hardship, mental, financial, physical, in order to start a new life for himself and his family. And throughout that time, he had behaved with courage and dignity, which was inspiring, and has served as a real example to me of how to behave, even in the face of extreme difficulty. Eventually, the rest of the family were able to join him, while my father, who had had a good managerial career back in Ivory Coast, took on a succession of menial jobs, such as caretaker, cleaner, security guard, anything to earn some money to provide for his family. The family managed to move into their own rented accommodation, but it was the tiniest of flats – a bedsit, actually – in a suburb of northwest Paris called Levallois-Perret.

During this time, because I had by now moved six times in the eight years I had lived in France, it was decided it would be better for me if I stayed living with Michel and Frédérique in Vannes, in Brittany, at least for the time being, until my parents got themselves a bit more settled. By the end of that school year, however, my grades were so low that the school told me I would have to do the year again. This system exists in France for those whose average yearly grades fall below a certain level, and it's really tough. You find yourself surrounded by kids who are younger than you are, and your friends move on while you have to slog through everything all over again. It's usually a very demotivating and depressing experience.

As my general attitude was getting worse and worse, my uncle and aunt decided, along with my parents, that a change of scene might be good for me. Off I went again, this time to spend a year in Poitiers in the west of France. I lived with a cousin who was studying law at the university there and who lived in a bedsit in a nice part of town, near the beautiful, historic centre. The idea, I think, was that he would be a good influence on me and I would rediscover my work ethic.

I was 14 years old, and although I had to start afresh yet again in a new school and re-do my year, somehow things did get better. I got on well with my cousin, but he was also out a lot, either attending lectures, working or socialising, so I had a lot of time to myself. I focused on my studies, my results improved and life felt altogether freer. From getting bad school reports in Vannes, I was now getting reports that said '*élève motivé*' (motivated pupil) and even '*très bon élève avec de réelles capacités d'analyse*' (excellent pupil with real analytical ability)!

The only downside was that, as well as promising my parents that I would do better at school, I had also promised my father that I would not play football for the entire year. He disapproved of my ambition to be a footballer and could see that it had been a distraction for my schoolwork, so out of respect for him, other than kicking a ball around a bit on my own, I literally did not play for an entire year. I know that might sound incredible, but that was the deal, and it never occurred to me to disobey him.

At the end of that year, my cousin graduated and went back to Ivory Coast, and it was only then that I finally moved back in with my parents in Levallois, almost ten years after leaving my country. When I said that we lived in a bedsit, people might imagine that it was a tiny one-roomed apartment in a drab block of flats in a not very nice suburb. They'd be exactly right. It was on the third floor. And it was *tiny*. About ten square metres (about 100 square feet). Immediately to the left of the front door was a small cupboard along the wall. Immediately opposite the door was my parents' bed, their few possessions stored away underneath in various bags. A few steps to the right of the door was a tiny kitchen area, and opposite that was the tiny toilet and shower cubicle, barely partitioned off from the main room. A small table, used for meals and homework, was folded up at night to make a bit of floor space. The one window was next to the bed. My mum had just given birth to my youngest brother, Freddy, so the baby slept with my parents, as did the next youngest of my siblings, Yannick (whom everyone calls Junior), who was about five years old. Where did the rest of us sleep? The rest of us – Danièle, Nadia, Joël and me – would roll out a mat (not a mattress, just to be clear) in the space where the table had been, between the front door and the double bed, and we would just squeeze up together and sleep. Not surprisingly, we would sometimes fight over who was taking up the most space! In any event, that's how eight people managed to sleep in one room, night after night.

Money was incredibly tight, the flat was very cold in winter, and I have vivid memories of walking the streets with my dad at 5 a.m. to help him distribute leaflets through people's letter-boxes, or going out at a similar time to help my mum in one of her jobs, cleaning a gym. But despite the hardship – and maybe because I was back with my family, or maybe because I was feeling more settled mentally and less rebellious – I continued to manage at school. So one day, I decided to approach my father.

'I would like to take up a sport again. Do you think that would be OK?' I asked, as casually as I could.

'Yes, maybe. Which one are you thinking of?'

'Oh, well, maybe, I dunno, maybe karate, or . . .'

'Or maybe football, perhaps?'

'Oh, well, yes, actually, yes, football would be good,' I replied, trying not to look too elated at his suggestion.

'Well, OK then.'

I was so happy.

I was allowed to buy myself a precious pair of football boots, and then wasted no time in turning up to train with the local club, Levallois, a well-regarded amateur team. After the first session they told me, 'Good, well played, come back and train with us next week if you can.' I couldn't have been happier! At first, they made me train with their Under-16 third team, which was fine, but soon they moved me up to their first team. And Levallois is where I stayed for the next four years, the longest I had ever been in any one place and in any one club.

Over the years when I'd moved from town to town with my uncle, I had either joined the junior teams of the clubs he had played for, or the local regional teams. But I had never stayed long enough to become part of a footballing academy, as most of my contemporaries had done in whichever countries they grew up in. I used to think that this was a disadvantage for me because I didn't have as good a technique as players such as Thierry Henry. He is only a few months older than I am but he went through the traditional route of a footballing academy and he consequently rose up through the ranks much faster than I did. Instead, although I had always been picked out and selected for teams, I had never had coaches to work with me for any length of time. Much of what I learned, I taught myself, partly by copying what my uncle did and listening to what he told me, but above all, by working harder than everyone else to become the best I could.

When I first started, I used to play in defence, usually at right back. I didn't mind this, because I got to take free kicks and corners, and could get involved physically. But before long, I was playing in attack, just as my uncle did, because that's where he thought I naturally belonged. 'What are you doing in defence?' he would say. 'Get up-front. In football, people only ever notice the strikers.' My years of emulating him and of working hard on my own were beginning to pay off.

I was now playing at Levallois, I was 15, and I was about to enter my last three years of school. In France that means going to the Lycée, which is a lot of work, in preparation for the Baccalauréat, the equivalent of 'A' level. My school told me that it would be really difficult for me to go down this route if I wanted to focus so much on my football.

It is at this stage that kids in France have to fill in a form, to be signed by their parents, saying what sort of jobs or careers they would like to have later on, because this helps the schools to advise what studies they should pursue. I put down 'football player' and handed it to my father to sign. He took one look at what I'd written and tore up the paper, throwing it to one side.

'I'm not signing that!' he pronounced, in a way that made it very clear there was no point in arguing. 'When you find a *real* job that you want to do, then you can give the paper back to me and I'll sign it.'

The next day, I came back with another form. This time I'd written '*boulanger*' (baker) on it.

'You're not funny,' he said crossly.

Finally, I found something else less unlikely to put down – to this day, I can't remember what – and he eventually signed it. Deep inside, though, I knew I would be a footballer, irrespective of what my father said. There was no question in my mind.

To keep him happy, I had to stay on at school, so I found an accountancy qualification that I could do until I was able to leave at 18. I picked it largely because I'd done a lot of research on which courses had timetables that might be compatible with the sort of training I wanted to do at Levallois, and the accountancy one, as well as pleasing my father, was perfect in terms of schedules. So everyone was happy but I'd been clever, I thought, to have worked this out. I have never told him why I picked that course, but I guess in the end he, too, was right, because it did turn out to be a useful qualification to have.

I would go most days to Levallois to train or to play. I was only really happy when I was on the pitch, and I could have spent all day there. The problem was that, soon after joining, my whole family moved to the other side of Paris, to a suburb in the south called Antony. The flat we had this time was much bigger, although we had to redecorate it from top to bottom to make it habitable. Still, there was no question of not going, even though, inevitably, another change of school was necessary. The biggest drawback was that it was now a huge trek for me to get to and from training, so I could only go once a week, and even then, with enormous difficulty. I knew the bus and train timetables off by heart, but would always be racing to catch the train home after training, knowing that if I missed it, I would not get home until gone 2 a.m., and would have to get up the next morning at 6.30 for school.

Sometimes, if my school results were bad, I would be grounded, so I could not go to training at all. Other times, I had chores to do at home before being able to go. But I was lucky in one respect. Our junior team coach, Christian Pornin, an amazing man, stood by me and did all he could to make life a bit easier. He would sit in rush-hour traffic to come and pick me up from the station before training, and would drive me back there afterwards if it looked as though I might miss the train. He seemed to believe in me, and I owe him a great deal for the trouble he went to in order to help me.

2

CAREER BEGINNINGS

SOON moved up through the teams at Levallois until I was playing for the Under-17s A team. The coach was Srebrenko Repčić, an ex-Red Star Belgrade striker, who seemed to see something in me, and helped me a lot with my technique and my moves, especially in front of goal. His training sessions were exhausting but, as with Christian Pornin, I owe him a lot because he inspired me to work ever harder, to learn from the greats (we used to watch endless videos of them) and to aim high. He was kind to me, as well, and would sometimes give me lifts to the station to make life a bit easier after a long training session. He instilled in me the notion that you only get one chance in life, and you have to make the most of it. I am very lucky to have known him and Christian Pornin at that stage in my life, because they believed in me and encouraged me. Naturally, I showed them a lot of respect by working hard, often training alone to improve my technique. I firmly believe that when you are respectful in life, you get paid back in kind. Similarly, if you are nice to people, they are often nice to you in return. I try to live like that, even if on the pitch it doesn't always come across that way!

These two coaches in particular saw my determination, which was not always obvious in others training with me at Levallois. There is no doubt in my mind that many of them were far more talented than I was. The difference between us was that I wanted it much more. They would turn up and train, but then they'd go out with their friends or girlfriends to the cinema or to clubs, and they would stay out half the night. The same would happen on days off. Sometimes they'd even go on holiday in the middle of the season. The net result was that when they turned up for training, they weren't always as fresh as they should be. They wanted to play football, but they also wanted to have fun.

I, on the other hand, only wanted to become a professional player. So although I did go out, my priority was always football. I hated losing, and, particularly when I was young, I would often cry with rage if we lost. It all meant so much to me; football was my passion, my life.

At the end of the school day in Antony, I would run to catch the train that would take me to training or to play in a game, and I would see my school friends standing there, hanging around, munching on their Big Macs (and don't get me wrong, I used to indulge as well, especially on the way home from training, as I rushed for the train), and I could hear them laughing at me. They were saying that I was taking myself too seriously, did I really think I was going to be a professional and play for PSG or something? But I had an absolute determination to succeed, and a total belief in myself. OK, so some of the guys I trained with had more natural ability than I had, but unlike them, I was willing to sacrifice all sorts of things in order to reach my goal. Actually, I didn't consider this a sacrifice, because it was something I wanted to do.

It's easy to forget now, with the amount of money that there is in top-level football, that twenty years ago the riches were not there to be had, especially in France, even in top-division football. I was not doing any of this for the money. When I finally graduated, aged 18, to playing in Levallois' first team, for example, I was paid about £175 if we won and nothing if we lost. So I was doing all this for the sheer love of the game, for the passion I felt, because for me, I came alive when I played. I lived and breathed football; it was where I could truly express myself. In fact, I remember my dad once coming to see me play and, afterwards, back at home, he turned to me and said, 'Who are you really, Didier? Who *are* you? Because the guy I saw out there, he was happy, talking, directing people, gesticulating, enjoying himself.' It was true. I was an uncommunicative teenager, and the football pitch was the only place I could be myself, the only place where I felt truly free. In many ways, that is still the case.

After a while, I began to want to search out opportunities elsewhere, to see if I could climb to a higher level. Levallois was great, but we were part-timers, mainly amateurs, playing in the lowest league, the National 2, the fourth tier of French football. I had also, by this time, met my future wife, Lalla, and although our relationship did not seriously start until I was 19 – partly because she lived in Brittany, so it was difficult to see her – she really encouraged me in my hopes to reach the next level in football. In fact, she has always been a really big factor in my life and my career, and I would not have achieved what I have without her incredible love and support. That's why I devote a whole chapter later in the book to her and to my family. In any event, I started sending my CV off to all the Ligue 1 clubs in France, hoping that one of them could at least give me a trial. Perhaps not surprisingly, most didn't even bother replying, while all the others simply answered 'No.' Some people might have been disheartened, but I didn't give up.

One day, when I was 18, my uncle told me he'd fixed up, through connections, for Rennes to give me a trial. Rennes, in Brittany, were, and are, a top-flight club, with a fantastic youth academy that has produced some great players, so I was really excited. I didn't tell Jacques Loncar, our first-team coach, or anyone else at the club what I was doing and went off to try my luck. By the second day of the trials, they had whittled down the original twenty-three players to the last two, including me. I was within touching distance of my dream. The next day, I even got to train with the A team, which included Sylvain Wiltord, one of the products of their youth system. I was beside myself with happiness.

Sadly, that elation was not to last. Someone from Rennes obviously called Levallois that day to get some more information on me. By the time I got home that evening, my secret was out and my dream was in the bin. Loncar basically told them I wasn't going anywhere. He also made it clear to me when I saw him the following day that he wasn't best pleased with my tactics, even though I explained why I had done this, that I was ambitious, and was desperate to try to get to the next level. After all, I was approaching 19 years old, and David Trézéguet and Thierry Henry, my contemporaries in age, had long since overtaken me.

Eventually, he accepted what I was saying and promised he would find me another club to try out for. Not long after, he proved true to his word and I was sent off for a trial at Guingamp, another top-division club in Brittany. The initial training went OK, I thought, but the next day, in a practice game with the first-team squad, I fractured my fifth metatarsal and had to retire injured. I couldn't believe my bad luck, and limped home, dejected, worried that I might have blown my big opportunity. When would I get another one?

The strange thing was, I so believed in myself that, despite this second setback, I still continued to think, 'One day, I *will* be there.' I always kept that faith. I'm not sure where that persistence comes from, but thank God I did, because out of the blue, the junior coach from Paris Saint-Germain, Dominique Leclerc, called up. Could I visit them at their training centre, Camp des Loges? This was a big deal. I explained about my broken bone and that I wouldn't be able to train with them, but that didn't seem to put him off and he was clearly very keen to sign me – I assume their scouts must have been observing me for a while. I had a medical and was passed fit to play within two months, so I was told that there was nothing to stop them signing me.

So off I went to Camp des Loges, situated to the west of Paris in a smart town called Saint-Germain-en-Laye, a world away from Levallois and Antony. Camp des Loges was an eye-opener for me, in terms of its sheer size, lavish facilities and quality of pitches. This was an historic, top-level club, and I was potentially going to become a part of it. Despite being a lifelong Marseille supporter, I couldn't let loyalty to my boyhood club get in the way of this amazing opportunity.

I was shown into a meeting room, and representatives from the club came to show me the proposed contract. I was unaccompanied – neither my father nor anyone from Levallois was there to help me, and I didn't have an agent to advise me. I was a long way away from getting one of those. This was the first contract I'd ever seen in my life and, to be honest, I was amazed when some of the details were explained to me. 'This is the contract we're going to give you,' one guy said, as he flipped through the pages. I would be a *stagiaire*, an apprentice, but they were proposing to pay me 7,000 francs a month (about £700), a vast amount for me at the time; *and* they were going to give me seven – yes, seven! – pairs of Nike football boots. I saved up to buy one precious pair of boots at a time, then took care of them so that they would last as long as possible. This was a huge deal. Not only would I receive all that, he added, but, 'We're also going to give you a car, an Opel Tigra, because yours is a special contract. We only have two *stagiaires*.' Wow. This was unbelievable!

Just as I was about to put pen to paper, the guy said, 'Just to be clear, this is only a one-year contract. If you perform and play well, we keep you. If you don't, at the end of the season, we let you go. Obviously, if you get injured, there's no guarantee we would keep you, either. In fact, as you're currently injured, there are a few things we have to change on this contract, so we just have to go away for a few minutes to do that – but we'll be back in five minutes.' And with that, they left me sitting there, mulling over what the guy had just said.

Suddenly, it dawned on me that this was going to be real pressure, high-level pressure of a sort I had never known before. Coming as I did from an amateur team that trained once or twice a week, then played fourth-tier games, this was going to be a huge change. It meant that, after one year, if I didn't perform to their expectations, I'd be back to square one. Worse than that, back to zero. Back to nothing. And that unsettled me deeply.

Time ticked on. Five minutes became ten minutes, then twenty. No sign of anyone. I was getting bad feelings about the situation. What was going on? Where were they? Were they changing their minds? No one seemed to show the slightest interest in me. I felt like a nobody. This was not a great start. Suddenly, I got cold feet. Really cold feet. 'OK,' I reasoned with myself, 'I'll give them five more minutes. If they don't come back, I'll leave.' It got to thirty minutes. 'OK, five more,' I bargained with myself. Thirty-five minutes. Forty. 'OK, enough, I'm off.' And I just got up and left, confused by what had happened.

'So, did you sign?' asked my dad when I finally got home.

'No, I didn't,' I replied sullenly.

'What? Why not?!'

'I didn't sign because they made me sit in this room for hours, and no one seemed to care or be interested, so I just left.'

'What? You should have waited, not just gone!'

'No, I got a bad feeling; I just didn't feel it in my guts.'

Even though Dominique Leclerc had clearly been very keen on me, the rest of the set-up felt wrong, almost from the start. If truth be told, I had never felt comfortable there. My father couldn't believe it.

'You're always crying because you have no opportunities, then PSG comes along and you say no?' I tried to explain what I'd felt, but I could tell he just didn't understand.

Then something amazing happened. A couple of days later, a certain Marc Westerloppe from Le Mans called me. I'd never heard of him. I'd never heard of Le Mans, to be honest, apart from the *24-heures du Mans*, the famous car race. But did I know they even had a football team? Absolutely not.

'We have a player like you, with the same profile,' he began. 'But he's getting old, and we'd like to replace him. We would like you to be that person, to play in our first team. I've never seen you play, but I've heard really good feedback, so I'd like to sign you.'

'But I can't play at the moment, I'm injured,' I replied.

'That's not a problem, don't worry. Come down and see us at least.'

This was amazing! He was really encouraging, and I liked what I was hearing, so I was quickly won over.

'OK, I'm coming. I'll be on the train tomorrow.' And that was that.

I went straight down there and saw the club, the whole set-up. Marc took the trouble to show me round the town, which is a really nice place in itself, and from the start I loved everything about the club and the potential lifestyle. It was a calm place, not frenetic like in Paris. Le Mans is about an hour by train from the capital, which for me was perfect – close enough to be within easy reach if I wanted to see my friends and family, but far enough away so I wouldn't be tempted to go back too often. I knew that if I had been training for PSG, I'd have had my own flat, and the next thing would be that my friends from Antony would descend on me, we'd all hang out together, I'd end up going out, and none of that would help me in my ambition to become a footballer. Here in Le Mans, I would have far fewer distractions. Plus they were offering the same money and supply of boots as PSG – adidas this time. Although the contract was also for one year, there were none of the uncertainties of the PSG one, linked to performance. Everything just felt right.

In addition, I liked Marc Westerloppe from the start. Something between us just clicked. He spoke very calmly and quietly, so much so that I often had to get close up to him to hear what he was actually saying. But there was an authority and a wisdom about him, which was fantastic, and I soaked up everything he said.

In contrast, a couple of years later, I played against a young player who had been signed by PSG on the same terms offered to me and at the same time as I would have been there. Unfortunately for him, at the end of that first season he'd been let go because he'd been injured, so that was the end of his PSG dream. That could so easily have been me, and my life would have been so different.

It was autumn 1997, I was 19 years old, and I was starting out in the academy section of a Ligue 2 team, a long way off being picked for the first team. I knew I was old in comparison with some of my peers, and way behind in terms of footballing development, but I was thrilled. As far as I was concerned, I was taking a big step towards achieving my goal.

For the first three months, I lived in the academy's halls of residence, near the training ground. I was still finishing off my accountancy qualification, so I had to go to college every day, sometimes until four or five in the afternoon, then train after that, often in the evenings. Actually, as well as pleasing my father by completing the qualification, it was a good way for me to do something other than just play football all day long. Those first three months felt a bit like living in student halls, because apprentices from the ELF motor-racing school lived there, too, so there was a real mix of sportsmen from different backgrounds, and that was good fun.

I quickly made friends with some of the other football apprentices, including Kader Seydi, whose room was opposite mine. He could have had a good career in football, but sadly he got a really bad knee injury, which ended his hopes and showed me how cruel the sport can be. The two of us started to hang out a bit with some of the pros in the squad, and that was really exciting. It felt special, like going out with guys a few years older than you at school. They had cars and nice clothes and they showed us how to have a good time in town. All this was a totally new world for me, and I have to say I enjoyed my new-found freedom, independence, and the small amount of money I now had, and I made the most of it!

What I also discovered at Le Mans was what it took to be a footballer. I had the raw potential and the skills, of that there was little doubt in my mind. What I certainly did not have, however, was the fitness, especially after being immobilised by my foot injury for several months. My body was completely unprepared for the shock of training every day. In the past, I could happily eat junk food on the way to train or play a game, and it didn't seem to affect my performance. I soon realised that was no longer possible, not when big physical demands were being made on me on a daily basis. One day, I'd be good, and the next day I'd be completely shattered, drained, unable to do a thing right. On my first session of jogging, I had to stop while everyone else ran on past me. My pulse was off the scale, I was drenched in sweat, and my levels of fitness were the worst of the group by a long distance.

Marc Westerloppe kept faith in me, though, and continued to give me advice and encouragement. Shortly after starting, I also came across Alain Pascalou, who was the first-team's physical trainer. Our paths had already crossed, but in difficult circumstances, and he never let me forget it. A couple of years previously, he had selected me for the regional Under-17 team of the *département* I lived in (the *Hauts de Seine* area that borders Paris), but because I'd not been doing well at school at the time, my father had forbidden me point blank to play. I'd begged and cried, but to no avail, so in the end, I'd had to respect my father and his authority and I had not turned up for the game.

Pascalou, despite knowing why I had pulled out, decided this time round not to let me off the hook. He was really tough on me, always yelling at me, telling me how hard he was going to make me work, goading me. 'Hah, don't you want to become a professional footballer? Be careful, you weren't good at school, you don't want to fail here as well, do you? You're going to have to be much better, otherwise you won't make it.' Stuff like that. Constantly. This sort of verbal aggression was new for me, and I hated it. I also assumed he hated me and I couldn't understand what I'd done for him to treat me like that.

Eventually, I realised that he was hard on everyone. He used to teach sports science at university, so although we were all a bit terrified of him, we could see he knew what he was talking about when it came to fitness, nutrition, looking after ourselves and getting the most out of our bodies.

In any event, between Marc Westerloppe and Alain Pascalou, there was a sort of 'good cop, bad cop' psychology going on, which in the end worked wonders for me. In both cases, and for very different reasons, it motivated me to try my hardest for them, to show them what I was capable of. For the former, I was desperate to repay his belief in me; for the latter, I just wanted to prove to him that he was wrong, and that I could and would succeed!

Unfortunately, since I wasn't used to this new physical regime, and I was putting so much strain on my body, I was regularly picking up injuries, and not just minor niggles or muscle strains, but major injuries that would keep me out for three months, six months at a time. Having arrived at the club with a broken metatarsal in my left foot, I began training in late summer. In October, bang, the same metatarsal broke once more, in essence because it had not had time to mend properly. I started training again, only to break a metatarsal in the right foot. This time, the doctors decided to put a screw in it at once, to help the healing process. Another two months' lay-off.

My most worrying injury was a fracture to my ankle and fibula right at the end of my first year. This was doubly worrying because not only was I unsure if I would make a full recovery, but also every year, in early May, everyone at the club would receive a letter informing them whether the club was renewing their contract or not. I was still on a trainee contract, and was desperately hoping I would be kept on. We were now at the start of May, I hadn't received a thing and I was beginning to get seriously anxious. That's when I broke my ankle.

I remember vividly being in tears as they took me off the pitch, not because of the pain but because of the fear – I hadn't received that vital letter. I was too scared to ask anyone, but I seriously thought this might be the end of the road for me, even though Westerloppe, who by now was the first-team coach, had previously told me I would be kept on. Now that this had happened, though, I was far from sure that would be the case. I imagined him and the other coaches, including Pascalou, discussing me among themselves, saying, 'Ah, that guy, he's always injured, we can't keep him.' Mentally, for me, it was a really difficult and uncertain time.

My parents came down to see me and to help, because by then I was living on my own in a rented flat in town. I could see my mother was worried about me, as she bustled about, cleaning up, stocking up the fridge and putting things away. I sat there on my bed, my leg in plaster, my crutches beside me, not knowing what my future held. Was I going to be heading back to Levallois after all this? Back to Antony? I couldn't even imagine doing that. I was desperate to show my parents that I could make it, I'd been right to persevere and when I'd told them I would succeed, I was right. I wanted to prove my father wrong – I *had* managed to do something with my life, even though I'd taken a different route from the one he had wanted. I also did not want to go back to the streets of Antony because I could see what sort of life awaited me there and it would not have been good for me. I'd seen what others had become. They'd lost all hope, and I couldn't bear the thought that I might be like that one day.

The next day, I hobbled down to the letterbox of my block of flats to see if there was any post for me. One letter. Clearly from the club. I tore it open, almost too afraid to read it. They were keeping me. Contract renewed. Indescribable relief washed over me. I was safe. I just needed to get better, then it would be back to work with a vengeance.

It was the summer of 1998, I was now 20 years old, and I watched my contemporary, Thierry Henry, celebrate as France lifted the World Cup trophy at the newly built Stade de France, amid scenes of football fever never before seen in the country. Henry was now a football superstar and international adulation was guaranteed. Meanwhile, there I was, on my sofa, my leg in plaster, still eating take-away pizza. What was I thinking at that moment, given the gulf in attainment between the two of us? Not 'you bastard', as some might imagine. No, my main thought was, 'I would *love* to be there! And one day I *will* be there.' I never lost that unshakeable self-belief, that blind faith in my ability to succeed.

3

PRO AT LAST

B Y the start of my second season at Le Mans, I was able to start training again. I was determined to work on my fitness, and not to disappoint Marc Westerloppe, and my efforts began to pay off. Soon I was playing in the reserves, and scoring goals. At one point, when the club was struggling against relegation, I even made the first-team bench, which I was really happy about, because it made me feel I was becoming part of the Le Mans story, and wasn't just some lowly apprentice.

At the end of the season, in the summer of 1999, I was finally offered that longed-for first professional contract. I was 21 by then, ancient by today's standards. Marc Westerloppe, my champion, had in effect promoted me and given me this chance.

To the club's surprise, though, I had acquired an agent by this stage, and one of the biggest agents of the time, no less – Pape Diouf. My friend Kader Seydi had a brother, Thierno, who worked for Pape. Thierno had quietly been following my career from its earliest days, even as far back as Levallois, and he watched me play at Le Mans quite regularly. As Thierno didn't yet have an agent's licence, he persuaded Pape to take me on. Le Mans were amazed because, in football circles, Pape was (and still is) something of a legend, especially in France where he looked after a lot of great players, including Marcel Desailly. My friends were even more amazed – in fact, they would laugh out loud when I told them he was interested and was going to sign me, especially because at that stage, I was still out with my ankle and fibula injury. Anyway, much to their disbelief he did sign me, and he remains a very special person in my life. Thierno became my agent and still is to this day.

Very quickly, I saw the amazing benefits of having someone like Pape to advise me. He explained to me that he wouldn't be calling me that often, maybe twice a month. I soon realised that was fine because when he did, he would devote two or three hours to me. He would talk to me, he would listen carefully to what I told him, and we would have really long, detailed conversations. He had so much wisdom, so much experience of life, of football, of business, that I soaked up everything he said. For example, he would gently say to me, 'When you're young, it's easy to rebel, to think you're right, or that it's someone else's fault that something has happened to you, rather than taking responsibility for it.'

When it came to football, if I complained about something, he would just say to me, 'Look, trust me, that's how it is.' At Le Mans or my next club, Guingamp, when I got a bit fed up and impetuously told him that I wanted to leave, he would calmly reply, 'OK, so you want to go? I can go and speak to another team – is that what you want?'

'Yes,' I'd reply, convinced this was the right thing.

'Firstly, your value will decrease,' he would then explain, 'because it's *you* who wants to go there, and they won't appreciate what you're worth as much as if *they* are the ones who approach *you*. Secondly, as a result, you will sign for less than you are on here. And the problems you have here, you will find them over there; or different problems. So, what do you do now? Try to find solutions. That's what.' For me, all this was totally new and totally essential to learn.

That initial season as a professional footballer was a steep learning curve for me, but somehow I managed to hold my own. More than that, I performed well enough to start earning a bit of a reputation among my opponents, who would be keen to cut me down where possible. Ligue 2 football is really tough and physical in France, so I was the not-so-happy recipient of a lot of knocks and crunching tackles in that first year. Sure enough, just when I was starting to think that I was getting somewhere, during a pre-season 'friendly' against Le Havre, I received another career-interrupting injury – another fractured fibula – followed by the inevitable surgery and rehab.

Unfortunately, that injury coincided with a loss of form by the team, and the results at the start of the following season, 2000–01, were disappointing. Marc Westerloppe's star began to fade. Suddenly, with no forewarning, it was announced one day that he had been sacked – end of story, and with no thanks for everything he had done for the club. This was a man who had taken the club from the brink of relegation and, within a few months, turned it round, enabling it to have a fantastic season; a man who had fostered and nurtured an exceptional team atmosphere. And now, just because the start of the season had not been good, he had been sacked. This man had changed my life, we had a very special relationship, he had continued to believe in me despite all my many serious injuries. And this was how he was being thanked for all his efforts, skills and dedication. I did not feel it was right, and I hated that he had been treated like this. This was the first time I had experienced this sort of situation. I now know, of course, that it is all too common in football, but at the time I was really upset by what had been done to Marc.

Before long, his replacement, Thierry Goudet, arrived at the club. Let's just say we got off on the wrong foot. If I remember rightly, I think his opening gambit to me ran along the lines of, 'Ah, so *you're* Drogba? Hmm.' I was just coming back from injury, the manager who had done everything for me had been sacked, and this new guy turned up, with another striker, Daniel Cousin, to make up for the fact that I wasn't yet fully fit, and spoke to me like that. It wasn't a good start.

I know that he'd heard a lot of stuff about me, not all of it positive. Some of that criticism was fair enough, because I was still young and inexperienced, but I felt he should have waited before saying anything, to see for himself before judging me, and to try to build a relationship before attempting to kill it from the start. Instead, he seemed to want to show he was in charge and to put me in my place. Again, I don't deny I still wasn't as professional as I should and could have been, but rather than trying to work with me to motivate me, I think he just wanted to cut me down.

I find it difficult with this sort of person – someone who doesn't seek the best in others, and is negative. I knew he didn't like me. That much was clear. So I found it hard to work with him, to prove to him that I was worth believing in. I tried, I really did. I kept on training hard, I never gave up, but still he would pick Daniel Cousin over me. I had no problem with Daniel, who is a good friend of mine, so there was no negative feeling between us. It's just that I firmly believed I should at least have been given a chance to show what I could do on the pitch, rather than sitting there match after match on the bench.

Matters finally came to a head at the end of the season. One day, I was on the subs' bench, the next, I hadn't even made the bench. I cried and cried, tears of anger and despair at the injustice. It was the first time since I'd been at the club that someone had done this to me, and that day is in my memory for ever. My team-mates, including Daniel Cousin, tried to console me but there was nothing they could say that helped. I just could not believe Goudet had, in effect, dismissed me from any future plans he had for the team. In the space of a few months, I had gone from being one of Le Mans' up-and-coming players, one who was beginning to attract a bit of attention in footballing circles outside the club as well, to one whose career was on the brink of evaporating. I was 23 years old, and my future hung in the balance.

Timing can be crucial in all careers, and shortly after this, a chance meeting turned out to be pivotal to what happened next in mine. At the end of every season, a big dinner – called at the time '*Les Oscars du foot*' – is held in a smart hotel in Paris. On this occasion in 2001, I was one of hundreds to attend, but I bumped into a former Le Mans striker, Réginald Ray, whom I knew well. Réginald had been a talented first-team player when I'd been at the academy, and when I stayed behind after training, he and I would practise together. I had really looked up to him when I was an apprentice and had huge respect for him both as a player and as a person.

'How's it going?' he asked me that evening.

'Not so well, you know,' I began, and I explained what was happening, how the manager didn't seem to be interested in me, that I had one year left on my contract but I knew they didn't want me. It felt good to speak to someone so experienced, and who knew the set-up at Le Mans. That's when Réginald gave me the best advice ever. It's not an exaggeration to say it changed my life.

'Look,' he said, 'try to be really, really committed for six months. Change your lifestyle for six months. Don't go out, eat well, train well. When you feel pain, stop; don't try to train through the pain. If after six months, this approach doesn't work, come back to me and tell me whatever you want. But for those six months, give it *everything* you've got.'

That's exactly what I did. Not only did I change my lifestyle, but I also blanked out all negative comments from the manager. I decided I would not let them get to me. Whenever he criticised me, I'd say, 'OK, yes, no problem.' I'd try to respond positively. I committed myself utterly to a new way of living.

My pre-season training went really well. I stayed injury-free – almost a new feeling for me – and I felt fresher and fitter than I had ever felt at the start of the season. I was back on the subs' bench, but at least I was now coming on, albeit for ten, fifteen minutes. And I would score. I was contributing, making a difference to the outcome of games. Even the manager couldn't help but notice.

'You know, Didier,' he admitted to me after a few games,

'let me tell you something. You don't need to play the full ninety minutes. For you, five, ten minutes are enough.'

'Well, OK, but you know that I would *love* to play for ninety minutes,' I tried to suggest.

'Yes, but you don't need to. Some people, they play ninety minutes and they won't do anything. You can play ten minutes and make a difference.'

'Yes, but I *want* to play for ninety minutes,' I tried again to point out. We carried on having these kinds of exchanges for a few weeks.

The fact was that, whenever I did come on, be it for five, ten or twenty minutes, I would grab those opportunities and give it my all. I don't know if it was down to determination or some sort of divine good fortune, but in each of the six games when I went on as a sub, I scored – and each game happened to be on national television. The best was when I scored two goals in fifteen minutes against St Etienne, who had once been a leading club in France, even though they were languishing at the time in Ligue 2.

Not long afterwards, during the winter break in January, Guingamp, a Ligue 1 club from Brittany, called. They were selling their striker to Paris Saint-Germain, they were fighting to stay up in the top division, and they needed a similar type of striker. Would I be interested?

At the time, I was stunned. I couldn't understand why they were looking at me, a mere substitute in a Ligue 2 club, but I guess they saw potential there. I had nearly signed a new four-year contract for Le Mans about a month before, but because I was not playing as much as I wanted, luckily I had decided to wait and see if anything else came up. For me, it has always been about the football, about being given the opportunity to play.

Strangely, Le Mans suddenly seemed keen to keep me. The president of the club advised me to go home and sleep on it, after which he assured me I would realise that it would be better for me to stay. Others were sceptical that I would actually make it in a Ligue 1 club, saying it would be a step too far for me. I did not hesitate, though. The next day, I went back to see the president and told him that even if he didn't want me to go, I did. So they could either let my agent, Thierno Seydi, talk to Guingamp, or we would just wait until the end of the season when I would be a free agent. He got the message.

Unfortunately, it was easier said than done to get hold of Thierno, who was accompanying the Senegalese team in the Africa Cup of Nations and was currently holed up in a hotel in Mali. It was impossible to get through to him. For three long days, I left messages on his phone and waited. No reply. I was getting desperate. In the end, I got creative. By this stage, Lalla, my future wife, and I had been properly together since 1999. Her father lives in Mali, so I called him and asked him to find out where the Senegalese team hotel was. Before long, I was able to call the hotel, explain the situation, speak to the team coach, Bruno Metsu, and ask to speak to Thierno. I managed to get through to him and after that he arranged everything between the clubs.

We were coming to the end of the winter break and Guingamp were desperate to sign me because they had a home game four days later against Metz and they urgently needed me to play. After speaking to Thierno and getting advice on how to handle things from Pape, I rushed up to Guingamp to discuss the contract, and I was very happy because it didn't take long for terms to be agreed.

In any event, I was now free to leave Le Mans. But Goudet had one final surprise in store for me. He banned me from the locker room and therefore from saying goodbye to all my team-mates. I had made so many good friends over the four years that to be denied a chance to say goodbye and wish them luck was both petty and disappointing.

I collected all my belongings that evening – almost under cover of darkness, once everyone had gone home – and was reduced to calling them, one by one, to say goodbye and to explain why I couldn't do so in person. As someone who had had my fair share of being taken away from friends and from stability when growing up, being forced to leave in this way hurt me particularly badly. I am an emotional person, so to this day, I dislike goodbyes, especially when they are imposed on me.

I will speak later about the wonderful influence of my wife and children but I should say here that as soon as she and her little boy Kévin moved in with me in January 2000 and our son, Isaac, was born in December of that year, my life changed for the better and I became a responsible husband and father. Having her in my life, as well as two young children to care for (and our beautiful daughter Iman was born in March 2002, soon after arriving at Guingamp), was the most perfect grounding and stabilising thing that could have happened to me at that point. I was nearly 24 years of age, I was maturing fast, both as a footballer and as a man, and moving to Guingamp proved to be the perfect next step for me and my family.

4

EIGHTEEN MONTHS IN BRITTANY, 2002–2003

OUR first night in this little Brittany town was spent in the station hotel, all four of us in the same room. Ligue 1 it might be, but Guingamp were far from being a glamorous wealthy club. No matter. We were happy, we settled in very easily, we had a nice little house, our wonderful daughter, Iman, was born a couple of months later, and I began to live my dream of being a top-division footballer.

I hit it off immediately with Guy Lacombe, the coach. Once again, when someone puts their trust in me, when people back me and give me a chance, I will give everything for them. I don't want to disappoint them and I want to repay their faith in me, so I work hard to show them that they were right.

Two days after arriving, I was picked to play the following day, away to Metz, on the other side of the country. No time to ease myself in gently. The problem was, I hadn't been training very hard in the few weeks before then, partly because it was the winter break in France, and partly because I knew

I was likely to leave. In addition, I was replacing a much-loved striker, Fabrice Fiorèse, the fans' favourite, who had just gone to PSG, and I inherited his number 11 shirt, so I had a tough act to follow.

Fortunately, Lacombe and several members of the squad were really supportive and welcoming, although in the case of Lacombe, he expected me to hit the ground running. He wasn't there to look after me and teach me what to do. As far as he was concerned, he had signed me as their first-choice striker, so I needed to be fit and ready. The player who was the most helpful was Florent Malouda. I had already come across him from my time at Le Mans, when he was at Chateauroux, but now that we were team-mates, Florent very quickly became one of my closest friends. In those early days, he constantly gave me tactical advice on the pitch, telling me how to pace myself and where to position myself so that I didn't run out of steam too fast. He looked out for me both on and off the pitch, and I was really grateful for all his help.

Although his generosity was amazing, I also noticed that in general the players from the squad were much more supportive of each other than had been the case in lower divisions. In Ligue 2, I saw a lot of players who acted as if they were their team's stand-out player. Perhaps they were trying their hardest to be noticed, in the hope that they might get transferred to a bigger and better club. Whatever the reason, I was really surprised when I arrived in Ligue 1 – and I saw this subsequently in my time at Marseille and Chelsea – and discovered that the true greats are usually very down-to-earth and simple, as if they have nothing to prove.

In the Metz game, I decided to run as if my life depended

on it. Unsurprisingly, after thirty minutes, I was dead. Nonetheless at half-time, although I had nothing to show for my efforts and we were trailing 1–0, I was quite happy with my performance. Lacombe clearly didn't share my view.

'This is not enough, Didier, you need to give more. You need to run more. You need to *do* more.'

'What?' I thought, taken aback. I nodded, outwardly agreeing with him, while thinking, 'How on earth am I supposed to do that? It's impossible. I'm already running and giving as much as I can, and I'm dead!'

Something must have clicked, though, because I scored an all-important equaliser two minutes after the start of the second half, and we went on to earn a valuable 4–2 away victory. I had made a mark, and even *l'Equipe*, the national sports newspaper, wrote about a 'Drogba festival' in its match report.

I continued in my efforts to please Guy Lacombe and to be the striker he had hoped I would be. He was a great tactician, and he taught me a lot about placement, movement, pace. Our results did not always follow, so over the next few weeks, he kept on at me, telling me that I still wasn't doing enough on the pitch and was not delivering the performances he was expecting. Maybe because his criticism was constructive rather than negative, I accepted it. It made me want to learn more and to work harder.

I scored three times in the twelve matches I played in that second half of the season – not amazing, but I felt I was progressing in my football, and making my mark on the team. Sadly, not all the supporters saw it that way, and one day, out of the blue, I received a letter at home – anonymous, obviously.

All it said was, 'Go back to your country, banana eater.' I was shocked and upset as I held the piece of paper in my hand. This was the first time I had come across such overt racism, and I couldn't understand why someone would do that, or why they had singled me out, given that we had a lot of black or foreign players in the team.

After my initial reaction, I soon decided that this stupid person had actually done me a favour. The letter put me in fighting mode and made me more determined than ever to succeed. I would show them that I was proud of who I was and what I had achieved. I also reasoned that this person had probably vented his disappointment at what I had done for the club thus far, and had tried to get at me in the cheapest, most obvious and cowardly way. I was well aware that, when I'd arrived at Guingamp, there had been a portion of the fans who had said 'Didier who?' when hearing of this Ligue 2 substitute coming in for their Ligue 1 favourite, Fabrice Fiorèse. Although I didn't feel the pressure to prove I was worthy of my place, nonetheless I knew that others probably thought differently. So while this letter was depressing in content, it actually gave me a strange sort of boost.

The end of the season became very tense indeed as we struggled to avoid relegation. The thought of going back down to Ligue 2 was awful for all the team. We hated the idea of letting down the manager and, more importantly, the fans. Plus Ligue 2 is a tough league with brutal, physical, nasty tackles. When you've got a taste for something good, you don't want to have to get used to the bad stuff again. In Ligue 1, there's good football, more respect, and we couldn't bear the thought that we might lose all that. I'd only just arrived at the club and I didn't want to go straight back to Ligue 2 football. Plus the team atmosphere was fantastic, a lot of my team-mates had confidence in me, and I felt supported. So when, in our last game, we clinched a tough 1–0 victory against Troyes to stay up, we were all elated. I can't remember how or why, but during the on-pitch celebrations I somehow ended up in my underpants! That's how happy we all were – just then, we didn't have a care in the world. We were so happy we felt like we'd won the Champions League!

That elation was not to last. Soon after, Guy Lacombe announced he was leaving. He'd been appointed to Sochaux, which was a step up for him. For me, it was a huge blow. When Lacombe was interviewed on French television, he said, 'There are two players that the French Ligue has to follow because they are the future of football in this country. One is Florent Malouda. The other is Didier Drogba.' My instant reaction to that was 'Me? Is that really me he's talking up like that?' But actually he had good foresight, because both of us did move on in a short space of time.

Once again, though, I felt that I was losing the person who was my champion and I was really thrown by that, not least because, as had been the case at Le Mans, the replacement, Bertrand Marchand, seemed critical of me. I didn't think he believed in me, or at least not as much as Lacombe had. Yet again, I got the 'you're not at the right physical level' speech, although to be fair, Marchand had already spotted me in his previous job as reserve-team coach at Rennes, and had said that I was a top-level player sleep-walking through my career, or words to that effect.

Our brush with relegation had created a really strong team

spirit, though, and I was encouraged and supported by my team-mates, even my fellow strikers, to train hard during the summer break and to keep believing in myself. Although I started the first game of the new 2002–03 season on the bench, against French champions Lyon, I was brought on for the last twenty minutes, when we were trailing 1–3. My experience at Le Mans of having to shine in a short time paid off handsomely, and in the last three minutes, we scored two goals, mine being the all-important equaliser.

From that moment on, I did not look back, scoring 17 goals from 34 games that season, plus four goals from three rounds of the Coupe de France, and I finished third best goal scorer nationally – not bad for my first full season at the top of the French game and at a club that was not big or historically successful. What was surprising to me was that it had felt easier to score in this division than in the division below. This was due to various factors. The first was that it was less brutal, less punishing physically. If I called for the ball, I had a better chance of receiving it, and although the pace was faster, with more bursts of speed required, if I was fit (which I was by then), I had a better overall chance of scoring. Another factor was that, by then, I had learned to read the game better and had a greater tactical understanding. It also felt easier to score in this division because I was finally getting some proper top-level experience. Lastly, I spent a lot of time studying the game, watching videos of players such as Thierry Henry and Raúl, trying to understand how they managed to get past opponents, however closely they were being marked. This latter element was vital, because as the season progressed and my goal-scoring got noticed by opposing teams, I realised that I was being closed down much more. I could see I was being taken seriously as a player, and as a result I no longer had as much space to run into as before.

Unfortunately, my tendency to get injured was not over, and I was out for a month that autumn with a cracked bone in my foot. I made the most of my time off, however, by doing some intensive fitness training, so that by the time I made my comeback in November, I was in peak condition, and this soon paid off, because I scored six goals in eight games. More satisfyingly, by the time the winter break came round before Christmas, we were sitting joint second, just one point behind leaders Marseille, which to us was incredible. We tried not to get ahead of ourselves, but some of the team started joking about (and dreaming of) European football. The fact was, everyone in the team was appreciated and supported, and this meant we were an incredibly tight, well-functioning unit. However, by the time we started again a month later, our opponents had sat up and taken note, and our results suddenly nosedived. Before we knew it, we had lost six games in a row.

We lost the first one against Rennes. That was OK, we thought. 'It's just a defeat, no big deal.' After the third defeat, we had a team meeting, to try to turn things around. 'OK, guys, we lost three games. Next game, we *have* to win, we have to change!' Out we went for the home game against Le Havre, not the toughest, but boom, we lost again. And again, and again. Six straight losses. From joint second position, we slid and slid, seemingly unstoppably, until we found ourselves in the lower half of the division. How fast our fortunes had changed. We could feel the spectre of the previous season hanging over us, when we had so narrowly avoided relegation, and we couldn't bear to imagine that we might be going down that route again, despite all our efforts and all our team spirit.

The next game was at home against the mighty Paris Saint-Germain, whose star player was Ronaldinho, no less. Our away game, the previous October, had produced a 5–0 rout by the Parisians and, for me, watching from the stands because of my injury, it had been particularly painful, given my history with PSG.

So we went into our game against them on 22 February – a date that is forever ingrained in any Guingamp supporter's or player's brain – more in hope of a victory than in realistic expectation of one. That is where football is so fantastic. The cliché of 'it's never over until the final whistle' rings true every now and again, and this was one such occasion.

We were fired up, we were hungry. In his team talk, the captain had spoken about getting even, nullifying our 5–0 defeat, showing character. We were up for it. In the tunnel, beforehand, I'd given a television interview in which I'd said that the main aim was to get into the game really fast and score as early as possible; taking three points would do us a lot of good, but what was important was to score fast. How ironic! There was indeed an early goal – but it wasn't ours. Within twenty minutes, we were 1–0 down. Not only that, but the goal was later voted Goal of the Season in France! Ronaldinho got hold of the ball, not far from the centre line and, other than a quick one-two with Jerome Leroy, he basically weaved past half the Guingamp team before scoring. Sometimes players are sad and pissed off when goals are conceded. On this occasion, I could only admire. I obviously couldn't clap, but in all honesty, that's what I felt like doing.

I just stood there thinking, 'Wow, that was a *really* good goal. Too good.'

The half-time team talk involved reaffirming the message that we had to stay strong mentally, not give up. Ten minutes later, PSG scored again. In all this time, I'd had several opportunities and they had all either come close or been saved. We were getting close, even though shortly after their second goal, Fiorèse, the former Guingamp favourite, now with PSG, nearly put a third one past us, which might have sealed their success. But for some strange reason, we just would not give up. We were urging each other on constantly, saying, 'It's impossible, we can't give up. Maybe we're going to lose, but we have to do it with our heads held high, and still fighting.' Within minutes, we finally pulled one back, thanks to a brilliant and unlikely high header by defender Auriol Guillaume from an inch-perfect cross. Guillaume jumped so high, in fact, and with such momentum that he ended up doing a full somersault on the way down before hitting the ground with a thump.

His leap gave us all wings. A few minutes later, in the sixty-eighth minute, I was able to blast one past the keeper to equalise. The ground erupted. The Roudourou stadium is small, with a capacity of about 16,000, but it is overlooked by blocks of flats and the balconies were overflowing with people. Between those outside the stadium and those inside, all cheering us on, I'd never seen or heard anything like it.

That was not the end of it. In the ninetieth minute, and after PSG had missed an easy opportunity, I managed to control a cross from Saci to score the unhoped-for winner. My shirt came off, a celebration dance was done with team-mates, and total madness broke out around us. That victory felt so incredibly sweet and satisfying. Firstly, on a personal level, their attempt to sign me a few years before was an experience that I had not forgotten; plus, I had not scored since Christmas and was desperate to start again. Secondly, the win was important on a club level. PSG had humiliated us badly four months earlier and we wanted to show the big, high-profile club that little Guingamp were nonetheless a team to be reckoned with; also, we were sliding fast down the table and badly needed a win to prove the doubters and critics wrong.

The final game of the season, away to Lyon, is also firmly etched in my mind, but for very different reasons. We had just won 3–1 at home to Monaco, a big result coming on the back of other great wins at Marseille and Lens. We were riding high, and the Monaco win – our last home game that season – meant that we celebrated hard and long at the team hotel that night. It was a crazy night, with lots of singing, dancing, drinking, and I think we left the hotel in a slightly different state from how we had found it. We too were a bit different – I remember my wife saying to me when I got home the next afternoon, 'What happened to you?' Possibly because I looked a bit green around the gills. In any event, that game had been a midweek game, so we were off the very next day down to Lyon for a final effort.

By beating Monaco, we had, in effect, handed the title to Lyon, but they still wanted to prove they were the best. In the dressing room, not long before the game began, we looked at each other, and someone said, 'Guys, if we lose seven, eight or ten nil, it's not our fault, right? Because let's face it, the manager was there, too, celebrating with us. We were partying with him, too, weren't we? So he can hardly complain.'

'Who said that?' I responded. 'We're going to win, guys!'

The atmosphere was so positive, we were still on such a high that we actually felt unstoppable. And we thumped Lyon 4–1, to their surprise. Florent Malouda scored two goals, and I scored the other two. Fantastic! It meant that we finished the season in seventh place, only three points off a Champions League slot, which was a real achievement for us, given the mid-season defeats we'd had, and given we had so narrowly avoided relegation the season before.

That game was important because Lyon were French champions, they played in Europe and many people would be watching it. Sure enough, within a few days, both Lyon and Marseille showed interest in me. Between being on a subs' bench to having these two big clubs chasing me, barely one season had elapsed. 'Ah, so this is how it goes,' I thought. 'This is *very* interesting. Once one team wants you, others sit up and take note. Your name is in the papers every day, and suddenly everyone is fighting over you.'

How did I decide who to sign for? My gut feeling. Pure and simple. Pape Diouf thought Marseille might be difficult for me. He was honest enough to say he wasn't sure the club were right for me. He'd had a lot of players go there and it was not an easy club to settle into. Expectations were high and there was a lot of competition for places. But – and it was a big 'but' for me – it was my absolute favourite team. I'd been a huge fan all my life. I had to try to stay rational, and not let my heart rule my head.

On the other hand, Lyon were the most professional and successful club in France at the time, going places in Europe as well. Would joining them not offer me more prospects?

Their president, Jean-Michel Aulas, is a class act and a true gentleman. He's a smart guy, and when I think of him, I smile. He knew how to connect with a player and do the right thing. I remember he sent some beautiful flowers to my wife, and she was very touched by the thoughtful gesture. 'Maybe we should go to Lyon,' she said. It was a shrewd thing for Jean-Michel to have done, because it showed that the club wanted the families to feel cared for and cared about. Florent Malouda was signing for them, and in some ways that, too, was swaying me in Lyon's direction.

Unfortunately, the manager, Paul Le Guen, was not quite so enthusiastic about me. On the contrary. He made no bones about it. 'Yeah, we already have this striker, and this other one too, and maybe . . .' and so on. He was hardly convincing. For me, when you start talking in 'maybes', it means you're trying to find excuses for the future, so that you can tell that player, 'I told you I didn't really need you.' It didn't seem clear where I would fit into his team. The president of the club clearly wanted me, but the manager didn't. In the past, I'd always gone to clubs because the managers or coaches wanted me, and I'd been close to them from the start.

In contrast, Marseille's manager, Alain Perrin, called me up directly and explained how he was going to use me within his squad. 'I want you to come to Marseille, and I want you to be my main striker, alongside Mido [the Egyptian player whom they had just signed].' He gave me a very clear picture of the team and where I would fit in. That was enough for me. Plus, if I'm being honest, I also chose Marseille for my own history. I wanted to be able to look back in years to come and say that I'd played for Marseille. I made a fan's choice, which might seem incredible to others, but in France, *l'OM*, as it is often simply called, is an iconic club. I wanted to be a little part of their history. For me, it would be a privilege, and a move that I had dreamed about as a boy.

Jean-Michel Aulas tried until the last minute to sign me, even after I'd confirmed to him that I had chosen Marseille. He even sent his special adviser, ex-striker Bernard Lacombe, to Abidjan where I was due to play an Africa Cup of Nations qualifier. We had a great meeting in the lobby of the team hotel, he was really convincing, and as a final, brilliant gesture, he left a Lyon number 11 shirt in my room – with my name on it. Very clever, and much appreciated.

I'd made up my mind, though, and nothing and nobody could have dissuaded me. I was incredibly sad to leave Guingamp, where I had made so many friends so fast. I had won over the fans, and that was really important to me. But I knew I had to seize this opportunity. I was 25 and time was marching on.

5

MY MARSEILLE DREAM, 2003-2004 . . .

GUINGAMP is a quiet town in Brittany, right in the north-western part of France, with fewer than 8,000 inhabitants. Marseille is the complete opposite. A huge port on the Mediterranean, it is the second city of France with 850,000 inhabitants, and is known for being bustling, noisy and multi-cultural. The Guingamp fans come from the area around the town. Marseille has fans all over the world. At the time, Guingamp's Roudourou stadium held about 16,000 people; Marseille's Stade Vélodrome, about 60,000. Those are just a few of the many differences between the two clubs.

The transfer was completed while I was on international duty, so I joined the team at the end of their pre-season training camp, ironically in Brittany, not too far from Guingamp. Immediately, I was helped to feel at ease. I shared a room with the captain, Swiss international Fabio Celestini, and he gave me some background information about coach Alain Perrin, his methods, and what he was like as a person. He also gave me good advice, just to do my thing and be myself. That allowed me to relax a bit. I was surprised to see Marseille fans everywhere. Their support showed me that the club's popularity was on another level compared with anything I had experienced before.

Fortunately, the attention was not on me as the new signing. Mido had just been signed from Ajax for €12 million, which was a record for an Egyptian player, so all eyes were on him, not on some guy who had just come from Guingamp and whose name a lot of people still couldn't pronounce. That suited me fine. I felt no external pressure, although I did feel some self-imposed pressure. Would I be able to play in this team? I was now part of the big time, and this was a new feeling for me. I was doing my best to look as though I fitted in, but deep down I felt different from my team-mates – a bit like the swan that looks as if it is effortlessly gliding along, whereas, in fact, it's paddling madly underneath the surface. That's what I felt like at the beginning – not out of my depth, just paddling madly to keep up.

That said, I cannot fault my team-mates. They were unbelievably welcoming. I was expecting a team full of big individuals, given the players who were there, and I assumed a lot of them would have the attitude that they'd done their job and, frankly, didn't notice or even care what people thought or felt. But they couldn't have been more different. For them, team spirit was vital.

This was summed up in one of the first training sessions back in Marseille. It was August and very hot, and because I hadn't done the pre-season with them, I wasn't as fit as the other players. We went for a run and I couldn't handle it. I was wilting under the midday sun, exhausted, my heart rate and pulse off the scale, and I started lagging further and further behind the rest of the squad. One of the defenders, Johnny Ecker, noticed, but rather than keeping going and just leaving me to stumble along, he tried to encourage me. '*Allez*, Didier, *allez*.' And when it was clear that even that was not going to enable me to keep up, he made everyone pull up.

'It's OK,' he said. 'We'll wait. We'll just follow you. You lead, we'll follow.'

And that's what happened. I was now dictating the pace. I was blown away by that attitude. In any other team, especially in lower division teams, that would have been unthinkable. It's sink or swim. If you're behind, you're behind, end of story. No one waits for you.

From the start, therefore, I felt welcomed and accepted, and that was a really good feeling. I got on well with Alain Perrin. Even though he was tough, he was also a good man and a good manager. You had to listen to what he said, of course, and he would tell you what he wanted you to do, but then he would give you the responsibility of going out and doing it. You were the one who was responsible for what happened on the pitch. 'It's not for me to perform, it's for you,' he would say. I would compare his style of coaching with Guus Hiddink's, but that style was not common in France at the time, so sometimes he would have problems with a few of the players who were used to relying more on their coach to tell them exactly what they had to do on the pitch. But my view is that, once you reach a certain level, you should *know* what you have to do. The coach will give you directions, but you are the one on the pitch, and ultimately you have to take responsibility for what happens out there. You should have enough experience not to need your hand held to that extent.

Alain Perrin's approach worked well for me, and he kept his word regarding my role within the team, which was to play up-front with another striker. He gave me the opportunity to perform. I started scoring goals from the start, in a friendly pre-season game, and just went on from there.

Life constantly throws up strange coincidences. Our first league game of the season was against none other than Guingamp, my old club, at the Roudourou stadium. The ink was hardly dry on the contract and I was back there, this time trying to beat them. I didn't actually score, but seeing many of my old team-mates and all the fans was not easy, because they very generously gave me a fantastic welcome when I stepped on to the pitch. I made sure I kept my emotions to myself, at least until the end of the game; otherwise it would have been difficult to concentrate and to perform. However, I have to be honest – although I had felt sad to leave Guingamp, I was elated to be a Marseille player.

I was given my favourite number 11 shirt. In the past that shirt number had been worn by club and footballing legend Eric Cantona, so to see it now with my name on the back felt like a particularly good omen. The first time I actually ran out on to the pitch at the Stade Vélodrome, I was almost overcome by happiness and had to try hard to contain myself. I remember seeing a huge banner at one end of the stadium with a picture of me and, underneath, the words, 'Drogba, score for us'.

The combination of having the fans chanting my name at every game, playing in such a beautiful giant stadium, knowing this club had so much history and I was now going to be contributing to it, all these elements never ceased to motivate and excite me. Foreign players who sign for Marseille are obviously aware that they are joining a great club with a great back-story, but if you grow up in France, *l'OM* has a special status. In the tunnel before every game, waiting to perform in front of 60,000 fervent fans, I used to experience a sort of out-of-body sensation. It felt almost unreal for me to be wearing that pale blue shirt, about to run out into this incredible stadium. In fact, for the whole of the season that I played there, that feeling never left me. Every game felt like the first. Every game felt special.

My first goal came in an away game to Lens in August, and I scored my first home goal in the very next game, a victory against Sochaux. Before long, whenever I scored, I broke into a bit of *coupé-décalé*, a popular dance in Ivory Coast and in the Ivorian community in France, based on Ivorian pop music. Those dance movements became my trademark as the season wore on, and the fans loved it.

Shortly after the Sochaux game came another milestone in my footballing career – the Champions League group stage. We had already qualified for it in August by beating Austria Vienna in the earlier round, albeit not very impressively, but no matter, we were through. We now found ourselves in a group with Partizan Belgrade, Porto and the mighty Real Madrid, and our first game of this group phase would be at the Bernabeu stadium in September. Their team contained more or less a roll call of all the best players in the world – in fact, it was almost ridiculous – from their captain Raúl, to Zidane, Ronaldo, Figo, Casillas and finally David Beckham, who had just arrived that summer on a huge transfer from Manchester United.

It felt slightly surreal that I was going to play in one of the absolute temples of football in the most prestigious European competition. The Champions League is the one I used to watch at home with friends on a Tuesday or Wednesday evening. We'd sit down in front of the television, with our take-away pizzas, and laugh and joke about which team we thought would win. Then the European anthem would play, and . . . So I remembered this when I walked out on to *that* pitch, in *that* stadium in Madrid and lined up with all these greats to hear *that* anthem. It was an overwhelming spine-tingling feeling. 'I made it, I made it,' I thought, still not quite believing it.

Surprisingly perhaps, instead of being totally overawed, the occasion made me feel at ease and strangely calm, as if I had an inner belief in our team – and in my ability to hold my own among this group of players. Maybe, also, I just felt I could relax and enjoy the occasion, now that I had made it to the pinnacle of European football, especially as, three days before, there had been a distinct possibility that I might miss it. I had twisted my ankle in training, and even the day before, when we were training at the stadium, I was still in pain. In the end, I was lucky. I was just fit enough to play – I would never have played if not – and it was almost not a shock to me when I opened our scoring in the twenty-sixth minute. Delighted, I ran to the corner flag to celebrate. Our many fans were cheering, but among the Real fans, it was a different story. I detected the unmistakable sound of monkey noises coming from their midst. It was a small minority but, all the same, it was very clear. I was shocked. And I will never forget thinking, even in my moment of glory, 'Wow, a big team like Real Madrid. I can't believe they've got fans like that!'

In the end, the Galacticos went on to win the tie 4–2, but we came away sensing we had played well, and this gave us great confidence for our next encounter, at home against Partizan Belgrade, which we duly won 3–0. Once again, I scored our opening goal. I was really pleased with my performance and how well the team had played.

My friends had been phoning me and texting me, ever since the Madrid game. My parents and family are not the sort to get carried away with their emotions, but my friends couldn't contain their excitement. 'So, Champions League, can't believe you're playing Champions League! What's it like then?' And like them, I couldn't believe it, either! Nor could I hide the fact that I was strangely amazed myself. 'Well, actually, it was . . . *good!*' And then I'd burst out laughing. It had actually been more difficult to play in Ligue 2 with the physical attrition that goes on there. In the Champions League, it's technique that's important, and timing, attacking at the right moment, having a good footballing brain, knowing when the other team is having a slight dip and grabbing the balance of power. It was all about reading the game and by then I'd started to understand these things, so it felt natural to me, and therefore easy.

We had two consecutive ties against Porto, who went on to win the Champions League that year, and were managed by none other than Mr José Mourinho. In the first leg, at home, I scored again, even though we went on to lose both that tie, 2–3, and the return leg in Portugal, 1–0. What pleased me most about the first leg was that I heard the defenders making some comments along the lines of the only way to stop me was to kick me. I must have been doing something right if they thought I was otherwise unstoppable. That comment, for me, was the greatest compliment they could have given me!

That was also the first time I met José – he came up to me in the tunnel, at the end, and jokingly asked me in French if I had any brothers or cousins who played football like I did.

'Actually, there are lots in Africa who are better,' I joked back.

'One day, when I can afford you, I will sign you,' he said, before we went our separate ways.

I didn't think any more of it, but through his scout, a certain André Villas-Boas, he stayed in touch, and André would come to watch my games, reporting back to his boss.

One of the things that was really starting to make a difference to my game was that I was in the best physical shape ever. This wasn't due just to the work I was putting in during training. This was down to two guys, Stéphane Renaud and Pascal Kerleau, with whom I had begun to work at Guingamp and who would continue to work with me right up until now (although Pascal left a few years ago and was replaced by Mathieu Brodbeck). Originally, they had been working with my Guingamp team-mate, Florent Malouda. I'd been amazed at his powers of recovery after a tough game, especially when we sometimes had to play three days later. He always seemed to be as fresh as a daisy compared with me. I needed five days to recover from a game, which obviously wasn't good, because if I was starting to train well only on the fifth day, the manager was hardly going to want to pick me for the following game. I realised I needed to do something to change. So Florent introduced me to these guys who were helping to prepare him, not only physically, but also technically and tactically. I started to work with them, too, and have continued to do so ever since.

Stéphane is a physical trainer, a sports physiotherapist, who specialises in exercises that can prevent injury and help recovery from football-specific training. This involves a lot of stretching. When I say a lot, this doesn't mean twenty minutes, but two, three hours or even more, if necessary, repeating the same movements, stretching all my muscles, and all my body's soft tissue.

Pascal comes from a more academic, scientific background and has a vast knowledge of physiology, biomechanics and the physical techniques required to perform at the highest level. Particularly in the early days of working together, we used to spend hours watching videos of games, analysing in great detail all the movements, tackles and techniques that, perhaps because I had never come through the youth academy system, had not yet become embedded as part of my muscle memory. But I learned how to tweak small but important parts of my game, how to read the opponents' body language, not least a goalkeeper's, how to make sure you evade the opposition at just the right moment, how you stay just outside their line of vision, how your success on the pitch can be down to a few vital seconds when you outfoxed the opposition, made that crucial pass, found that split-second gap through which to run or pass. All this involved hours of analysis, hours of practice after training, and hours of physical training and stretching back home.

In addition, I would usually see an osteopath once a week to complete the work that I was doing. Some people thought this was excessive and pointless, but I was committed, and believed totally in the benefits of what they were bringing me, borne out by the fact that, since hiring them towards the end of my time at Guingamp, my fitness improved no end, my goal-scoring increased and my footballing career took off.

My 'fitness team' never interfere with anything that is being done at the club, nor with its training philosophy. They are always seeking to work *with* the trainers, and to help me to be better for the club. In the same way that basketball super-stars, such as Michael Jordan and Kobe Bryant – whom I have always admired – have their own teams of physios, my approach is now catching on with other top players in other top teams.

The reality in football is that, even in a top team, there might be three physios, but there are still twenty-two to twenty-four players in a squad. With the best will in the world, those physios can spend a maximum of ten, twenty minutes with a player before being required to help another. To a large extent, it has to be a 'one size fits all' approach. I realised that my body, which had been forever getting injured when I was younger, needed to receive some more specific, tailored help if I wanted to achieve my full potential.

So my 'fitness team' followed me to Marseille – and then to Chelsea – and the extra work soon started to pay off, which motivated me to keep going. I've always had to work really hard at my football. I'm the first to acknowledge that I'm not the most talented, but I could see that my efforts were really helping me to reach the level I wanted – and the one that was expected of me.

Unfortunately, the team's results were not equal to expec-tations. We had started well, having finished second in the league the previous season, and were actually top of the league at one stage in September, but then results gradually started to suffer. We finished third in our Champions League group and failed to get through to the knock-out phase, losing our focus on the French championship in so doing. During this time, Alain Perrin somehow lost the confidence of the team and he stopped communicating with us. Fabien Barthez was signed on loan from Manchester United after existing goal-keeper Vedran Runje had criticised the team's tactics against Madrid – I don't know if those two events were connected, but you have to wonder if they might have been. In any event, by the time the winter break came around, there were defi-nite tensions between Perrin and some players, not helped by the fact that our captain was injured. One day I remember saying to one of the assistant coaches that there was no senior player in the team to turn to for advice, no one to look up to for guidance, no leader. He turned to me and said, 'Well, you'll have to do it!' Me? Be a leader at Marseille? Come on! In the end, I felt I had no choice, and it felt quite natural for me to step in and try to unite people. So I started to organise lunches with a few players after training, or the occasional dinner, just to bring players together and to help us rediscover team spirit. It was fun, and we got to know each other and each other's families much better, and all this helped enormously during a period of instability where we lacked leadership from the coach.

When Alain Perrin was eventually sacked in early January, after one defeat too many sent us down to sixth in the league, I was genuinely sad because he is someone I had – and continue to have – a lot of respect for. Although I was not surprised at his departure – we felt it had been coming for a few weeks – I was shocked that it was done in a brutal manner. I was learning, though, that this is the norm at all levels of football. At the time, I felt that he got little thanks or recognition for everything he had done for the club. After all, he'd led them to Champions League qualification for the first time in four years, and the club had been runners-up to Lyon the preceding season. But that was clearly not enough, and our indifferent autumn, together with the atmosphere in the dressing room, evidently made it impossible for him to stay.

In his place, reserve-team coach José Anigo was appointed. Marseille born and bred, close to the fans, he lived and breathed *l'OM*, and was a much more direct, sociable, friendly type of personality. José immediately developed a bond with the players and remotivated us. I made it clear to him very fast that, even though I was sad that Perrin had left, I was totally committed to him and was very much here to do a job. In the past I had suffered when my champion had left a team and a new manager or coach had taken over who had not been keen on me or my style of play. So I was determined to show him that he could totally count on me and that I would give everything I had in order to help the team. As a result, our relationship got off to a good start. It was time for a fresh start, for me, and for the team.

6

. . . AND HOW IT ENDED

OK, so we were no longer in the Champions League, but we were now qualified for the UEFA Cup, and we wanted to show the new coach, as well as the owner of the club and the fans, that we could respond positively and perform. A new captain was appointed, Algerian Brahim Hemdani. I started to get involved in organising warm-ups during training and continued to try to bring the team together. In a way, given that I was in my first season at the club, it was odd that I had such a high-profile role within the squad. It's not as if I'd had any previous experience of top-flight clubs and so could say, 'Listen guys, at Juventus, or Barcelona, or PSG, this is how we used to do it.' Yet I was one of the guys who would speak up at meetings, whom others would turn to, and, when we weren't playing well, would ask, 'Now what do we do?' Even players who were more experienced than I was would seek out my advice and guidance. On the pitch, my influence reached the stage where one of my team-mates, Philippe Christanval, told me one day that, to be honest, I was the one holding the team together and if I played well, the team played well. No pressure!

I spent a lot of time at La Commanderie, our training ground, just chatting to everyone who worked at the club, trying to make them feel part of a bigger picture, to give them a real sense of belonging to one big family. For me, it was – and remains – important. We, the players, who are fortunate enough to play for these great clubs, have a duty and responsibility to give back some of the help and love we get from the people who work there. They are rarely thanked or noticed, but contribute hugely to a club's success.

My role within the club, as well as my efforts on the pitch where my goal count continued to rise, soon got noticed by the fans, and by the start of 2004, my popularity was such that I could no longer set foot outside without being mobbed. Any attempt to walk down to the local boulangerie to buy the morning baguette for breakfast turned into a half-hour outing. Fans would want to chat, get an autograph or take photos – pre-selfies, on bad phone cameras. All this was completely new to me. At first, it was fine, and I enjoyed all the attention, but it got to a point where one day I just thought, 'Stop. Enough. This is not me, I don't want this. I don't want to put my family through this. Why are people crying for me, screaming for me, almost crashing their car [as happened several times] when they spot me driving alongside them on the motorway?' It was getting out of hand and I didn't want that sort of life. Also, I felt like saying to them, 'I'm not the person you see. I'm a *really* simple guy. I'm just a normal person from Ivory Coast. I don't deserve your adulation.'

The club had a sports psychologist and I decided to have a chat to him. I told him what was happening, and how it was starting to affect me. He explained to me that I had to find a way to absorb that sort of attention, to accept it; also that, not only was it part of the responsibility of playing for a big team such as Marseille but it was also an inevitable by-product of being successful within that – or indeed any other – team. I couldn't live the rest of my career avoiding this, in a bubble. This was life-changing, and I had to accept it. Above all, I had to focus on playing for myself, because if I did so, the results would follow, the goals would come and fans would be happy. That was the priority – by playing for myself, and performing, I would end up pleasing others. It took me a little while to digest what he told me, but I understood what he was trying to explain, and from that point on, I began to adapt and to acknowledge that, with success comes responsibility – respon-sibility towards others and to yourself. It's not always been easy over the years, but gaining awareness of that at the time was at least the first step towards making peace with the life I now had.

I was destined to stay at Marseille for just one season, but I felt such a commitment to the club and to the fans, that, ever since, when people discover I was there for so little time, they are always shocked. 'One year? It felt to us like you were there for five years!' But that means that from day one, I had an impact. I received so much from the fans, and as a Marseille fan myself, I wanted to give them everything I could. I had scored goals at Guingamp and had a high profile, both with the fans and within the team, but Marseille was different. It allowed me to grow. Marseille is the club where I finally became a man, and a leader of others.

I was not the only leader, I must be clear. As soon as he arrived, Fabien Barthez found himself in this role as well.

Fabien had been signed in October but was not eligible to play until January. He came with a huge reputation. He had been a World Cup winner in 1998, a European Championship winner in 2000, and he had just helped Manchester United win the 2003 Premier League title. He was actually re-joining Marseille, having played for them very successfully in the 1990s, so he was already a crowd favourite. Fabien was not someone who spoke just for the sake of talking. In meetings, he would sit and listen while everyone else gave their opinion. Just like the Godfather, Fabien would wait until everyone had said their piece, then he would come in with a few choice words, and everyone would sit up and take note. Sometimes, in team meetings, I would jot down some of the things he said and did, and we would subsequently discuss issues together. He never sought to be the centre of attention, but somehow commanded it nonetheless. Fabien was a big influence on me, and I learned a lot from him and the way in which he conducted himself in the few months that we overlapped at the club.

In the last sixteen of our UEFA Cup campaign, we were drawn against Liverpool, who were managed at the time by Gérard Houllier. It's not that I needed motivating, but the thought of playing at Anfield, in front of the Kop, on the day of my 26th birthday (11 March) made the first leg extra special. And what was the best birthday present I could have wished for? To score a goal, of course, which is exactly what I did. Amazingly, this was the first goal scored at Liverpool by a French team in twenty-seven years, since St Etienne scored way back in March 1977. Bob Paisley had been the manager at the time, and the team had included legends such as Kevin

Keegan and Emlyn Hughes. So here was I scoring for a French team for the first time in a generation. After the game, which we drew 1–1, the whole dressing room echoed to the loud and raucous chants of 'Happy Birthday', a moment that Houllier and his men strangely failed to appreciate or share with me. No matter, it's a memory that I hold very dear, among the many I have of playing against Liverpool.

A 2–1 win in the return leg, to which I contributed a vital penalty, pushed us into the next round where we stormed past Inter Milan with two wins – I scored the crucial only goal in the home tie. Once again, we had managed to get past one of the great European teams, one that contained both Fabio Cannavaro and Christian Vieri.

Newcastle United now stood between us and a place in the UEFA Cup final, and we all knew that the talismanic Alan Shearer, a god up on Tyneside, would do everything he could to help his team to beat us. He was 33, but still a highly effective, powerful player. In the end, we managed to hold them to a 0–0 away draw – a personal disappointment because I'd hit the crossbar and failed to convert a couple of opportunities, but at least it meant we were still in the frame.

The home leg was looming and, despite suffering from a slight groin strain, I felt strangely calm and determined. I knew what I had to do. I put a lot of pressure on myself, but I also knew how much others were counting on me to perform and to give them the victory the club was so desperate for.

My prayers were answered and I scored two really important goals, one in each half, the sort I used to dream about when I was a kid. We had made it through to the final in front of our deliriously happy fans. All I can say is that thousands and thousands of people filled the streets of Marseille that night, car horns blared, flags were waved, and singing and dancing went on until the early hours, including a lot of demonstrations of *coupé-décalé* by the locals!

Three days after the Newcastle game, we had to play Monaco away in the league. The manager decided to rest me, because the Cup final was ten days later, but with fifteen minutes to go we were 1–0 down and he put me on all the same, hoping (in vain, as it turned out) that I could make a difference. We were defending a corner kick and I jumped, but as I did so, a defender kneed me violently, though unintentionally, in the hip. As soon as it happened, I felt the pain searing through me, and as I landed, I knew I was in trouble. I was in so much pain that I saw stars and couldn't move. My leg was temporarily paralysed.

I was whisked straight to hospital in Monaco, but nothing showed up on the scans and X-rays. Nonetheless, I couldn't walk for the next five days. I was given regular anti-inflammatory injections in the hope that the pain would subside but with the final fast approaching, it became a race against time.

As a mark of how important the final was, not just for the club, but for the city as a whole, on the morning of the team's departure for the game in Gothenburg, against Spanish champions Valencia, several of us paid a visit to the Catholic basilica of Marseille, Notre Dame de la Garde. It's one of the city's landmarks, high up on the hill and visible from all around the area. It is viewed as keeping guard over the city and its inhabitants, so I came to present one of my OM shirts as an offering, and hoped that this would maybe give us a bit of divine good fortune in our forthcoming game. This was not the first time such an event had taken place. In 1993, the team had done the same before their Champions League final against AC Milan in Munich. In any event, my shirt was readily accepted and it hangs, properly framed, next to the OM pennant, to the right of the basilica's entrance – but sufficiently high up to deter anyone from making off with it!

I started the final pretty well, despite being in pain every time I ran, and playing at about 50 per cent capacity. Before long, however, I was floored by Argentinian Roberto Ayala's stray elbow, which flew out. We were the better team at the start but Valencia fought back, and the game was evenly balanced when, on the stroke of half-time, Fabien Barthez brought down their centre forward, Mista, in the box. The referee, Pierluigi Collina, judged Fabien's foot to have been too high, and he was sent off. It didn't seem to me to be such a flagrant tackle and, given the importance of the game, and the fact that we were still not yet halfway through it, I thought Collina was wrong to send Fabien off and, in effect, kill the game. But Collina was the world's most high-profile referee at the time, and he was adamant, when I complained to him, that he had no choice but to follow the rules. In any event, Valencia scored from the penalty and, after that, it was game over. Within fifteen minutes of the start of the second half, they scored again, and although we had some good opportunities to score, and kept running and trying until we were half dead, we never managed to pull back the deficit.

Valencia, to be fair, were a good team with a very good manager, Rafa Benítez, in his last season before joining Liverpool. Although they were better than us on balance, we certainly felt we would have been capable of beating them on the day if I had been able to perform at my best and if a few things had gone our way. It was the end of our dream of winning a trophy and a huge disappointment for players and fans alike.

We still had one more game to play that season, the last one of the Ligue 1 season. We were lying in seventh place, much lower than we wanted, but the team we were due to play on that final day were desperate. They *had* to win to avoid relegation. The name of our opponents? Guingamp. It was a complete coincidence. Not only had my first game for Marseille at the start of the season been against my former team, but the last one was as well, and it would be my new team that would decide their fate. This was not a comfortable situation for me, to say the least, but I had to stay professional and play as if I didn't care who the opposition were. I didn't score, but we did beat them 2–1, condemning them to Ligue 2 football the following year. At the end of the game, I hugged my former team-mates, several of them in tears. I remembered how, only two years before, at the end of my first season with them, we'd had to fight to the death to avoid relegation, and it had come down to the last game of the season. That time, we had won. This time, it was not to be, and I really felt for them – after all, that could so easily have been me.

At the end of the season, I was voted Player of the Year in France by the French equivalent of the PFA, the UNFP. This was a huge honour, and a big surprise to me when I heard the news. Yet again, it felt like just the day before I had been on the bench at Le Mans, so to be given this award was slightly bewildering, even though it's true that I'd scored thirty-two goals that season, and was the league's third most prolific goal scorer (Auxerre's Djibril Cissé topped the table). I think, though, that the award was given to me partly because I was a new face in French football, and partly because I'd had a particularly big impact in European games, scoring six goals in the Champions League (despite Marseille featuring in the group stages only) and five in the UEFA Cup, in which I'd scored in every round except the final.

That award felt very sweet, given that, aged 26, I was hardly a youngster. But I never forgot that I was part of a team and my success had been facilitated by my team-mates. No player is ever bigger or more important than his team. What happened next showed me that, however successful, loyal and attached a player is to that team, no club is ever going to let that stand in the way of an irresistible offer.

I first heard that a club were interested in me in March or April of 2004. It was after a press conference – I can't remember on what occasion – and a French journalist came over to speak to me.

'Oh, I heard something on the grapevine. Apparently, an English team has made an offer for you,' he said.

'Really?'

'Yes, and it's for a *lot* of money! And apparently the club is ready to let you go.'

'Ah, don't worry, I'm not going. I'm not going *anywhere*,' I responded, jokily. 'You have my absolute word on that.'

I didn't take what that guy said remotely seriously. I just wandered off and thought no more about it. After events unfolded, I did think back to that brief exchange and wondered ... maybe I was already being talked about after all. José

Mourinho had not yet arrived at Chelsea, but maybe, given that I knew he was interested in me, he was already telling the club that he would like to sign me, not as a condition of him joining, but nonetheless, as a definite early wish for me to be part of his set-up as soon as he arrived. Who knows?

Right at the end of the season, I signed an extension to my contract with Marseille. As far as I'm concerned, when I do that, I'm committed to a club. In other words, I don't sign and then go elsewhere. At the start of July, I was in Cameroon for an important World Cup qualifier game, and was doing an interview with a journalist, discussing all my plans for the following season at *l'OM* – what I wanted to achieve, how I wanted to beat the great Jean-Pierre Papin's goal-scoring record of thirty league goals in a single season, how much I wanted to be their greatest-ever player, help them to win the league, and so on.

After the game, which Cameroon won 2–0, Pape Diouf came to see me in my hotel room. Pape was now *l'OM*'s general manager and so could no longer be my agent. His visit was a surprise, because he never normally came to see me play international games.

'I need to talk to you,' he announced, purposefully. I actually had no idea why he needed to see me so urgently. 'There's this team that's made an offer for you, and the club is ready to accept. It's going to mean a very good salary for you.'

'No, I don't want to go. I've just signed a new contract, and for me, when you sign, you sign. You don't mess people around.'

'Well, you have to go, because the club wants you to go.'

'What's the club?'

'Chelsea.'

'I don't want to go. I gave my word. I'm not going.'

'Yeah, but the president is ready to decide today.'

'I don't care. It's not even for the money. I don't want to go. You can tell the president that even if Chelsea double my salary compared to here, I'm not going. I don't want to go!' And with that, I left. End of discussions, as far as I was concerned.

I was really agitated, really angry. I felt cornered, trapped and betrayed. The news was a huge body blow. I just could not believe what I had been told, and was incapable of taking it all in at the time.

The next day, I flew back to Paris. As soon as I landed, I went to the nearest newspaper kiosk to buy *l'Equipe*, the daily sports newspaper. Its front-page headline was: 'Didier Drogba, he's leaving', or words to that effect. 'OK, hold on. I've obviously missed something!' I told myself.

When I spoke to Pape again, he urged me to accept, because it was too good a chance to refuse. It would make me and my family financially secure for ever. I again explained that I was not motivated by the money. For me, being part of a family, which is what the club felt like, was more important than earning vast amounts of money. In my mind, I wanted to be a one-club player, to be to Marseille what Paolo Maldini had been for AC Milan, for example. Perhaps because of my childhood, when I had been regularly uprooted and separated from my parents, what I craved above all else was a sense of stability and belonging, and in the Marseille family, I really thought I had found it. Now, yet again, it was being torn away. I called José Anigo, the coach.

'What's going on, José?'

'I'm afraid I can't say anything.'

He was obviously under instructions not to say a word, even though I was pretty sure he would be really disappointed to be losing his key striker for the upcoming season.

I couldn't even talk to my wife properly about this, because I was finding it impossible to be objective about the pros and cons of the situation. Whenever we had discussed my moves in the past, the decision had been clear-cut. Each time I had left a club – Levallois, Le Mans, Guingamp – even though I had been sad to leave, I had felt ready for the next stage. Now, just as we were finally settled – we had a lovely house over-looking the sea, the kids were happy, the weather was great – I was proposing to uproot everyone and take them into the unknown. We'd be going to another country where none of us spoke the language and where we had no idea if things would work out. My wife had always been wonderfully supportive, but I knew that she would not be keen to leave. After all, she had never even been to England, so it would be a huge step for her.

As soon as I got back to Marseille, I went straight to see club president Christophe Bouchet and insisted once again that I did not want to go anywhere.

'In two or three seasons' time, yes, fine, but I'm not ready to go right now.'

'Ah, well, yes, but you see, we're not sure that the offer will still stand in one or two years' time,' he pointed out. The penny suddenly dropped.

'Oh, so *you* think that I'm not able to reproduce what I did last season. Is that it? You're thinking that I was lucky to have that kind of season, and you want to cash in on me now? OK, well, if that's what you think, then I guess your decision is made and I *am* going.'

With that one sentence, he had given away his real reasoning. That was enough for me. He had revealed that he didn't actually have faith in me. It has always been psychologically vital for me to know that those I play for believe in me completely, so I knew in that instant that I now had no option but to leave. It wouldn't have mattered which club had come asking. Chelsea, AC Milan, Juventus, Real Madrid, it would all have been the same. The way Bouchet had put it, I felt betrayed, stabbed in the back, and I had to leave.

The deal was almost done by then, anyway, so there was very little left to arrange. The transfer fee was about €37 million, about £24 million at the time. At the time, José Mourinho was criticised for spending so much on an unknown French striker, but he just replied, 'Judge me when he leaves the club.' Some of my former clubs, including Vannes and Tourcoing where I played as a kid, and Levallois and Le Mans, received pay-outs as part of the deal. Levallois received what for them was the huge sum of €675,000 (about £450,000), which helped them, among other things, to build a much-needed new stadium.

As an aside, I was incredibly honoured that they named it after me, and in October 2010, I made an emotional return there to inaugurate it and to meet and play against some of the kids who now played there. I also met up again with one of my former coaches, Srebrenko Repčić, who had been so formative in my development, and so supportive of me at a time when life was undeniably tough. It's so important that these amateur clubs survive, because that's where you learn some important lessons in football and in life. You

As a toddler, at home in Abidjan.

At school in France, enjoying some painting.

My mother, Clotilde.

My father, Albert.

My uncle, Michel Goba, also a footballer.

I played for Levallois Sporting Club just outside Paris from 1993–1997. They later named their ground 'Stade Didier Drogba'. A huge honour.

Playing for Le Mans, not long after signing my first professional contract in 1999, aged 21.

Le Mans coach, Marc Westerloppe, who supported me so much in my early years.

With close friend, Florent Malouda, at Guingamp.

Greeting ex-Guingamp team mate and friend, Blaise Kouassi, 2nd August 2003. My first game for Marseille was against my former team!

Marseille vs Porto, Champions League, October 2003. The night I first met Jose Mourinho.

On a training run with fellow Marseille team mates, left to right: Sylvain N'Diayé, Fabien Barthez, Laurent Batlles.

6th May 2004, against Newcastle United, UEFA Cup semi-final, 2nd leg. Being congratulated by coach José Anigo after I score my second goal.

6th May 2004. The fans celebrate after I score the first of my two goals in the UEFA Cup tie against Newcastle United.

February 2005, Millennium Stadium, Cardiff. We win the Carling Cup against Liverpool, my first trophy with Chelsea, and my first ever as a professional footballer.

This photo needs no words.

July 2005, in New York during a pre-season tour to USA. L-r, William Gallas, Claude Makelele, Shaun Wright-Phillips, me, Geremi, Lassana Diarra, Carlton Cole.

October 2005, outside the Presidental Palace, Abidjan, with my mother, Clotilde, after President Laurent Gbagbo congratulated the team on qualifying for the World Cup Finals.

February 2006, Africa Cup of Nations quarter final, v Cameroon. Striking the winning goal to win 12–11 on penalties.

October 2005, meeting President Laurent Gbagbo to celebrate the Ivory Coast team's first-ever qualification for the World Cup Finals in 2006.

February 2006, Africa Cup of Nations. Fans celebrate in the streets of Abidjan after hearing we had beaten Nigeria in the semi-finals.

March 2007, dressed in traditional robes, I am honoured to accept the award for African Footballer of the Year.

June 2007, paying a visit to my beloved grandmother, Hélène, surrounded by other family members.

November 2009, with manager Carlo Ancelotti. He played a big part in me having the best season of my Chelsea career.

FA Cup final, 2007, the owner of Chelsea FC looks happy after his team win the trophy for the first time since he bought the club.

FA Cup final 2007. The first of many goals in the new Wembley Stadium.

learn to share, to be part of a team, to rely on and respect others, and those values can sometimes get lost in professional sport.

A press conference was organised soon after at the Stade Vélodrome at which I had to say my goodbyes. I was on the verge of tears for the entire time. I could hardly bear to attend my own press conference, and was still trying to make sense of what had happened in the previous twenty-four hours. I went through the motions, mumbling the usual platitudes about what a great opportunity it was for me, but my body language was completely at odds with the situation, given that I was going to a bigger team, with better prospects, and for more money. I should have been smiling; instead, I sat there, hunched forward, head down, not wanting to engage, clearly unhappy for the entire conference.

Afterwards, I went into the dressing room and shed tears of pain. I felt pushed away. 'You have to go,' the club had said, in effect. Given the choice between the money and me, they had chosen the money. That was so painful to think about and it upset me greatly. I went out onto the pitch one last time. No fans were there, chanting my name, and it was unbearably silent. I turned round and walked out of my adored club, tears still flowing. I couldn't go home in that state, so I got in my car and drove. I drove along the beautiful coastline, to the beach, and just sat there, on the sand, for what felt like ages. I was trying to understand what had happened to me. It had all happened so fast. The press conference had been arranged even though all the details on the contract hadn't yet been fully ironed out and I hadn't yet officially signed it. But it was considered a done deal, thus the apparent need to announce my departure. Football was a business, I realised, and there was no point in fighting it. I just had to accept the inevitable.

I got back in the car. By the time I got home, it was evening. My agent, Thierno Seydi, had arrived and was staying over because we were supposed to be flying to England very early the next morning so that I could sign the contract. I couldn't bear to pack – my wife had to do it for me. In the middle of the night, unable to sleep, I suddenly went downstairs to see him. 'I'm not going, it's no good. Speak to my wife, I'm not going!' I knew deep down it was too late to back out, but I hated the feeling that I had lost control of my destiny. That was the cause of the outburst, plus a little part of me was clinging to the thought that I was now a free agent. I didn't belong to Marseille any more but I didn't belong to Chelsea, either. Maybe I could just sign for somewhere else? The truth of it was that Chelsea didn't mean a whole lot to me at that stage. Of course, I knew it was a big club, José Mourinho had just been appointed, which caused great excitement, and it clearly had big ambitions. But for anyone living or playing in France, the English team to watch was Arsenal, full of French or Francophone players, and managed by Arsène Wenger. The twenty-first Ligue 1 team, it was sometimes called, the one that had just secured the 2003–04 season in incredible fashion by remaining unbeaten throughout. Although Chelsea had been Premier League runners-up, they still didn't mean anything much to the majority of footballers playing in France.

My last-minute tantrum was short-lived. I duly got on a very early flight and arrived at Farnborough airport on a private jet, laid on by Chelsea's owner, Roman Abramovich. He was there to welcome me, along with José Mourinho, who immediately put me at ease by speaking to me in French, one of the many languages he speaks.

'How are you, my friend? You're a good player. But if you want to become a great player, you have to play for me. Marseille is a good club, but for you to become a better player, you have to play for a great club, like Chelsea, and you have to play for me!'

He was clearly saying that he thought I had potential and wanted me at the club. I felt I could trust him, so my instant reaction was, 'OK, I think I've found someone who understands me.' His belief in me was all I wanted to hear. I was ready to sign.

7

BECOMING A BLUE,
2004-2005

THE meeting was brief in the end, and other than shaking hands with Mr Abramovich and José Mourinho and sorting out a few details of the deal, nobody lingered. It was a strange way to discuss the signing, but I was too wrapped up in my own emotions to analyse the situation much at the time. Pape had also flown over but was acting as Marseille's representative. It was strange to see him on the other side of the table.

However, that first day at Farnborough, although I did not spend much time with José, the few words he had spoken to me when I arrived had made me understand the man he was. So as I left, I hugged him and thanked him in a way which, he said afterwards, made him realise that our bond was different. It wasn't the normal bond there is between a manager and a player. That was because, as José said, I knew that by going to Chelsea he was changing my life forever. I also felt that we were both going on this Chelsea adventure together, we were starting at the club at the same time, and that created a link that has stayed with us to this day.

The actual signing took place a couple of weeks later in London. This time, I was staying. I chose the number 15 shirt (the day of my son Isaac's birthday). Damien Duff still had the number 11. A quick photo call was arranged, handshakes, and that was it. Thierno and Pape said goodbye and good luck, and left for Marseille. I felt like a kid again, saying goodbye to my parents, all those years before. I took my bags up to my room in the Chelsea Village hotel, right next to the stadium. It was a great room, with a view of the ground, but it was a really lonely first night. My family were still in France because there was a lot to organise before leaving for England.

By the time I signed, it was the end of July, and I was immediately required to go on a pre-season tour to the USA with the squad, leaving the very next day. My introduction to the squad literally took place on the coach that was taking us to the training ground, which at the time was out near Heathrow airport, in Harlington. The summer had been a busy transfer time for the club. Arjen Robben had arrived from PSV Eindhoven, Petr Čech from Rennes, and Ricardo Carvalho arrived from José's old club, Porto, a week after I did.

My initial problem was that I didn't speak English. My command of the language extended to the pointless sentences that all French kids learn at school, the best known of which is the extremely useless exchange, 'Where is Brian?' 'Brian is in the keetchen.' Surprisingly perhaps, that phrase rarely came in handy in my first few weeks at the club.

I clambered on to the bus, and just like the first day at a new school (of which I had some experience), I kept walking, shaking a few hands as I went. Actually, there were a few familiar faces – Frenchmen Claude Makélélé and William Gallas, Cameroonian Geremi, and Petr Čech, whom I'd played against at Rennes. Even though I didn't know them personally, I felt comfortable with them because they all spoke French, so I went and sat with them and spent much of the journey to the US in their company.

The day after we arrived, there was a training session, my first with the squad. As usual, I looked around, didn't say anything, tried to work out what was going on, what the team dynamics were, who the various people were. I noticed a tall strong guy who looked so young, and who walked and carried himself in such a way that I assumed he was from the reserves. 'That's interesting,' I thought. 'They've obviously brought him over to get a bit of senior squad experience.' Towards the end of the session, I asked another player who the young guy was. 'It's the captain!' he replied, laughing. 'John Terry.' That's how little I knew about the team – I hadn't even recognised their new young captain!

That first training session was an eye-opener in so many ways. I remember turning up to board the bus holding my trainers, which I assumed I would shortly be wearing.

'Where are you going with those?' the manager asked.

'We're not going to run?' I was surprised.

'Bring your football boots,' he answered, 'because you're playing football. Everything I do is adapted for the game, and is related to the game – and the game does not involve wearing trainers!'

This was new for me. In France, it was the norm for pre-season training to involve 5- to 10-kilometre runs, often through the woods, supposedly to improve our stamina. Only after that would we start to touch the ball a little bit. I had always hated those runs and often used to struggle with distance-running training. José, instead, trained in a completely different way – as he had in Portugal – so his methods were new for the whole squad. We did a lot of work specific to the game itself – passing, tackling, running, braking, accelerating, changing direction. Whereas in France, it was more, 'OK, you need to be physically fit in order to play,' here the emphasis was on being *football* fit. No need to run around for miles. Actually, to some, it may seem that the stamina-runs approach is more tiring and better for you. In reality, it's just more boring and, I believe, less effective. You work much harder with José's approach than if you're jogging round for an hour or more. There's nowhere to hide – you have to keep chasing the ball, breaking into short, explosive runs, changing direction constantly. Aerobically and anaerobically, it's much harder, but also much more fun.

The first three or four sessions were difficult, and quite a few of us had a lot of adapting to do, but they were stimulating, new, and I really enjoyed them. The manager himself was different from any other I'd known. When we were not training, he would laugh, joke, talk to us. But once training got under way, he became deadly serious. Make no mistake, he was here to win trophies, so there was no room for messing around when we trained.

When I signed, José Mourinho had promised me that, after the tour, I would be given a short time off, so as soon as we all got back from America, I went on holiday with my family for a week. In theory, it should have been idyllic, but in reality it was the worst holiday ever because I was very tense, and could only think about the forthcoming season. So my mind was in the opposite of relaxed mode.

When I re-joined the squad after my family holiday, I was surprised to discover that the training facilities at Harlington were not those I had expected of a Premier League club with big ambitions. That was all about to change, because Roman Abramovich, who was in his second season of ownership, had already made it a priority to invest in new facilities, so we moved to the Cobham training ground the following year. In the meantime, the existing facilities, which Chelsea had been using since the 1970s, were so old and in need of repair that sometimes we would finish training, only to discover that there was no hot water. Even Guingamp had been better than that.

Similarly, when it came to helping me to settle in and find somewhere to live, Chelsea were not the impressive organisation they are now. Gary Staker, the player liaison manager, did all he could to help, but to be honest, he had too much to do to help me find possible houses or show me round south-west London. So I either relied on other players to advise me, or did it myself. This was not easy, given my playing commitments and my poor command of English, and often after a hard morning's training, I was too tired and couldn't face the thought of visiting a load of houses, especially as I didn't even know where I wanted to live. Should I live near the training ground, in Chelsea Harbour, or near the future training ground, knowing we were moving there relatively soon? I remember being introduced to one property agent by the club, and it soon became clear that he thought the £24 million transfer fee had gone directly into my own pocket. All the houses he showed me were way out of my price-bracket, with prices ranging between £8–10 million. I tried to explain that I had bought my house in Marseille just the season before for about £500,000, but he just looked at me, confused. Maybe he thought I'd got muddled up with the exchange rate, or that the figure had got lost in translation, and what I really meant was £5 million.

Initially, I stayed in Chelsea Village, because the hotel was literally next to the stadium. I could look out of the window and see fans below, and on match days, I'd get woken up at eight o'clock in the morning because they would already be arriving and I could hear them chanting. During the first few weeks, my wife and kids came over regularly to visit, but it was not easy for them, even though we were living in a hotel suite. It's not home, and when you have three children – Isaac and Iman were three and two years old respectively, and Kévin was nearly a teenager – that sort of arrangement doesn't work for very long. Eventually, after much searching, we did find a lovely house about ten minutes from the Cobham training ground and fifteen from a good school for Kévin, so it was in a perfect location and we stayed there very happily until we moved to our current house a few years ago. But those early weeks were definitely hard for all of us.

The start of this first season was a mixed affair, both for me and for the team. I was really pleased to score my first Chelsea goal in my third game, against Crystal Palace, but I was also reintroduced to the physical nature of Premier League football and received what I call a 'nasty' tackle. Everywhere else in Europe, when that sort of foul happens, you go down and the referee gives a yellow card. In England, when you get fouled, you have to stand up and shake the guy's hand! It makes me laugh now, but at the time, it was a big culture shock and let's just say that I took a long time to get used to it.

I then had to wait another month before scoring again, this time away to Middlesbrough. Chelsea were struggling to keep up with title holders Arsenal, who got off to a great start and were top of the table. Physically, I was being hampered by various problems, and I ended up missing several weeks during the course of that first season after surgery for a groin injury. This didn't help me to feel established within the squad. It didn't help, either, that I was still pining for my beloved Marseille. I believe you have to be mentally 100 per cent committed to play at your best and, certainly at the start of that season, I don't think I was fully committed, if I'm honest. How could I have been, given the circumstances of the transfer?

Chelsea's fortunes did start to improve as the autumn progressed, and by early November, we were finally top of the Premiership, a position that we were not to relinquish for the rest of the season, while title favourites Arsenal suffered a terrible run of form.

One of the undoubted low points of the season, both for the team and for me, came in our Champions League quarter-final against Barcelona at the Nou Camp at the end of February. We were leading 1–0, looking good. Early in the second half, after what I still maintain was an innocuous challenge on their goalkeeper, the Swedish referee made what I think was the wrong call, and showed me a red card. As ever, in these situations, that gave them a huge advantage and they went on to win the tie 2–1, which most people thought they had been lucky to do.

Afterwards, the common view, even among non-Chelsea fans, was that I should not have been sent off, but the damage was done. Anger among our supporters towards the referee went stratospheric and reached a point where he received actual death threats, leaving him unable to referee the return leg (which we went on to win 5–4 on aggregate).

I was determined to make up for my sending-off when we played the Carling Cup final against Liverpool at the end of February, a mere four days after the events in Barcelona. As it was, I was grateful that the manager selected me, because this showed he had faith in me, despite what had happened in Spain. This final was a chance to repay his belief in me, and to show the Chelsea supporters what I could do on a big occasion. It was also my first opportunity to win a trophy of any sort. The fact was, I had never been in a team that had won anything at all in my entire footballing career, neither at amateur nor professional level. So this game was a big deal for me, and I felt under a lot of pressure to perform.

The team as a whole also felt a lot of pressure. As the manager had pointed out to us at the start of the season, you could count on the fingers of one hand the players in the team who had actually won an important trophy, particularly a league title. So to show other teams that we were a force to be reckoned with under his guidance, it was essential that we started off by winning this trophy.

Liverpool no doubt felt pressure as well. They too had a new manager, Rafa Benítez, so one team was managed by the most recent UEFA Cup-winning manager, and the other by the latest Champions League-winning manager. That big coincidence undoubtedly added to the rivalry that day between the two men and their teams, rivalries that continue to this day.

The final, played at Cardiff's Millennium stadium, started off disastrously for us when John Arne Riise scored for Liverpool after just forty-five seconds, which was a record for a final in the history of that competition. It wasn't the sort of record we were keen on. We hadn't even had time to settle down and organise ourselves, yet suddenly we were playing catch-up, chasing in order to stay in the game. We kept going, though, kept fighting. We were ahead on possession, but still not getting that vital equaliser.

The last ten minutes of the game were approaching when we were awarded a free kick. Paolo Ferreira took it. The next thing I knew, Steven Gerrard had sent it into his own net with a back header. Terrible for them – total relief for us! That goal was probably worth two because suddenly it gave us renewed hope, freed us up and allowed us to start to dictate the game more. In extra time, we continued to be the better team, although no one broke the deadlock in the first half. Then, just after the re-start, I scored, turning the ball in from close range. This was the first of nine goals I would go on to score in major finals with Chelsea and it was a moment of sheer joy, a chance to atone for Barcelona and to show everyone that I could be counted on for the big occasions. Five minutes later, we sealed our victory when Mateja Kežman scored, and although a minute after that Liverpool pulled one back, it was too late, and we could not be caught. Final score: 3–2.

For all sorts of reasons, that victory was very special to us all. We had just lost two big games in a row – the one in Barcelona, and before that the FA Cup fifth round against Newcastle – so although we were top of the league, suddenly we had felt destabilised. Winning this trophy was a way of putting things right, of reasserting ourselves, and a way of announcing to the world that we were now a force to be reckoned with. It also indicated a real shift in the balance of power between us and Arsenal, up until then our more successful London rivals. From the moment we overtook them in November to reach the top of the league, the balance of power shifted in our favour, where it has stayed ever since, but winning that trophy was definitely a very symbolic way of conveying that message loud and clear.

From that moment on, we became really strong. Of course we were disappointed that Liverpool got their own back for the Carling Cup defeat by beating us in the Champions League semi-final (before going on to win the trophy in Turkey in that historic game), but we played that game just a few days after clinching what for us would also be an unforgettable victory – Chelsea's first-ever Premier League title. Whether that played a part in the fact that we weren't able to score at Anfield, after a 0–0 first leg at Stamford Bridge, I don't know.

In any event, in our minds, winning that title away at Bolton Wanderers remains one of our most memorable moments. For a team that had never won it before, it was such a big psychological achievement and a further sign that we had arrived. For me, it was a key moment in my career. I had won individual awards in France, even in Africa – goal of the season, player of the year, and others – but I had never won a trophy. Now, I had won two, including a league title in what is considered to be the toughest league in the world.

I remember, José had been clear to us at the start of the season: if we did exactly what he told us to do, played as he wanted us to play, and put our trust in him completely, we would win the league. For sure. That's the sort of statement that makes people accuse him of arrogance. That's not what it is, though. It's confidence. If we won all our games against the smaller teams, and either won or drew against the big ones, then the title would be ours. Simple as that. It seems obvious, but I don't think every manager thinks that way, or, at least, doesn't break it down and explain clearly how to go about achieving that aim. That season, that's exactly what we did. Not only did we beat all the smaller teams, we also beat Manchester United both at home and away, and drew in both our games with Arsenal. In total, we lost one game during the entire season – away to Manchester City – and won the title with a record 95 points. Even our critics had to admit that that was an achievement.

When I look back now to my first season in the Premiership, I can say it was a season of some highs, but quite a lot of frustrating lows. The move to England had been harder than I'd expected. I had a lot to adapt to both in terms of the language and the team's way of playing, and my family had a difficult time adapting as well. The fans were not won over by my contribution. My season's league goal tally was a modest 10 (16 in all competitions), a long way behind Golden Boot winner Thierry Henry's 25 (31 in all competitions). I'd had various injuries that had interrupted my assimilation into the team, and I'd had no time at the start of the season to acclimatise myself to the culture of English football.

I had been shocked, for example, by the relentlessness of

the Premier League, and the pace at which the games were played, week in, week out. In my first full week at the club, I was thrown in at the deep end, with three games in one week. In France, that happens rarely. In England, it happens several times every season. Clearly, if the manager has a big enough squad, he can rotate the players. But injuries are so common that, even with a big squad, players often have to turn out when they are either really tired, or not actually fully fit. As a result, the notion of 'playing through pain' is a common one in England.

The physicality of the English game was another element that had taken me by surprise in my opening season, although I had already been introduced to it to some extent when Marseille had played against Newcastle and Liverpool the previous season. I remember vividly one throw-in. I tried to go towards the ball, when suddenly a defender came out of nowhere and smashed into me. I just looked at him, in shock, then looked at the referee, expecting him to blow the whistle. No whistle – just play on! In France, that would have been a clear-cut foul, but not in England.

The reason that injuries are not more prevalent is that there's a way to go into contact with another player. Although injuries are part of the sport, and no player ever wants to end up injured, I would never personally hang back because I thought I might be risking injury. When you see a tackle coming, there are ways to avoid problems, and you also don't go into a tackle that you're not sure of, even though, of course, we all sometimes misjudge them.

There were, however, some great times in my first season. My team-mates had really welcomed me, and William Gallas,

Claude Makélélé and Geremi in particular had become great friends. We had a lot of laughs together, and some memorable poker evenings in hotels around the country, when travelling to away games. My English was slowly improving, so I was getting better at communicating with others.

First and foremost, though, lifting those two trophies were the highlights of that season. They definitely helped to compensate for the difficulties I was still experiencing, which centred around adapting to the English game. Those trophies kept me going because, at times, I did wonder if I was ever going to succeed in England and at this club. The Carling Cup, in fact, had been such a big deal for the club that before our return leg against Barcelona in the Champions League, we had actually presented the trophy to the fans. I was suspended at the time, but I remember being out on the pitch with the team, parading the trophy in front of the fans. They were so happy. Moments like that gave me the strength and encouragement to carry on.

8

DO I STAY OR DO I GO?
2005–2006

I HOPED that my second season would feel more comfortable, personally and professionally, than my first, and scoring both goals in our season-opener Community Shield win against Arsenal was about as perfect a way of starting as I could have wished.

During the summer, José Mourinho had recalled Argentinian striker Hernán Crespo from AC Milan, where he had been on loan. At one time, Hernán had been the world's most expensive footballer, when Lazio bought him from Parma for €56 million (about £35½ million) in 2000, and he had an incredible reputation as a goal scorer. At first, I was happy with the arrangement, but it soon became clear that the manager was putting us in competition against each other. Rather than using us both together, he would more or less alternate between the two of us. I would play one game, score, then Hernán would play the next; or one of us would start a game and be taken off in the second half if we hadn't scored.

The next game, things would be reversed. I think he was trying to get the best out of us by pitting us against each other, trying to motivate each of us to try even harder, to surpass the other. It was never explained to us, but after about three games we each understood what was happening, and we knew what we had to do.

As it happened, we got on very well, so it actually got to the stage where we laughed about it. There was never a sense of rivalry; on the contrary. For example, if I scored in a game, Hernán would come up to me and say, 'Very good! Great performance.' The next game, he would play and score, and it would be my turn to say to him, 'Man, how did you score that goal?!'

In the end, though, it got frustrating for both of us. It's always been better for me to play regularly. It gives me a rhythm, and keeps me match-tight. Also, the thing was, the manager had used this 4–3–3 system quite a lot, and had won many big games with it. When he wanted to be a bit conservative, that was the system he favoured. But he also had the players to be able to play 4–4–2, which is what suited me best. So one day, I went to see him.

'José,' I said, 'you know, it's very difficult for me to play like this. I'm a striker and I don't score enough goals because I'm always between two defenders, and it's very tough.'

On top of that, I'd been away for over a month, playing in the Africa Cup of Nations, where we'd been really disappointed to lose to Egypt in the final in a penalty shoot-out. Much as I loved it, and it was a huge honour to represent my country, the competition was always a big challenge because it meant that every two years I couldn't have a full season. I would play until the end of December, then miss all the games in

January and early February. I remember, just before going, that José told me jokingly to 'have a good holiday'! I think he meant that I would be missed, and that he wished I wasn't going. In any event, when I re-joined the club in February, I was very tired – hardly surprising. Meanwhile, in my absence, Hernán Crespo had been scoring a lot of goals, so I basically had to fight for my place once again, and playing alone against two defenders was therefore not a good thing for me.

One of the manager's many qualities is his ability to listen, and that's exactly what he did. He listened to my opinions on how I was being used and I like to think he took them into account. In any case, he obviously weighed things up, because he decided to change the system and put Crespo and me up-front together in a 4–4–2 formation. Once he did that in the second half of the season, and once I got regular starts, the goals began to come. In the end, as the season progressed, I felt much more as I had done at Marseille. Our new system gave me more freedom and made the difference between being inconsistent and feeling comfortable.

Unfortunately, although I began to feel more at ease on the pitch, I was still not feeling accepted by our own fans. By early March, we had been knocked out of the Champions League by Barcelona in the last sixteen, which was really disappointing for fans and everyone at the club, after the previous year's semi-final. In each leg, either I came on for Hernán Crespo, or he replaced me, in a return to the 4–3–3 tactic, which did not work since neither of us scored. We had already been knocked out of the Carling Cup by Charlton Athletic back in October, surprisingly early, and so were now placing our hopes on the FA Cup and on defending our Premier League title.

In March, two back-to-back games almost derailed my entire season and made me seriously question everything. First of all, we played Fulham at Craven Cottage. They were struggling against relegation, and were desperate to get a good result, which gave the game extra importance from the start. The home fans were soon furious when their side were denied a penalty within five minutes of the start (the right decision when replays were shown). They scored in the seventeenth minute, though, and seemed to be dominant, which led José Mourinho to change the team around, take off Joe Cole and put me on to play up-front with Hernán Crespo. By the second half, playing now with a 4–4–2 system, we had worked our way back into the game.

That's when I received a long pass from a team-mate. I controlled it, ran, went round their goalkeeper, Crossley, and scored what I thought was the equaliser. Immediately, though, mayhem broke out as the Fulham players surrounded the referee, Mike Dean, and appealed for handball. Given the position of Mike Dean relative to where I had been, it would have been impossible for him to know what had happened. At first, he appeared to give the goal. Then, with all the Fulham fans and players going crazy, he walked over to the assistant referee, had a discussion and disallowed the goal. Had he been influenced? He claims not. Whatever the rights and wrongs of that decision, it stood, and I was criticised in the press for what had happened. The controversy in the game didn't end there because William Gallas was sent off in the ninetieth minute for a bad tackle on one of the Fulham strikers.

If I thought that was a bad moment, it was nothing compared with what followed. We played Manchester City away, and I shall never forget either the game, or events afterwards. The game itself started well for us. We were clearly the better side, although we were not managing to score. I was paired up-front with Eiður Guðjohnsen, and finally, in the thirtieth minute, he sent a through ball to me that allowed me to score my thirteenth goal of the season. So far so good. My second came a mere three minutes later, when I fired in the ball from six yards. As in the Fulham game, arguments broke out at once. The City defenders were saying that I had controlled the ball with my arm. They were so angry that their captain, Sylvain Distin, continued verbally attacking the referee, Rob Styles, even after the half-time whistle had gone, which earned him a yellow card. As he'd already received a yellow card for his protestations at the way I had scored, this second yellow got him sent off.

That was not the end of the controversy. In the closing stages of the game, their defender Richard Dunne and I got tangled up. I was dribbling past him, he tried to turn and lost his footing. As he did so, his arm went up behind him and hit me on the face, and one of his fingers went right into my eye. It was so painful that I couldn't continue. I was lying there on the ground in agony. My eye started to swell up, and I was having real trouble getting up and carrying on. The crowd didn't know what had really happened, but they all started to boo me, and not just the City fans – our fans, too. I was so shocked. I couldn't believe that it had come to this, to be booed by our own supporters. I could understand if they had booed me because I was not performing, but I was giving everything for my club, doing everything I could to try to earn the fans' support. Just before the final whistle went, the announcement was made that I was man of the match. Cue more booing. What an irony – best player, but unloved by both sides. That really hurt.

The media, of course, went crazy. Was it a handball? Did you really get hit in the eye? The pack of journalists were hungry to hear what I had to say. A BBC *Match of the Day* reporter cornered me, soon after the game, wanting to know exactly what had happened. He spoke very quickly. I was having trouble even following what he was asking, because, although my English was better, it was still not very good and I used to struggle to understand. My mistake, in the heat of the moment, was to be honest – and naïve. So when he asked me if it had been a handball, I said, 'Yes, it was a handball.' But I also said, in reference to the Fulham game, 'This is part of the game. I try to score, and if the referee sees the handball, there is a re-start. He didn't see it, so for me it is part of the game.'

He then asked me if I dived. And this is where things went wrong and, I believe, got lost in translation – not for the first or last time. So I said, 'Sometimes I dive, sometimes I stay up. In football, you can't stay up all the time. I don't dive, I play my game. If they are not happy with this and don't want me to play, I don't play.' Needless to say, only that first, very media-friendly sound-bite got used. And re-used, and re-used. Until that 'Sometimes I dive' became a phrase that defined me.

This episode was a very painful way for me to learn that the British media – certainly at the time – are tough. I had been used to giving interviews only to the specialist sports newspapers *l'Equipe* or *France Football*. Together with television and radio journalists, they only ever reported on the actual football game. That's it. No extras. No controversial or difficult questions. Whereas the British media were completely different. I learned my lesson the hard way and I learned it that day. My answer was headline news in every possible media – TV, radio, newspapers, internet.

I also hadn't factored in, when replying to the questions, how much of a role my English must have played in how my words were interpreted, nor how I was perceived by the media during those first few years. My English was still very French, very stilted. I didn't have the range of vocabulary I do now, nor the subtlety of expression. If I'd had to answer the questions in French, it would have been a very different story. I would have been able to explain myself much more clearly. As it was, I was just trying to keep my answers quite short, not get too bogged down in long sentences, and often felt myself hampered by my lack of command of English. It definitely affected how I was able to express myself that day.

To his enormous credit, Arsène Wenger stood up for me, saying that I was under the spotlight a lot, but that he liked my attitude. He added, 'He is not an unfair player. Maybe he gets shoved and pushed as well and no one sees it.'

I agreed with him completely and still do. All strikers, especially those who, like me, grow up on the Continent, play that way, so it was normal and I wasn't doing any more than many other strikers, but I was definitely getting more attention. Also, as Arsène said, I think people thought, 'Ah, he's tall, he's strong,' so sometimes I felt I needed to show it a bit more in order for referees to believe I had been fouled. I admit it took me a while to adjust to the English way of playing and the English football culture, so in the first couple of seasons, it's true that the diving issue regularly arose. But in the end, I adapted and was a better player for it.

In any event, after the Manchester City game, I was so fed up that I spoke to my agent, Thierno, and to Pape Diouf.

'I'm not happy, I'm upset,' I told them. 'The team is good, we're winning trophies and titles, but I don't know if I want to stay here.'

They both listened, and I think they felt a bit responsible for the situation I was finding myself in, so they didn't dismiss my complaints outright.

I also spoke to my wife. I listen to what she says. She never imposes her views or insists on anything, but I always listen to her before making a decision based on what will be good for the family as a whole.

'It's difficult for you,' she said. 'It's difficult for us, too. But I think the kids are happy here, so . . .'

What she was indicating was that she would support me in whatever I decided but she also hoped that we could all stay together here in England. I thought about what she said and decided to stay. Looking back, staying was definitely the best decision for all of us. At Chelsea there was a plan, an ambition. We were now training at our new Cobham base, and although at first we were still using pre-fab huts, by the time it was finally finished, the facilities were incredible, and it was clear the owner was prepared to back us fully and do whatever was needed to help us be successful on the pitch. Plus, it's not as if I was on the subs' bench. I was playing regularly, I was scoring, and was clearly part of the manager's plans for the future. I just needed to win over the supporters.

So I came up with a plan. Firstly, I would have a really good rest, as soon as the season was over. Then I would go to the World Cup in Germany and perform my best for my country, after which I would make sure I had a *really* good pre-season. The pre-season preparation defines everything. Most of the time, when I had a good pre-season, the season was great. Having a good pre-season means training well, not getting any injuries, being able to repeat session after session, not being tired, not being dictated to by my body, but instead being able to dictate the pace at which I trained. That summer, for the first time since I had joined Chelsea, I wanted to have the sort of pre-season that *I* wanted, not the sort that my body allowed me to have.

That was the plan anyway. In the meantime, there was the small matter of our next game, against West Ham, just two days after the problems at Manchester City. Our 4–1 win was particularly satisfying for me, because I did my talking on the pitch. We had gone 1–0 down and were down to ten men after seventeen minutes. It wasn't looking good. But not long after, I scored the vital equaliser, then set up the second goal for Hernán Crespo. Afterwards, José Mourinho showed how much he backed me and wanted to silence the critics by announcing that 'Didier should go home, switch on the TV, listen to the pundits, buy every single paper tomorrow and listen and read to see if the same people who wanted to kill him have now the common sense to say what he deserves.' That certainly made me feel better!

Coming into April, we were still on course to win the double. An FA Cup semi-final against our eternal rivals Liverpool was scheduled for the end of the month at Old Trafford, the new Wembley stadium still not being finished. A New Year loss of form had lasted until mid-March, but we were now imposing ourselves once again in the league and we were on course to retain our title. What we really wanted was to bring home the FA Cup as well. Sadly, that was not to be. The Reds scored two goals, one in each half, before I managed to pull one back with a header in the seventieth minute. We had our chances, but Liverpool were the dominant team that day.

We were very disappointed, obviously, but there was no time to wallow. We had a vitally important home game against Manchester United the following Saturday and we needed to draw in order to secure the Premiership title again. We were really motivated and within five minutes we were rewarded when William Gallas scored with his head off a Frank Lampard corner. United fought back, and Rooney had several chances to equalise. The game was finely balanced, and in the second half it all got pretty tense until Joe Cole scored a fantastic solo effort just after an hour's play. That settled our nerves, although we never took anything for granted because Manchester United continued to attack right until the end. Our third goal, by Ricardo Carvalho, was just what we needed to feel secure, and the final score didn't really reflect how well Manchester United had actually played.

I'd had another difficult season, and still didn't feel accepted by all the supporters. The media had decided on an image of me, it seemed, and that made it harder for me to win people over with my football. As with the previous season, although there had been good moments, there had been bad ones, too, the lowest point being without a doubt the Manchester City game. But I had decided to stay and to do everything I could to make it work. Retaining the Premier League title helped to convince me that my future really was with Chelsea. It felt good to be able to celebrate that trophy with my team-mates, and being able to do so in front of our fans, and against our Premier League rivals, made it even sweeter.

Although in the end we won the league easily – after that game we were actually 12 points ahead of second-placed Manchester United – it had definitely felt harder to win second time round. We had started in incredible fashion with 15 wins out of 16. By early 2006, with an 18-point lead, everyone had assumed the title would be ours. Then we'd stalled, our results suffered, while our closest rivals, Arsenal, Liverpool and Manchester United, had improved and started to catch up. The latter even went on a ten-game unbeaten run, so we had been relieved when we secured three wins in a row in April against West Ham, Bolton and Everton before securing the title at Stamford Bridge.

By the end of the season, we were still eight points clear, and had equalled our previous season's record number of wins – twenty-nine – so it was a comfortable margin, but so often in those last few weeks of the season it had not felt that way. It proved to me that when there is pressure and expectation, a win feels even better and more enjoyable. Our consistency showed once again that we were always going to be a contender for trophies and titles. José Mourinho must definitely have thought that, because during the trophy-winning celebrations, he threw his Premier League medal into the crowd, making someone very happy. Presumably, he planned on winning more . . .

9

A GOLDEN SEASON, 2006–2007

THE summer before the start of the new season was strange. There was the World Cup in Germany, for which Ivory Coast had qualified for the first time ever, so that was something which in advance I couldn't wait to be involved in and which I will talk about later in more detail. Unfortunately, though, the tournament turned out to be a harder experience for me than I had hoped and it left me unsettled and emotional about everything, something which I maybe didn't realise at the time.

At Chelsea, I had the support of José Mourinho, and was getting to know my team-mates better, which meant they knew me a bit more off the pitch, as well as on it. That helped me to feel more comfortable among them. I had scored 16 goals in total, 12 in the league, second to Frank Lampard with 20 (16 in the league). That was fine, and I was very happy that Frank had done so well, but I felt as if I was underachieving, and that was very frustrating. I am someone who is eternally dissatisfied with his performance, and I knew

I could have done better – especially if I'd been selected more consistently.

The media and some of the Chelsea supporters were still critical of me and, truth be known, I still felt unsettled. During the summer, one person in particular put a stop to all that, and convinced me once and for all to stay. Yes, José Mourinho had always been incredibly supportive of me, as had other team-mates, but the guy who single-handedly convinced me to stay was Frank Lampard. I am sure that, to this day, he doesn't realise the impact of what he did that summer. One day, just after the World Cup, I was having a short family holiday in Marrakesh when I received a text message from him. Strange, because I didn't remember ever having been texted by him during the entire two seasons I'd already been at Chelsea. I looked at the message, and I remember it to this day: 'Hi DD, I hope that you're staying, because we have to win the league together, and we have to win the Champions League together!' I just stared at the phone. Frank wasn't the sort to talk a lot. He's really calm. He's a leader, but he leads more by his goals, by what he does on the pitch, not by words. Along with JT, he was the boss of the team. And the two of them, plus Petr Čech, were players that I had a special bond with. But Frank is a really smart guy, and although he and I had never discussed my situation or what I might have been thinking, he had obviously understood. He just *knew*. For me, receiving that text was absolutely decisive. It felt really powerful. It was proof that I was wanted – not that the team or the club didn't want me before, but I needed someone to tell me. The fact that he had gone to the trouble of contacting me meant a huge amount. So much in fact – and I have never told anyone this – that I kept the phone for a long time, just to be able to keep that message! That's how special it was. And that's how special Frank Lampard is.

That was the day that freed me as a striker. I went on to be top scorer in the Premiership that season, winning the Golden Boot, and I felt unstoppable. That was the day that freed me, gave me wings, allowed me to show what I was capable of. The need to feel wanted, loved and valued by others has always been a vital motivating factor for me, and that single message was the catalyst that I needed for my career at Chelsea to take off.

It just shows how important the psychology of a player can be in his success or failure. Some people think, 'You just have to play, stay focused, no matter what's going on.' But I reply that that is impossible, certainly for me. Football is a sport of emotions. We are not robots, we are human beings. We cannot separate out how we feel about ourselves, or what is going on in our lives, from what we do on the pitch. Well, I can't, for sure. To play well, I need the affirmation of others that they want me to be there. Once I get that, I am capable of anything – and in return I will give them everything!

The summer transfer season had been busy for Chelsea. Hernán Crespo went out on loan again and we signed Andriy Shevchenko from AC Milan, Michael Ballack from Bayern Munich, Salomon Kalou from Feyenoord and John Obi Mikel from Norwegian club Lyn. In addition, Ashley Cole joined us from Arsenal, while my good friend William Gallas travelled in the other direction. Although Ashley went on to make a huge contribution to the club, William's loss was felt, both at team level and by me at a personal level, because we were very good friends.

Andriy Shevchenko had an incredible pedigree – captain of

Ukraine in their first-ever World Cup showing, where they had reached the quarter-finals; twice top scorer in *Serie A*; Champions League winner; and 2004 European Player of the Year. Before the season started, the team, including the new signings, had a meeting with José Mourinho during which he announced, 'Didier, you know that I like to play 4–3–3, but we're going to start with 4–4–2, with both of you up-front. If it works, we carry on like this. If it doesn't, I go back to one striker.' That suited me fine. So when we started playing, I did everything I could to make sure the two-strikers system worked out. The result was that I started the season as I had finished it, scoring goals.

Immediately, I felt my relationship with the fans improve. My English, too. I was now able to make jokes in English – that's always a test of how good you are in a foreign language. If you can make jokes in it, you're doing well. And as a final piece in the psychological jigsaw that I needed to perform, I was given the number 11 shirt!

I learned so much from Andriy Shevchenko. He was also such a nice guy, so modest. It was actually strange to be playing along-side him because I had been such a huge fan that, when I was on the PlayStation with my son, I would always be Shevchenko – and now, here I was, playing in the same team as he was! To be honest, I have always been very lucky in my career. Whenever I have been in competition with a striker – from Daniel Cousin at Le Mans to Hernán Crespo, Andriy Shevchenko and others at Chelsea – I have never had a negative rivalry, always a positive one. Maybe it helped that the team spirit was good in those teams, but in any event, I was really happy when Andriy joined.

It was a shame for him that he was injured when he arrived because he was never really able to perform at the level he had been used to and the one we all knew he was capable of. He scored some important goals for us, but not as many as he would have expected to. I think the fans found that difficult to accept after a while. But when we played together, the pairing worked well, and we found a way of communicating, on and off the pitch.

Within the team as a whole, I was starting to find my place off the pitch as well as on it. People always wonder how we got on, and if I'm being truthful, human nature being what it is, the group of French-speakers did tend to hang around together, the English-speakers as well, and the Portuguese-speakers, but it was never done in a divisive manner. It's just that you naturally stick together if you share a common language and culture. So at lunch or dinner, for example, the team was often split into three or four tables, each with their own language. José, of course, could converse with all of us in each of those languages!

Roman Abramovich would sometimes come along to a training session or into the dressing room for a few minutes. He's a very shy and reserved person, so whenever he appeared, he was always very discreet and would mainly observe, shaking our hands and exchanging a few words with us at the end. You could see from his face that he was happy with the team and with the results, but he definitely did not throw his weight around or act as though he owned the place – even though he did! Over the last few years, I have come to know him a little more and to spend some time with him, but in those early days, I had very little opportunity to get to know him.

My season got off to its best start ever – five goals in the first five games, six goals in the first seven. The season as a whole was going well, and it soon became clear that our main challengers were going to be Manchester United. I think we just lacked a bit of final toughness to grind out wins even when we were not playing at our best, and that cost us the title that season. We managed 24 wins, against Manchester United's 28, but it was our 11 draws versus their five that made the difference. We lost too many points in games that we could have won.

In cup competitions, it was a different story, maybe because we didn't have to keep winning week in week out in the way that's necessary to win the Premier League. In any event, our first final was the Carling Cup, in February, against Arsenal. This would be the last final to be played at the Millennium stadium in Cardiff.

The build-up to the final had focused on whether Arsène Wenger would field a team of relative youngsters, as he had done in earlier rounds. He made a comparison between some of these inexperienced players who had great potential and unknown singers on *The X Factor* who went on to great success. And he added that, 'The game of Chelsea is based on experience and power, ours will be based on mobility and movement.'

Wenger was true to his philosophy. His team's average age on the day was 21. There were kids in there. Theo Walcott was 17 at the time, as was Armand Traoré. Abou Diaby was 20, and Cesc Fàbregas was 19. The big experienced guys, such as Thierry Henry and William Gallas, were not even in the squad. They relied on Kolo Touré and Philippe Senderos for experience.

In contrast, we had our usual big guns, and fielded in essence our first team, full of experienced, physical players. I remember the day before the game, we were saying among ourselves, 'If we lose this game, against those *kids* . . .!' For our confidence, at that stage in the season, it would have been crushing. So we were determined not to lose.

At the start, they surprised us. In fact, they were all over us. We didn't see the ball, and they had several good chances. Then, in the twelfth minute, Theo scored, sidefooting a shot past Petr Čech. It was his first goal for the club and the Arsenal fans went completely crazy. Meanwhile, we were in disbelief. This was really not looking good! I had hardly touched the ball in the first twenty minutes.

Then, just at that moment, Michael Ballack sent a pass down on the right-hand side of the penalty area and, after going round the defenders, I shot it past Manuel Almunia to equalise. That was one of those goals that tipped the balance between two teams and everyone knew it.

In the second half, we started to overpower them, push them off the ball and take control of the game, physically and strategically. Suddenly, halfway through that half, John Terry was accidentally kicked in the head by Abou Diaby, who was attempting to clear a ball. It was immediately clear the injury was bad because John fell to the ground, temporarily knocked out. He was stretchered off fast and taken straight to hospital. We did not know how serious his condition was but we became even more motivated because we really wanted to win the game for the sake of our captain.

Time was ticking on, and finally our efforts paid off. In the eighty-fourth minute, Arsenal lost possession, Michael Essien passed to Arjen Robben on the left, who then crossed it to me in the penalty box. I remember anticipating what he would do and managing to evade my marker, Senderos, to head home a fantastic, really satisfying goal – and the winner. Not only had I scored both goals in what turned out to be our 2–1 win, but the second one of those became one of my all-time favourites against Arsenal and it always gives me a lot of pleasure to think back on it!

As I ran to celebrate with my team-mates, all I could think of doing was drawing 26 in the air with my fingers, in recognition of our captain's shirt number. Amazingly, considering how horrible John's injury had initially seemed, he discharged himself so fast from hospital that he was actually able to make it back to the stadium in time to join in our celebrations. He's a hard man, is JT!

The FA Cup final against Manchester United was another game we could not contemplate losing. We had handed them the Premiership title two weeks before, by drawing against Arsenal in early May, which left us seven points behind United with two games to go. The next game had been at home – against them – but because both teams were more interested in the FA Cup final a few days later, few first-team players were on the pitch that afternoon and it was a low-key game, rather than the big match it would normally have been.

The FA Cup final was the first to be played at the new Wembley stadium. As a kid, I had dreamed of playing at Wembley, so seeing that beautiful new stadium for the first time and having the opportunity to play there was very special. I had won a few trophies by now with the team, but none at the home of football. In all honesty, though, I was a bit disappointed not to have played there when the famous twin towers were the symbol of the stadium.

Just before the game started, when we were all out on the pitch, I felt the need to tell my team-mates something, which maybe surprised them. Kick-off was seconds away.

'Guys,' I said, 'I just want to say, well, maybe you're not, but I am nervous; and I'm scared. I don't know, this feels strange, but I'm scared. But I give you my word, I will give everything for this game. I will give *everything*.'

It was true. I did feel different, playing for the first time at Wembley, in this enormous stadium – at 90,000, its capacity is almost 20,000 more than the Millennium stadium in Cardiff – the name of which is known all over the world. However, I think I articulated what everyone else was feeling, because I knew my team-mates, and I could see they weren't behaving as they normally did, even before big games. They weren't talking, moving or behaving like they usually did. So I just thought I needed to say something.

Afterwards, JT confirmed to me that I'd voiced what everyone had been feeling, and that it had been really helpful. What's amazing to me, when I look back on that small incident, is that it showed I was comfortable enough at Chelsea and within the team to be able to admit that I felt vulnerable. A year before, that would have been impossible. But now, finally, I knew that my team-mates had faith in me, the same way as I believed in them. And that was a big difference. I could really say what I felt. That's how good I felt at the club.

As it turns out, the Manchester United players probably felt the same as we did. It wasn't the best game, so maybe everyone was a bit nervous and anxious to win at the new Wembley. Plus, it was the first time in over twenty years that the final had been contested between the winners and the runners-up of the Premier League. For each side, the stakes were high. Our opponents were chasing the double, and with the Carling Cup trophy already ours, we were desperate to take home a second trophy that season.

By the end of normal time, it was still 0–0, with neither side being dominant or looking very likely to score. Extra time began, and I started to have cramp. This was not good. I ran over to the side of the pitch and called to the manager, 'You need to make a change because I can't run any more. I'm done.' He was having none of it.

'No, no. You don't need to run. Just stay there, just stay there. You will score. Just focus. Just one ball and you will score!'

And then my prayers were answered. Yes, all this time in my head I had been saying, 'Ah, please God, please God, give me one goal, just one goal!' Again and again, imploring him to give me that one opportunity. Suddenly, in the 116th minute, four minutes before the end of extra time and having to go into a penalty shoot-out, the ball came to me from John Obi Mikel. I gave it to Lampard, he passed it back to me, and I just put it past their goalkeeper, Van der Sar. Goal! End of game. We had won the FA Cup. I had scored my first-ever goal against Manchester United in three years of trying, and I had scored the first-ever FA Cup final goal at the new Wembley. It was a very big deal for me, a very big deal indeed. That game was everything I could have hoped for – well, without the cramps!

What happened at the end of the game symbolised in many ways my relationship with José Mourinho. After the whistle went for the end, we were all celebrating on the pitch before the actual presentation of the trophy, when I realised he had left the pitch. I ran down the tunnel to look for him and found him in the dressing room on the phone to his wife. I told him that if he didn't come out with us, the team wouldn't go and collect the cup. 'We are only one. You can come by your own or I will carry you there!' I told him. For me, there was no question: he was a central part of Chelsea's success so he had to be with us when we received the trophy, otherwise it would be meaningless. On a personal level, his presence was also important: he was an essential part of my story at Chelsea and my life in general, so I wanted to share that moment of celebration with him, otherwise it would feel empty.

Together with the Carling Cup, that final turned me into a big-game winner at Chelsea. It cemented my relationship with the club and with the fans. I had scored thirty-three goals that year, more than double my previous season's total. Twenty of those goals were league goals, and I duly won the Golden Boot award that year, which just capped an amazing season. Now I was a dedicated Chelsea player for life.

10

MADNESS IN MOSCOW, 2007–2008

JOSÉ Mourinho had brought me to Chelsea and, although there had been a few moments when things did not always run smoothly between us, he had always remained an incredible supporter of mine. Bringing me to Chelsea had been a priority for him. When he was at Porto, he told me that he had been watching me at Marseille, and was impressed by my attitude on the pitch, my effort and my performances. He had defended and supported me off the pitch over my three seasons at Chelsea because I had always battled hard for him on it. Over those years, he had been quoted as saying that, with me, he 'could go to every war'. I felt a huge debt to him and, along with Frank Lampard, he was one of the key reasons I did not leave the club during the first two seasons. I'm not sure that, deep down in my heart, I would have wanted to leave a club managed by someone who believed in me so much. There was also a real closeness and understanding between us because we had started our adventure at Chelsea at the same time, so that gave us a special relationship from the very beginning.

Since the day I joined the club, wherever I go, people always want to know about José – Why is he such successful manager? What is his secret? One of his many qualities is that he brings a winning mentality to all the teams he manages. Chelsea, for example, already had good players like JT and Frank Lampard. Then he brought in me and Petr Čech, and we were both already good players in the French league. He also brought in Mateja Kežman and Arjen Robben from Holland, as well as Ricardo Carvalho, Paolo Ferreira and Tiago from Portugal. He turned the whole squad into players who only thought about winning. We had complete belief in our ability to get results. And when he left, that winning mentality stayed with us. It's a bit like riding a bike. Once you know how to do it, you never forget, it stays with you forever. And that is what he does with his players, at whichever club he is at.

What José did with me, was give me a belief in myself, in my ability, that made me want to work my hardest and give everything for him. Some people said I was like a son for him, but I knew that if I didn't perform, I wouldn't get picked. He never selected players for sentimental reasons, or out of favouritism, which is good. If he liked you, you knew it, but that remained outside football. On the pitch, if you played, it's because he believed in you, so you knew you deserved your place, and I really appreciated that.

He's really supportive of his players and tells them if they have played well. Even if someone else has scored the winning goal or scored a hat trick, he'll still go up to a defender, for example, and tell him that as far as he was concerned he was the man of the match. That's important for a player because it makes them feel appreciated and valued. Defenders or midfielders don't always get the glory, but they are just as important to the final result as the guys who score the goals. That sort of thing then creates a lot of player loyalty towards him.

He always did that with me, even if I hadn't scored. If he thought I'd played well all the same, he would tell me, he would encourage me. José has always supported me, especially during my early years at Chelsea when I was coming in for a lot of criticism. Even when he was criticised for buying me, an unknown player, he was clear – he said 'judge him when he leaves the club'. That belief in success says everything about José. We have a great working relationship, and I am sure our story is not over, that in the future we will work together again, but more than that we have a real friendship which is rare in football and means a lot to me.

Unfortunately, by the start of the 2007 season, the situation with José at the club was difficult. The owner and the manager are both big personalities, and they each knew what they wanted to achieve. It's just that they had different views on how to achieve it. The owner wanted to win the Champions League as well as the Premier League. The previous season, we had won neither, and I think that was a big problem. The manager, on the other hand, was trying to protect the image of his team, and of some players, I think. We knew he was under pressure and that at the start of the season some friction existed between the owner and the manager about how to regain our momentum. As I said, they're both human, they both had different ideas, so these things happen.

Also, I believe things often come in three-year cycles, and

we had arrived at the end of just such a cycle. We had won two major domestic trophies the first year; the second, we consolidated, winning the Premiership again. The third year had maybe been disappointing because, although we had won the Carling Cup and the FA Cup, we had lost in the Champions League semi-final and come second to Manchester United in the Premier League. That third year is the most difficult – you have to cap what you have done before, otherwise you're going backwards.

By the start of this season, the fourth that José had been in charge, I think we had started to reach a point where it was sometimes harder for his message to get through. We wanted to hear it, we tried, but somehow we had lost a little bit of what had made us special. And we only needed to lose a few percentage points of performance for our results to suffer. For me, I hadn't been able to play in all the games because I had a knee injury. Even when I was playing, I was not fully fit, so I couldn't really perform at my best. I felt bad that I couldn't help José. I felt I was letting him down and that I was partly responsible for what was happening to him – even though logically I knew that was not the case.

José was given a chance to show that he could still produce his magic, but in September, we had a couple of average results: a 2–0 loss away to Aston Villa and a 0–0 home draw with Blackburn Rovers, leaving us fifth in the table at that stage. We then played the Norwegians Rosenborg at home in the Champions League and drew 1–1. That game must have been the final nail in the coffin.

The following evening, there was a screening at a cinema next to the club of *Blue Revolution*, a documentary about the previous five years, since the owner had bought the club. Afterwards, as José and I were returning to our cars, I asked him what was going on. He just said, 'It's finished for me,' and drove off, his face showing no emotion. I stood there in shock, completely lost for words. Even if the situation had not been good in the last few weeks, I hadn't seen this coming, and I couldn't believe that he was actually leaving.

The next day, the announcement was made that José and the club were parting company. José came to see us in the changing room at Cobham to say goodbye. We were all there, the news hadn't yet sunk in, and he made an amazing speech. He thanked all of us for helping him so much over the years, he said he would never forget about us, we were all fantastic, special players. He wished all of us and our families good luck. It wasn't a long speech, just a few minutes, but it was a really hard speech to listen to for all of us – even now, I get shivers down my spine just thinking about it – and we were all very emotional, including José. He's an emotional guy – it's not surprising, because everyone can see how he is during a game – and it was obvious that he was very sad to be leaving.

When the moment came to say goodbye to me, he hugged me very hard, and I started to cry. I couldn't help it. I'd experienced several managers or coaches leaving, many of whom had been incredibly important to me, my development and my career, but José's departure was without a doubt the hardest of all for me. It affected me badly, to the point of leaving me in tears, and that hadn't happened before. But this man had changed my life. I had a unique bond with him, a special relationship. Plus, it's in my nature to feel great loyalty to people who believe in me. Not for the first time, someone who had been a major part of my life was being wrenched away and was no longer going to be a part of it.

After that day, I decided to change, to remain more emotionally detached from such situations. I learned to handle them differently, or rather not to put myself in such a situation where I might risk feeling similar emotions. José's departure also confirmed to me that football was a business, and there was no room for emotions when difficult decisions had to be made.

I went straight to see the owner. I asked him why now? Why had he not made the change at the end of the previous season? I was very calm, but I just wanted to talk to him and to hear his thinking. He replied that he had wanted to give José a chance to see if things could change at the start of the season. I have enormous respect for him, so I understood what he told me. 'As long as I'm here, as a player,' I assured him, 'I will always be professional and give my best, because I belong to the team.' We shook hands and, as far as I was concerned, that was the end of the matter.

In the dressing room, the initial period after José's departure was not easy. Some of us thought that a few players in the squad hadn't done all they could on the pitch to help his cause, and for the first time ever, this brought out some bad feelings among the group and certain things were said. I'm not sure if we were right to think this, but in any event, there had never before been any disagreements among us, so this new situation was clearly not good for the team, and we had to talk things through until matters were resolved. In the end, we are professionals, and we knew that we had no choice but to get on with things and to work hard for our new boss,

Avram Grant, who had been named as the new manager with immediate effect.

His appointment was not really a surprise because he had arrived during the pre-season period in the summer to be the new director of football and he was already involved in the training sessions on a daily basis. Avram was very smart – he kept on Steve Clarke, José's assistant. José had described him as the best assistant in the world and it was true, he was really good. In October, Henk ten Cate, Frank Rijkaard's assistant at Barcelona, was appointed. So Avram, who didn't have experience of top-level football, especially Champions League football, had surrounded himself with top-quality, highly experienced assistants. It was a good combination and it worked well for us.

Avram was also smart because when he wanted to work on one specific element, he would say to one of his assistants, 'OK, today, we're going to work on pressing,' (for example), and Steve Clarke would come up with a training session based around that. As a result, we really enjoyed the training sessions. They were different from what we'd had before, so the novelty made them both fun and stimulating. Avram was always very calm, very relaxed, and he gave us players a lot of responsibilities on the pitch and a lot of freedom, knowing that he had Steve Clarke and Henk ten Cate behind him to keep us on track and focused. The team he had was full of experienced players, such as Michael Ballack, JT, Frank Lampard, Claude Makélélé, Michael Essien and me, and we were able and willing to take on that responsibility. It's not as if he was dealing with youngsters who needed to be told what to do. So we all got behind him and tried to make things easier for him when he took over.

I was coming back from injury when Avram took charge, and in my first game back, against Fulham, I managed to get sent off after picking up two yellow cards. My first Premier League red card – that was a shock. I'd been at Chelsea for three seasons, won everything except the Champions League, and José's departure had undoubtedly affected me. I was playing and remained completely committed to Chelsea because I was a professional, but try as I might, I couldn't avoid thinking that things had changed. My heart wasn't in it in the way it should have been.

After the Fulham game, we won a Champions League group game away at Valencia in which I scored. I played well, but I felt detached. My mind wasn't clear. In mid-October I travelled to Innsbruck for a friendly between Austria and Ivory Coast. While I was there, I did an interview with *France Football,* and told them that I didn't know if I'd be at the club the following season. Looking back, I guess I should not have given that interview but at the time, I didn't think I was saying anything that surprising. I felt it was time for a change. José's departure was a factor but not the only reason, and I was just being honest.

Henk ten Cate was not happy when he heard on the grapevine what was about to hit the newspaper stands. As soon as I got back to England, he challenged me. 'Why did you give this interview? You have to apologise in front of your teammates,' and so on. I felt I had nothing to be embarrassed about.

'My friend, you don't know me!' I replied calmly.

'Maybe, but you still have to do this!'

'OK, OK, no problem.'

We were about to start training. I could see Avram and

Henk talking, and then the manager announced to the assem-
bled squad, 'Ah, Didier has something to say.'

'Oh, OK,' I said. 'Guys, as I said in the interview, I don't know
what is going to happen at the end of the season, but as long
as I'm here, I'm going to be professional; and I hope you're
going to be the same and give everything for the club. Just
like I will. That's it. End of story.'

For me, there was no story, but the club thought I had
stepped out of line, and felt obliged to issue a press release
confirming that I was committed to the club until 2010. And
just to show I meant what I said, in the next game, away at
Middlesbrough, I scored, and in a gesture of how strongly I
felt towards the club and the supporters, I kissed the badge
on the shirt by way of recognition and celebration. This was
the last time that there was to be any talk of me leaving the
club for several more years.

The season itself was a good one but, for the first time in
the four years since Roman Abramovich had bought the club,
we ended it without actually winning a single trophy. We lost
in the FA Cup quarter-final to Barnsley, were runners-up in
the Carling Cup to Tottenham and, for the second successive
year, were runners-up to Manchester United in the Premier
League. That was painful, especially as the title was decided
on the very last day of the season. We needed to win against
Bolton, and United needed either to draw or lose against Wigan.
Instead, we drew 1–1 and they won 2–0. Actually, looking back
now, I think we really lost the league when we drew 4–4 away
at White Hart Lane in March. We'd been leading 3–1, then 4–3
until Robbie Keane equalised with two minutes remaining.
The loss of those two points turned out to be decisive.

So, since we'd lost out in all domestic competitions, our only hope of a trophy was the Champions League. In the semi-finals against our big rivals, Liverpool, things went according to plan for me. I had a really good game in the return leg at home, scoring two and contributing to a 4–3 aggregate win.

We were now through to the final and desperate to win, especially as the game was being played in Moscow, on Russian soil for the first time. A win there would have extra significance for our owner. Our opponents in that final were our other big rivals, Manchester United, whom, surprisingly, we had never previously met in Europe. They were as desperate as we were to win, because 2008 marked the fiftieth anniversary of the Munich air tragedy, and they had been open about wanting to bring the trophy back in memory of those who died. For both teams, therefore, the stakes were high.

For me, too, winning the competition was a big deal because I thought I could then be happy that I had won everything there was to win with Chelsea.

For the final, we arrived two days early in order to be really settled and prepared for the game. We wanted to do everything right for a match that, for the owner, was such a symbolically big game. But things don't always go the way you want; you can't always control a situation. For me, I was very affected at the time by the news that my maternal grandmother, to whom I was very close, had been admitted to hospital in Ivory Coast, and was not expected to live much longer. During the two-day lead-up to the game, I was constantly on the phone to my mother, who was at her bedside, and she was telling me that the news was not good. I had been so close to her when I was little and now she was dying. During the game, I couldn't concentrate. I found it really difficult to put it out my mind, and I was constantly on edge. Maybe if I hadn't had these personal problems going on in the background, things on the pitch would have turned out differently. But we are human beings, and people don't necessarily realise we cannot always detach ourselves from what is going on in our lives. That said, I also believe in destiny – that final was not our final, it was not meant to be. It was Manchester United's final.

The game itself started reasonably quietly, both teams trying to get into their stride. In the twenty-sixth minute, Cristiano Ronaldo scored with his head from a pass by Wes Brown. I nearly equalised a few minutes later, but the score remained the same until almost half-time when Frank Lampard scored, following a deflection off both Nemanja Vidić and Rio Ferdinand, which wrong-footed their goalkeeper Edwin van der Sar.

The second half was goalless, although we were the more attacking side, coming close when a long-range shot of mine hit the post. In extra time, tension was rising, and we were unlucky not to score when a Lampard shot hit the crossbar. At the other end, JT saved us by heading a Giggs shot off the line. Time was ticking on, and I was getting more frustrated because I was not performing in the way I wanted. I could also see that both Ferdinand and Vidić were tired and were even trying to stretch time out, as if they were playing for a penalty shoot-out. I spoke to the manager pitch-side. 'We need to play with two strikers and we will score. Me or Nico [Anelka], or someone. But we need to play with two strikers.' All evening, we had played with only me up-front, but this was not the system that suited me best. The manager didn't listen to me.

Nico was on, sure enough, but as a winger, leaving me alone against the two United defenders. This gradually became more and more frustrating because I knew that we were so close to scoring and finishing the game.

Four minutes before the end of extra time emotions, frustration and instinct got the better of me. We had a throw-in, after the game had been stopped to treat players for cramp, and Carlos Tévez was slow to give us the ball. There was arguing between a few players, then, it all happened so fast, Vidić gave me a push and, as an instinctive reaction, I just flicked my hand at his face. It wasn't hard at all, but with the referee standing nearby, it was an instant red card.

I felt as if I was in a nightmare. I couldn't believe what had just happened. The walk back to the dressing room was so long, so incredibly long, and the whole way I kept thinking, 'This could be my last game for the club!' All sorts of other thoughts were crowding my mind, and I could hear booing coming from our own fans. I knew I was responsible for this, and it was absolutely horrible. I will never forget those feelings.

By the time I reached the tunnel, it was almost time for the penalty shoot-out. I couldn't go back to the dressing room, so I stood there, in that tunnel, completely alone, waiting for the shoot-out to begin. From where I was, I could just see the pitch. United won the toss, and the penalties were taken from the end where their supporters were sitting.

It was a very strange experience, watching on my own, seeing what was happening on the pitch, hearing the noise from the fans, while I was standing there in silence. I was like an outsider, looking in.

The weather was terrible. The skies had opened and a huge downpour was soaking the pitch. The first penalty-taker was Carlos Tévez, and he scored easily, sending Petr Čech the wrong way. Next up was Michael Ballack. Again, no problem. The next two, Michael Carrick for United and late substitute Juliano Belletti for Chelsea, made it 2–2. Cristiano Ronaldo came up for his kick and, as he often did, he stopped halfway into his run-up, I think maybe to put the goalkeeper off. It may have ended up putting Cristiano off, though. In any case, Petr managed to guess correctly and dived to his right to save the kick, while Cristiano covered his face in shock.

Meanwhile, the rain continued pouring down. Frank Lampard showed his usual courage to score and put us 3–2 ahead. The next three kicks, from Owen Hargreaves, Ashley Cole and Nani, all found the net, although on more than one occasion, the opposing goalkeeper got a hand to the ball. The score was 4–4. Our captain could win it for Chelsea. Everyone remembers what happened next. JT slipped when he planted his standing foot as he was about to shoot, and the shot hit the outside of the right post before flying wide. John immediately sank to the ground, his head between his knees, devastated.

Now it was sudden death. The tension was unbearable. At that stage the whole thing becomes a lottery and a test of the mind more than a test of football.

United's Anderson was first off, followed by Salomon Kalou for Chelsea – 5–5. Ryan Giggs coolly put the ball in the net and then it was Nicolas Anelka's turn. He'd already won the Champions League with Real Madrid, he was a very experienced player, he was a good penalty-taker, so we were very hopeful. So many things were going through my head at that moment, it was almost impossible to keep watching. Just before he was due to kick, Van der Sar pointed to his left, as if he was taunting Nicolas to shoot where the previous six Chelsea players had done. Did that make him change his mind? Was it gamesmanship? In any event, the goalkeeper guessed correctly, dived to his right and saved Nicolas's shot. We had lost, United had won. Perhaps it was simply destiny, and it was always going to be their night.

I turned around and went straight to the dressing room and there I sat, on my own, in numb disbelief, trying to under-stand and wake up from this nightmare, realising that there was nothing to wake up from and that this was really happening. I sat there for what felt like a long time. Then Roman Abramovich came in with his young son, who was about 9 or 10, and the boy was crying and crying. Of course, my reaction was to give this poor kid a hug. 'One day, I will win the Champions League for you,' I promised. But it was tough to see that child crying, thinking I couldn't make things all right for him.

I learned later that JT was sobbing for a long time on the pitch after the game and Avram Grant had tried, without success, to console him. Plenty of others were in tears as well. My red card prevented me from going to collect my runners-up medal after the game and Avram Grant gave it to me quietly later that evening. This was just as well. I didn't want to be there, and was spared the whole awful ceremony with the medals and trophy presentation. Apparently, as soon as the manager got back to the pitch after the presentation, he threw his own medal into the crowd. He was not interested in keeping it. I wanted to throw my medal away as well, but my wife persuaded me not to. Even today, though, this medal means nothing to me. People say, 'Oh, but you were still finalists,' which is like saying that I should be happy to finish second. Pierre de Coubertin may have said the important thing is to participate, but I'm sorry, I'm not of that view. Maybe it's fine to finish second when you never expected to be there in the first place, but for us, no, it was 100 per cent not fine.

Eventually, when everyone started coming back to the dressing room, nobody was speaking, it was very silent. A few people came up to me, asked me what happened and how I was doing, but I just replied, 'It's OK, it's too late, it's too late.' I was shattered, emotionally and physically, and I just wanted to get away from Moscow as quickly as possible. It was an example to me of how thin the dividing line is in sport between success and failure, between history being made and cruel loss. Avram Grant was a kick away from being hailed one of Chelsea's greatest managers, but in the end, within a couple of days, he had, unsurprisingly, lost his job.

Meanwhile, as soon as we got back to England, I took a holiday. We went as far away as we could, just my wife, my family and me. Then, just as I was starting to recover a little, I got a call from my mum – my grandmother had died.

11

TWO MANAGERS, ONE TROPHY, 2008–2009

THE 2007–08 season had been a difficult one with some highs, but plenty of lows. It had also been one long struggle with injury. I had developed a knee problem and eventually, in January 2008, I'd had surgery on my meniscus, just before going to the Africa Cup of Nations. In normal circumstances, I should have waited one month before starting to train again, but I had not had the luxury of time, and just ten days after surgery, I was back running. After that, I was never able to have the time off to regain full fitness, and for me to perform, I need to be 100 per cent fit. I came back from the tournament with a swollen knee and basically struggled through the rest of the season as best I could.

As a result, during the summer of 2008, before pre-season training began, I really tried to take care of myself. I went to see a knee specialist and tried to rest my knee while doing exercises to help it to recover. But when I came back to London after the summer break, I realised I had put on 3kg, that's

6½lb, in weight. That's not much, ordinarily, but given my knee was still not right, I could not afford to carry any extra weight at all.

In June, speculation about who would succeed Avram Grant ended when Luiz Felipe Scolari was appointed. He was coming straight from managing the Portuguese national team, after they'd lost to Germany in the quarter-finals of the European Championship. His big claim to fame, of course, was that he had managed the Brazilian team to victory in the 2002 World Cup. He had pedigree, for sure, and was the first World Cup-winning manager to take charge of a Premier League club, so people expected a lot from him. The tabloids called him Big Phil, and he had a reputation for tough talking. The problem was that, although he could talk, he could not speak English, at least not at first, and he needed the services of an interpreter whenever he had to speak to us personally. Scolari had brought a fellow Brazilian, Flávio Murtosa, to be assistant manager and that made communication even more complicated, especially when Steve Clarke left in September. Although the manager really tried with his English, during the whole time he was at Chelsea I felt it was difficult for him to get his message across because of the language barrier.

When I returned to London in advance of a pre-season summer tour to Malaysia and Hong Kong and realised that my knee was still not good, I went to see the manager. It was my first proper meeting with him, and I told him I couldn't train properly, so would not be fit to go on the tour. The first thing I needed to do was work on my recovery, either in a specialist centre I knew of where they would really focus on the injury, or here in London. At first, he said OK, no problem.

But the next day, he contacted me to say that he'd changed his mind, and I had to go to Malaysia. I didn't understand the U-turn, nor the manner in which it was delivered. He could have said, 'OK, let me have a think,' and then told me no, and explained why. In the end, it was decided I wouldn't go on the tour, but that incident didn't exactly set things off on the right footing.

Once pre-season training started in earnest, Scolari's training methods came as a shock to us, and to me in particular. It was back to European-style 5-kilometre runs before we even touched a ball. Given my build, my body, my style of play, this was not good. Plus, I hadn't trained like that for years, not since my days in France. So I couldn't manage his training sessions at all – my back was in agony within a couple of kilometres of setting off. I could hardly walk, never mind run, and would have to pull up before the end. I think Scolari just decided I didn't want to work with him. This was wrong, and throughout his time there, I always tried to play my way back into favour. In any event, from the start I was overlooked in favour of Nicolas Anelka. I didn't have any problems with Nico, quite the opposite. We were really close friends then and remain so to this day. Within a few weeks, though, it was clear I was definitely no longer first-choice striker.

The result of Scolari's training regime was that, because our sessions were of low intensity, we were fresh as daisies at the start of the season, compared with other teams who had been working very hard in pre-season training. Obviously, he really believed in what he was doing, but the reality was that the hardest part of the sessions was the 5-kilometre run, not what we did after it. We might have been aerobically fit, but we were not *football* fit. Then, because we hadn't had that early, physically intense preparation, we started to dip after two or three months and it was our turn to become really tired, whereas other teams were better able to keep going. That scenario happened every time we had an inadequate pre-season, and it happened this time round.

The problem, as I saw it, was that Scolari had no previous experience of Premier League football and of the enormous physical demands it makes on players. The proof of that came one evening early on in the season. I remember we were staying in a hotel before a game the next day, watching Liverpool against Manchester United. The game, needless to say, was *very, very* intense.

'These two teams, they will *never* finish the league like this,' Scolari said to me. 'After five games, finish, they will collapse.'

'No, no,' I replied. 'This is the Premier League. It's like this *every* weekend, all season.'

'No, no, no,' he insisted. I dropped the matter because I could tell he didn't believe me.

In the autumn, it wasn't the other teams that started to slide, it was us, dropping points and achieving one win in five games in the run-up to Christmas. At the same time, I was coming back well from my knee injury, my fitness had improved and the manager picked me for my first game back, a Boxing Day game at home against West Bromwich Albion. I scored in our 2–0 win, and was very happy with my performance. The next game was on 28 December against Fulham. We drew 2–2 and I had an average game, which is not surprising given I had been out for a while, because it's tough to play twice in three days when you're not match fit.

Early in the New Year, after a poor game in which we drew at home against Southend in the FA Cup third round, we lost 3–0 away to Manchester United, and I was not happy with my performance. At one stage, I had a chance and shot but completely missed the target, to the extent that I started laughing in an embarrassed way. It wasn't that I found the situation funny, quite the reverse, but I think Scolari must have misinterpreted my reaction, because he started criticising us publicly, and me specifically, saying we were not going to win the league playing as we did. By then, despite his public denials, he had fallen out with senior players, such as Petr Čech and Michael Ballack, and the atmosphere in the dressing room was therefore not what it should have been.

The crisis between him and me came three days after the United game when I was left out of the squad to travel to Southend for our FA Cup third-round replay – not even dropped but left out altogether. This had never happened to me at Chelsea, not even to make the squad. So I went to see him, just to have a chat, not to start a fight. I just wanted to know where I stood.

'No, you're not coming with me. If you want to leave, it's time to do it.'

'So you don't think I can help the team?'

'Well, I didn't select Deco either.'

'Yes, but Deco is injured. I'm not.'

'Look,' he finally admitted. 'You're not part of my plans, and you're not going to play for me again until the end of the season. So if you want to leave, now is a good time. Speak to your agent. We're in January, you have time until the end of the month to find a club and to leave.'

I knew he basically didn't see a role for me at Chelsea, and he was trying to find a way of getting rid of me. What he really wanted was to bring Adriano, who is Brazilian, from Inter Milan to Chelsea.

'It's OK. If you want Adriano to come, I can go to Inter.'

That much was certainly true, because the manager there was none other than José Mourinho, so I would have been very happy to go there.

When I left the meeting, the first thing I did was call Mr Abramovich and explain the situation via one of his assistants.

'I understand if the manager doesn't want me to stay,' I went on, 'so I would like the club to facilitate things for me if I have to go.' But the assistant answered straight back.

'No, you're not going anywhere. Who said you were going? Nobody has said anything about you leaving the club!'

'Oh, OK,' I said, taken aback by his tone and categoric denial. Still, at least I knew where I stood – I didn't have the manager's backing, but I obviously had the club's.

I want to make it clear that I never had a personal problem with Luiz Felipe Scolari. I know that he tried, he really tried, to make things work at Chelsea, and he made big efforts to learn the language, but in the end, I think the footballing culture was just wrong for him. From the beginning, it wasn't the right fit. These things happen to the best of managers.

Our last game with him in charge was in early February, a 0–0 home draw against Hull. He left the next day, and an interview with *France Football*, which came out a few days later but which had taken place before that game, revealed just what he thought of his players and their inadequacies. He claimed that he did not have the right players, especially on the wing, to play a 4–4–2 formation, the one that also suits me better, and therefore he couldn't play me up-front with Nicolas Anelka. Although I understood why he'd wanted to do the interview, that sort of backward-looking criticism was not, in my view, a good way to end the relationship, however difficult it had been.

During Scolari's time at Chelsea, I decided to take control of my relationship with the media and the fans. I felt I was often misunderstood, there were so many untrue stories appearing about me in the media, stories that were mistranslated, and which made me unhappy because I felt misrepresented. So I decided to take control of my media relationships by hiring a PR agency specifically to help me in that way and they have been amazing. Right from the start, I have been able to communicate with fans and media much better and I still work with the same agency. That decision was a turning point for me, especially in my relationship with the fans.

In any event, once Luiz Felipe Scolari left, Guus Hiddink, the manager of the Russian national team, was appointed temporary manager with immediate effect. As for us, from having been a team that was supposedly not fit and not performing, we became a team that worked our way back up the league to finish third, reached the Champions League semifinal, and won the FA Cup. We were the same group of players, so in my view, there had clearly been a problem earlier in the season.

As soon as Guus Hiddink arrived, it felt good. We really respected him, he had a great track record both at club level, with PSV Eindhoven, and at national level, with the Netherlands, South Korea and Russia. Also, he spoke English, which for us was great. The first thing he said to us when he arrived was, 'This team is not fit.' It was that obvious. Aerobic fitness was one thing, but we clearly lacked essential football fitness. That changed at once, and he worked us hard to get us back into the sort of shape we should have been in.

He also set about rebuilding the team's confidence, including mine, which had been shaken during his predecessor's time at Chelsea. He told me to stop running around all over the place, as I had been trying to do in my efforts to fit into the team. 'You're a striker, you don't have to do that. Just stay up there and finish the actions.'

As a result of his different approach, and his communication methods, my morale immediately improved, and I started playing and scoring goals once more. I was desperate to show that I wasn't finished, and the manager's arrival gave me renewed motivation and energy. My team-mates were happier as well and, as a result, we reeled off four straight wins in Guus Hiddink's first four games. Things were definitely looking up.

We wanted to win a trophy for the new boss, and to show how much we had improved during the second half of the season, so the Champions League semi-final loss against Barcelona was really frustrating. I firmly believed we were once again one of the best teams in Europe, full of experienced players. The first leg, away, had ended 0–0, so for the return leg, we felt big pressure. We couldn't help thinking of the previous year's final, and how close we'd been to winning the trophy. This was our chance to finish the job off this year.

It was not to be, though we came as close as it was possible to come to winning without actually doing so. Michael Essien's fantastic ninth-minute goal from 20 yards gave us great hope. The next eighty or so minutes were spent trying to increase that narrow lead. We were the better team. Barcelona were unable to get a single shot on target and also had Abidal sent off in the sixty-sixth minute (wrongly, probably) for fouling Anelka as he ran for goal. That was one of several incidents that made this game as famous for its refereeing decisions as for the actual football. We had four separate penalty appeals turned down by the Norwegian referee, Tom Henning Øvrebø, and each one, I thought, was an incorrect decision. The most clear-cut, ridiculous one, in my opinion, was when Gerard Piqué clearly handballed in the penalty area, yet the referee, who was standing nearby, waved the appeal away. How he could not have given a penalty is something that I still don't understand. In fact, even during the game, as decision after decision went against us, I started to think, 'What's going on? How can that be?' One mistake, OK; two, maybe; but *four*, in such a big game? What on earth was going on? I think the referee was out of his depth.

About ten minutes before the end of the game, I was substituted. I had been limping but, as far as I was concerned, I was not ready to come off. If the manager had asked me if I'd wanted to come off, I would have said, 'No, I'm OK, wait a bit. I'll let you know if I can handle it.' I knew that if I left the pitch, it would allow defenders Piqué and Dani Alves to put more pressure on our team. But it was too late. I saw the board go up with my number on it, so I had to come off. I was really frustrated about that, so I had to go to the changing room to try to calm down a bit.

I'm not psychic, but I just knew in my guts that something

bad was going to happen. I just felt it. Eventually, I came back out and sat on the bench, watching the final minutes tick by, just praying, praying, praying. The clock moved on to the ninetieth minute. Maybe, maybe, we could hold out after all. Suddenly, the ball was played on to Iniesta outside the box, he struck it cleanly and it soared straight into the top of the net, past Petr Čech. Boom. Equaliser. Bye bye Chelsea.

There was a final, terrible refereeing decision when a Michael Ballack ball hit Samuel Eto'o's arm in the penalty area and again we were denied a penalty. The referee had been right next to the incident, but still that made no difference. Final score, 1–1, Barcelona win on aggregate.

As soon as the final whistle went, everyone went crazy – fans, players, everyone. Barcelona were going crazy with happiness, but we were left really angry at the huge injustice of the evening. I admit I lost control, and marched straight on to the pitch to start shouting at the referee and anyone else who would listen, saying that the whole thing was a disgrace (there may have been the odd F-word added in, just to make things clearer). I was beside myself, and getting a yellow card at that stage (and later, a three-match suspension) hardly registered. What did register was the unfairness of the situation, how hard and how well we had played, only to be denied by someone else's errors. I was also thinking of my promise a year ago in Moscow to bring the Champions League trophy back to Stamford Bridge, and that for us to get to a final would have been a fantastic turnaround after the first half of the season. I had started the season with a manager who told me I was finished, I couldn't run and I was lazy, so what better way to prove he'd been wrong than to get to the final. All these thoughts were running through my mind as I launched into my verbal attack.

I obviously regret using some of the words that came out of my mouth in my outburst, but I don't regret the feelings I had at the time, because I still believe they were justified. I truly believe that we were denied our victory. The fans understood my reaction, because I was expressing everything they felt too. They didn't want to see their players shrug their shoulders and stroll off the pitch without a care in the world, they wanted to know the players felt the same injustice at the situation as they did. Also, what people don't always understand when they're watching these sorts of incidents in front of their televisions is that, on the pitch, our emotions are intensified. We are so committed to our team and to our club, the stakes are so high in those big games that sometimes, yes, we lose control. I'm not saying it's right, but it's difficult to understand fully unless you have been in that situation.

We had one final trophy left to play for – the FA Cup, where we were through to the final, against Everton. In the semi-final, we had beaten Arsenal 2–1 and I'd had another of my moments when I'd scored the vital goal that made the difference. I always say, it's fine to score goals, but it's the ones that matter – the equalisers that change the game, the winners just when no one expects a goal – that are important in your career. And I have been lucky enough to score a fair few goals that mattered. I'm always thinking in games, 'It's time to make a difference, it's time to do something, that's what I'm here for.' Often, you get just one moment, and you have to seize it.

As a result, I spend my time praying during games, asking God to help me, asking him to show me. People might be surprised at how often this happens, but my faith drives everything I do, both on and off the pitch. I really, truly believe there is something, someone, helping me to be, not just a better player, but a better person. That is more important than anything to me, especially now that I am coming to the end of my football career. I was brought up in the Catholic faith, we all went to church, and God has always been in my life and that of my family. As a young man, I was not practising – going to church, praying – but my belief in the power of God never left me. Then, around 2008, 2009, I started to rediscover a closeness to God, to communicate with him, to have conversations with him. And that includes speaking to him during games, which might sound funny or strange to some people, but anyone who has seen me looking up to the heavens or crossing myself, that person will realise this is true.

The game against Arsenal was just one of many instances – but it is a good example – when I experienced a really powerful example of God's help. It was an average game, the score was 1–1, and I was not playing well. I was trying to force things but nothing was coming off. I had no spark. We were into the final ten minutes of the game when I started to speak to him, asking him to show me how to play better, to show me how to score. Five minutes later, six minutes from time, a high ball from Frank Lampard sent me off down the pitch, I ran round Łukasz Fabiański and scored our long-awaited winner. I was almost shocked! I know that some people will think, 'Ah yes, but he scored because at that moment, the ball came to him,' but I really believe there is something. This sort of incident has happened several times – in the 2012 Champions League final, for example – and I feel very lucky to have my faith in my life, not just for these moments, but for the wider things it brings to me as a human being.

The FA Cup final was our last chance to win some silverware that season and we really wanted to prove our critics wrong, as well as reward our manager. The game itself was historic because Everton's Louis Saha scored after twenty-five seconds, the fastest-ever goal in FA Cup final history. It's not a good start to the day when you are playing catch-up almost from kick-off, but once again, I scored the important goal – the equaliser, the one that gave us hope. That header in the twenty-first minute put us right back into the game, and enabled us to start playing more fluidly, enjoying the fact that we were playing at Wembley, our fans were there, and this was a special day. The goal was the turning point for us, and Frank Lampard's seventy-second minute left-foot winner won us the Cup. What had been an emotional, at times difficult season for us ended on a real high. At one stage, in April, we had still had a chance to win the Premier League, the Champions League and the FA Cup. Although in the end we managed to win just the last of those trophies, we felt it was an achievement that we had even been in the running for the other two – not bad for a team that had been written off by some at the beginning of the year. So we savoured our win that day. Actually, I think that was part of the secret of our success – we never took any victory for granted. We enjoyed each one, because each one felt hard-won, precious and very beautiful.

12

THE ANCELOTTI YEARS, 2009–2011

T HE event that outshone the FA Cup win at the end of May was the birth, earlier that month, of my beloved son, Keyran. My wife and I had waited a long time for this happy event, so it felt almost miraculous to be welcoming this healthy, beautiful baby into our family and we felt truly blessed.

Keyran's arrival set the mood for what turned out to be not only a great summer but also my best-ever season. Is that a coincidence? Maybe not. I certainly felt happier and more settled than I had for a while.

This was also due to the arrival at the start of June of our new manager, Carlo Ancelotti. As planned, our temporary manager, Guus Hiddink, had left the club at the end of the season. Ancelotti had twice won the Champions League, as well as many other trophies, so a lot was expected of him.

At the end of the previous season, there had been a lot of rumours about my own future at the club. Some people there undoubtedly wanted me to leave. Their view was that I wasn't the kind of player that Chelsea needed, not so much in terms of footballing skills, but more because of the image and bad reputation that I was giving the club. Although the majority of fans loved me because of my performances on the pitch and everything I had contributed to winning for them, a small number didn't understand that my reaction to events on the pitch was always caused by the fact that I showed my feelings and my emotions, as well as my love for the club. I was always ready to fight for the club. My reaction after our Champions League loss to Barcelona at the end of the season showed exactly the same level of frustration as felt by the fans. If a camera had focused on them, the same words would have been read on their lips because they all thought the same as I did, if not worse! I'm not proud of what I said or did, but it showed how much I cared.

Guus Hiddink, who had always been one of my supporters and had been instrumental, in the few months he'd been with us, in restoring my confidence, understood me well. As a result, he was one of those who, at the end of the season, wanted me to stay. So he spoke to the owner – who had never stopped supporting me – and to his assistants. They listened and made it clear that I was definitely part of their plans for the future.

My first encounter with Carlo was a sign of things to come because he got things off to a good start by calling me, during the summer while I was on holiday, to introduce himself and to let me know that he was looking forward to working with me. That was a really impressive thing to do, I thought. He didn't need to do that. He could have just waited until he saw me for the first time and said, 'Hi, how are you?' like most people would have done. But no, he took the trouble to call me – and presumably others in the team – and that showed respect for his players. So I was really pleased that he was coming to Chelsea. Here was a class act, a big coach with a lot of experience, someone who could maybe help us finally to achieve our Champions League dream.

There were no 5-kilometre runs for him in pre-season. It was the same sort of training that we had done with Guus Hiddink, partly because the latter's fitness coach had stayed, so the drills and the training were completely football-adapted.

In the absence of any international competitions that summer, I was able to have a holiday and then get down to work with some really good, effective pre-season training. As before, if I had a good pre-season, it usually meant that the forthcoming season would be a good one. That summer, for the first time in a while, I was actually pain-free – the knee injury was finally better – and this allowed me to push myself physically to the limit, which felt really liberating. As a result of all this hard work, I was very fit by the start of the season, and immediately back to the form I had shown at the end of the previous one.

Although we had gained Nemanja Matić and Daniel Sturridge in the summer transfer window, the team was basically a settled one because we were still the same core of players who had been there for the previous three or four seasons. Team spirit was amazing, there was healthy competition for places, which is good, and all in all it was a very different feeling in the dressing room from the one a year before. The players I was closest to were those I called, jokingly, 'my African brothers' – Salomon Kalou, Michael Essien, Nicolas Anelka, John Obi Mikel and of course Florent Malouda, whom I had known for such a long time, since we used to play together at Guingamp. I was instrumental in getting Flo transferred from Lyon to Chelsea, under José, because I really wanted him to experience a club managed by such an incredible guy. I wanted Flo to see the methods José employed, the way he motivated his players and instilled in them a sense of loyalty towards him and towards the club.

I was like a big brother to these players at the time, because I had been there longer than they had, so felt I knew the club well. At the same time, however, I have always been friends with everyone. I'm happy to sit with anyone and everyone – I was really close to JT, Frank, Petr and spent fantastic moments with them – and I always try to be the bridge between different groups, to try to make people feel comfortable and relaxed. Younger players often ask me for advice or information, sometimes just on small things, and I try to help whenever I can. Even players from other clubs have called me for advice and I hope I have been of help. It's important because I remember being in their position, feeling out of my depth and overawed when big names were in the team, and pleasantly surprised when they turned out to be approachable and normal. So I try to be like that myself wherever possible.

As a team, we didn't socialise much outside football. We were away so much during the season that when we were home, those of us who had families tended to spend those precious moments with them, rather than going out with team-mates. That said, if we'd had a good win, we might go out in a small group. José Mourinho always said that, even if we didn't win, if we knew that we'd given our all on the pitch, we could still go out occasionally for dinner, for example, but we couldn't go mad in a nightclub. So although we did go out to clubs, it was to celebrate something like a birthday or a big win, not as a matter of course. We were professionals, so we tried not to get into trouble. Partly thanks to social media, we had to be very careful, even when off-duty. That's something you just have to accept is part of the life of a sportsman. There's no point in complaining about it; you just have to get on with it.

In any event, we had a fantastic start to the season, winning the FA Community Shield after a penalty shoot-out against Manchester United, as well as our first six league games. It felt as if we were back to our winning ways – and I was back to my scoring ways. I was forming a great partnership with Nicolas Anelka, and by Christmas I had scored 18 times in 21 games, which for me was unhoped for, considering my situation a year before.

Our biggest disappointment that season – as well as mine – was when we lost to José's Inter Milan in the knock-out stages of the Champions League in March. For him, it was easy to play against us, because he knew us all so well. Clearly, though, it was also really important for him to win, to get one back on his former club. For us, it was different. Although we knew José and his assistants, we didn't actually know his players, so José being their coach gave us no particular insight. We just knew that he would stop at nothing to ensure his team had the upper hand. After losing 2–1 in Milan, we lost 1–0 at Stamford Bridge, which for us felt like a tough loss.

The owner was not happy, either. He called a meeting with us and basically said that now we were out of the Champions League, it was important we did the double, no ifs or buts. It came as no surprise, I guess, but it was just as well we delivered!

I scored a vital winner in our 2–1 away win against Manchester United in early April. That result put us back on top of the table and in control with five games remaining. The title was a very tight race between us and Manchester United, secured only on the final day of the season – they beat Stoke 4–0, but we beat Wigan 8–0, our biggest-ever league win, to finish one point clear of our rivals. It was strange that, given how close the title race had been, we broke many records in winning it: we scored 103 goals that year, which was the most in our club's history; we were the first Premier League side to score 100 goals; we were the first English team ever to score seven goals or more in a game on four different occasions; finally, we finished with a goal difference of +71, a record for English clubs. So even if the finish was close, we certainly won it impressively and with an attacking style of football. In addition, the victory felt especially sweet because we were able to deny Manchester United a fourth successive Premier League title!

For me, the final league-winning game against Wigan had been special because I'd managed a second-half hat-trick, which, in effect, handed me the Golden Boot for the second time with 29 goals, ahead of Wayne Rooney's 26. That felt really satisfying, especially as I'd scored a lot of what turned out to be important goals. Among the highlights were two goals at home against Arsenal, bringing my total against our London rivals to 12 goals in 12 games – a number that I must say had a nice ring to it.

Apparently, Arsenal had been interested in signing me when

I was at Marseille, although they never made an actual offer and I wasn't really aware of it at the time. Arsène Wenger says that he knew I was a good player even when I was at Le Mans but he never took things further. But that's life; sometimes it just takes you one way rather than another. In any event, my second Golden Boot showed my critics that they should not have written me off. What a turn-around I'd had in the last twelve months!

A week after winning the league title, we went to Wembley for the FA Cup final, aiming to win the double for the first time in the club's history. Sadly for our opponents, Portsmouth, they were in a very different position from us. Managed by our former boss, Avram Grant, they had gone into administration earlier in the season and, as a result, they had been relegated. Did we feel sorry for them? Yes. Did that change our attitude when we went into the game? Absolutely not. This was a big opportunity for us to create history, so we certainly weren't going to let sentiment get in the way of our task. In those sorts of situations, you might commiserate with the opponents at the end of the game, especially if you have friends in the other team, but otherwise, you're 100 per cent professional.

The 1–0 score doesn't really give an indication of the sort of game it was, especially as it was still 0–0 at half-time. In the first half, we managed to hit the woodwork five times. In the fifty-fourth minute, Portsmouth were awarded a penalty, which Petr Čech saved, while we were awarded one late in the second half which, surprisingly, Frank Lampard missed. Fortunately, it didn't matter in the end because by then I had scored our one and only goal – a perfect free kick, struck clean and low from a long way out, it cut straight through the wall and shot right past David James who, even at full stretch to his left, could not get near it.

I was yet again the match-winner, and had scored in all five Cup finals (Carling and FA) I had played in with Chelsea, and all six of my Wembley appearances – again, not bad records, and definitely something to savour afterwards. Those weren't records I was aware of at the time, because I was only ever interested in scoring for the benefit of the team, but it was certainly nice to hear about them subsequently. My goal in the final was my thirty-seventh that season in all competitions, the second highest in the club's history, and I was really proud and touched to be voted Player of the Year by the Chelsea fans. It had been a long time coming, but it was certainly worth the wait!

I will always remember season 2009–10. It was a really special year when I felt fulfilled, professionally and personally. My body felt good, my football felt easy. There have been times in my career when, however hard I worked or tried, I could not score. That season was the opposite. Sometimes, I wasn't even looking for goals and I scored all the same. It felt so easy, like a power shower – you barely press the button, no effort required, and the water just flows!

Unfortunately, that feeling was not to last. South Africa were hosting the World Cup in 2010, and Ivory Coast had qualified, much to our excitement, especially since this was the first time the tournament was going to be staged on our continent. As I will explain in a later chapter, we had some preparatory friendlies in Switzerland and, in one of the games, just ten days before the start of the World Cup, I broke my right arm very badly. The thought of not playing in this long-awaited tournament was not one worth contemplating, so I had immediate surgery, and, with my arm in a cast, I went on to play as best I could.

Straight after our participation in the tournament ended, I took a much-needed two-week holiday. I was exhausted after the season I'd had, followed by the dramas of the World Cup. That holiday was not enough, especially as I had further surgery straight afterwards, this time for a hernia, which had been bothering me since about 2004. It seems surprising, but I had, in effect, played with this hernia ever since then and previous surgery had failed to get rid of the problem completely. Although the 2009–10 season had been my best, I had actually had to take anti-inflammatory medication every time I played, which was not good, and not a long-term solution to the problem. In fact, the hernia was causing me more and more pain, so I decided to go under the knife for the second time that summer. As a result, I had to miss most of pre-season training and, as had happened in the past, a bad pre-season meant that the season itself was never as I hoped it would be.

I started off well enough, scoring a hat-trick in the first game of the 2010–11 season against West Bromwich Albion, and we won our first five league games. It looked as if we were set to continue our dominance of the previous season. But fairly soon, results started to falter, while by early October I started to feel really exhausted, as if I was running on empty. I kept saying to the management team that I was tired and needed some days off, and that maybe those two operations had taken it out of me more than I'd realised. Nobody listened.

As far as they were concerned, I was fine, and I was just over-reacting to how I felt.

Eventually, I went to see Carlo and insisted that I needed four days off, minimum. 'OK, fine,' he agreed, reluctantly. Off I went to Abu Dhabi, in search of some sunshine and relaxation. Almost as soon as I got there, though, I started to feel really unwell, so I came straight back. A couple of days later, I was supposed to train with the fitness coach. I dragged myself off to the training ground, but within five minutes, I was sweating, cold, shivering. 'I cannot run, I cannot do anything, I have to stop!' I pleaded. They couldn't understand it, thinking I was just being lazy. I insisted. 'Look, why would I lie to you? I want to get fit, I want to work hard and feel better. Why won't you believe me?' They looked at me and started to think that maybe I was not making it up completely. So they allowed me to go home to have my much-needed rest. But I was still being selected to play and so I struggled on, playing in three league games and even a Champions League home match against Spartak Moscow. It was a terrible month. I knew something was very wrong, but nobody seemed to believe me. I was clearly unwell, and played the Champions League game with a high fever, but I felt I had no choice, since everyone was doubting what I was saying.

At home the next day, I lay on the sofa, unable to move, and I have never felt so ill in my life. My teeth were chattering – literally – and I was hallucinating. My daughter, who was ten at the time, came in from school, took one look at me, and said, 'Dad, are you OK?' and I remember saying, 'Yeah, yeah, I'm fine!' It makes me laugh now, because it must have been so obvious I was anything but fine. Anyway, I'd been for blood tests and the very next day the results came back, showing I had somehow caught malaria. To this day, I'm still not exactly sure when and how I caught it, because although I'd been to Ivory Coast a few weeks before, I'd flown in and out in the space of two days. But clearly I'd been suffering from malaria for about a month, since I'd first started to feel unwell. To be fair, the club had sent me for blood tests initially, but apparently there was not enough parasitic activity in my blood at that stage to diagnose malaria. It had needed the disease to take hold more strongly before the tests could confirm what was wrong with me. I think that I must have been bitten at a time when I was already tired and my immune system had consequently been fragile.

In any event, although I was immediately given medication to cure the problem, enabling me to play not long afterwards, it completely ruined my season. Some days, I'd feel OK, others less so, and as I was 32, people inevitably started to think, 'Ah, he's not what he was before, he's over the hill.'

The January transfer window coincided with this period, and suddenly Fernando Torres was signed, partly because I had been ill and was still not back to full fitness, and partly because, as they told me, they wanted to start preparing the succession, the time when I was no longer around. 'OK, I'm not done yet, but hey, no problem!' I felt like saying. I understood the club's point of view, though. They had to anticipate, and I had to accept.

Fernando Torres, or Nando, as I call him, was signed from Liverpool for a British record-breaking fee of £50 million and as soon as he arrived, the manager completely changed the system to accommodate him. Before then, we were playing with two strikers, the system that I prefer, and that suits the team best, too, I think. But I wanted him to fit in, so I had to change the way I was playing. I went a bit wider, or dropped back a bit more, like a fake number 10, and he would be on his own up-front. For the previous two years, I had been playing centrally up-front and alongside Nicolas Anelka and finishing the moves. We were now adapting in order for Nando to fit into the team, and that didn't really work.

It didn't help, of course, that he arrived injured. He'd spent a long time injured at Liverpool. He'd even played the World Cup injured. So when he came to Chelsea, which was a massive move, he knew he was not fully fit. Also, moving within the same league from one major club to another, and trying to work his way into a group of players who had been together for so long, and who had had so much success together – that must have been really really tough for him. Finally, with all due respect to Liverpool, at that club, Steven Gerrard and Fernando Torres had been the kings. At Chelsea, there were twenty-two kings. So I really felt for Nando, because I knew how difficult the situation was for him. To a lesser extent, I'd been there, but I certainly knew what a big transfer meant in terms of the pressure of expectation.

At Liverpool, the team was geared around him as their main striker. It wasn't that others couldn't score – they could – but they fed him the ball, they structured the team around him with the aim that he would score. That's not how it was at Chelsea. I'd been in a similar situation at Marseille – I was scoring a lot of goals, I was the king. Then I came to Chelsea, and suddenly, instead of thirty-two goals, I was scoring half that number. Still pretty good, but as a striker, that took some adjustment, and I think Nando found that difficult as well. The fact is, it took him three months to score his first goal.

In the meantime, we were no longer in the Carling Cup, having suffered a third-round exit at the hands of Newcastle back in September. We had lost in the fourth round of the FA Cup in February to Everton, and the defence of our Premier League title was proving difficult, with Manchester United emerging as favourites to recapture it. The Champions League quarter-final tie against our biggest English rivals was going to be a show of strength between the two teams.

'When are we going to win the Champions League?' I remember Carlo asking me, a few days before the first leg.

'Well, put the team around me, and we will win the Champions League,' I replied.

It sounds a bit arrogant, written like that, but I was confident that I knew what we had to do to win. He didn't really answer me, and sort of mumbled a 'yes, but no, but' and so on. 'OK, no problem,' I replied. I would accept whatever he decided.

I was picked for the first leg, at home, in early April. Unfortunately, I didn't play well, and it ended in a 1–0 win for United, with Wayne Rooney doing the damage after twenty-nine minutes. For the second leg, I was on the bench – not what I had planned for my 300th appearance for Chelsea! Not surprisingly, I was very frustrated, also because I knew I could still perform and get a result out there. Instead, he picked Nicolas Anelka and Fernando Torres, which was a gamble, given that Nando had not yet scored for us. When Javier Hernández scored the opening goal for the opposition just before half-time, Carlo immediately turned to me and said,

'You have to go in.' I was upset, of course, that we were now in this position. 'Ah but it's late, and now you put me in!'

I warmed up during half-time and went on straight after the start of the second half when Nando came off. I immediately got stuck in, forcing Van der Sar to make a couple of important saves. Then, in the seventy-seventh minute, I chested down a pass from Michael Essien, ran at goal and struck the ball hard and low past the United keeper. I had given us hope – finally! We barely had time to celebrate, though, because in the space of a few seconds, in their first attack after our goal, Ji-sung Park scored, sending us out of the one trophy we still had never won, and the one that the owner had very much set his sights on bringing home.

It was clear that time was up for the manager. By mid-May, Manchester United were once more Premier League champions, with us finishing nine points behind. As ever, when a season is not going right, some players had started to complain about the manager, about not getting picked. The fact is, Carlo Ancelotti is a really good manager, but more in terms of being a really good coach, someone who picks the teams and sets out the tactical system. Maybe he should have had someone next to him who could shoulder the burden of all the problems with the players when they weren't happy, who could handle the personal side, leaving him to focus only on the football element.

To some extent, assistant managers do that, and it's true that we had lost a great assistant manager, Ray Wilkins, back in November. The job of an assistant manager is to be close to the manager but also close to the players, to understand their feelings, to know when to talk to them and what to say when they're disappointed or frustrated. If a player is not selected, for example, the first person he would normally approach would be the assistant manager, not the manager. The assistant manager may, of course, say, 'Go and speak to the manager,' but if he is good and confident in his role, he will first try to explain what the problem is. Maybe the player needs to work on an aspect of his game, or the manager is trying out a different player. In any event, the assistant manager is the mediator, and maybe Carlo Ancelotti could have done with having less of the 'managerial' element to handle, not least because he's too nice a guy. He wants to please everyone and it's impossible to do that.

Carlo was sacked at the end of the season. Two days before, he came to see me.

'I'm really happy to have worked with you, Didier, and I'm sorry we didn't always agree on things. I want you to know it wasn't personal.'

'Ah, don't worry, I know that,' I replied. 'It's football.'

Two years before, he'd gone to the trouble of calling me before the start of the season to say hello. This time round, he made sure he said goodbye on good terms. In both instances, he didn't need to do that. But then, as I've already said, he's a class act.

13

AVB AND RDM, 2011-2012

I N June, our new manager was announced – André Villas-Boas, or AVB as the British media soon called him. He was my sixth manager since joining the club seven years before. In the four years since José Mourinho had left, in September 2007, this was our fifth manager. I had heard rumours before the end of the previous season that they were hoping to appoint André and I was really happy when his arrival was confirmed because I knew him well and considered him a friend. We went back a long way. When I was at Marseille, he was one of José Mourinho's assistants at Porto and often came to watch me play and then reported back to José on my performance. He followed José to Chelsea, then Inter Milan, and we had stayed in touch all this time by text message, which was nice for me. As a manager in his own right the previous season at Porto, he had achieved amazing results – the team had won the Portuguese Premier League undefeated, with a twenty-point margin, and the UEFA Europa Cup. This made him the youngest-ever manager, at 33 years of age, to win a European competition.

So he certainly came to Chelsea with all the right credentials, and I was full of hope that he would be a great manager for us. I wasn't worried that a friend was now going to be deciding whether I played or not. For me, if the friendship is real, we should be able to separate the personal from the professional. He should be able to be honest and straight. If he does not pick me, he should be able to say, 'OK, I'm not picking you because the other guy is better, or because I want to play a different system,' and even if I get upset, I should be able to accept that it's simply a professional decision, delivered clearly. For me, it should be a simple situation, so I was not worried.

When he arrived, he appointed Roberto Di Matteo as assistant manager, so Roberto was returning to the club he had played for as a midfielder for six years. André's training methods were exactly the same as José's, which we were very happy about. For those of us who went back to those days, it was a return to what we knew. However, we also learned unofficially that he wanted to get rid of a few people whom he regarded as ageing players, such as Frank Lampard and Ashley Cole – and me. That's his right, because the club needed to keep moving forwards, but he shouldn't have kept those players at the club while he was trying to make his revolution. Although we weren't going around complaining, it had an impact on the rest of the squad if we weren't happy.

It was the last year of my contract at the club, whereas André had signed a three-year deal, so I think he felt in a stronger position than I was in, relative to my role in the team, so he didn't discuss it when he arrived. For the first game, against Stoke City, I was on the bench, and Nando was in the starting eleven. I thought I might at least get to play the second half, given that whenever I played against Stoke I either scored or created a chance. So I was disappointed when he put me on for the last ten minutes only and the game ended 0–0.

Later that week, I went to see him.

'I would like to know where I stand, André, and why you are using me for only ten minutes.'

He replied that when he'd first seen me in pre-season, he'd come away thinking, 'Wow, Didier is still Didier, there's no competition, he's still the best.' Then, as the pre-season progressed, he'd decided that, in fact, it was Nando who was better in everything.

'No, I don't think so,' I replied. 'If you want to be honest and fair, the best in pre-season was Nico [Anelka]. Not Nando, not me. So if Nico starts, for me, that's not a problem.' I then asked him to be honest with me and to tell me where I stood. He avoided giving me a clear answer. Well, it was an answer of sorts, I suppose.

André decided to rotate the team. I would play one game, Nando would play the next, then Nico, and so on. For a player like me, who needs a rhythm and frequent, regular games, that was not good. I think other strikers prefer this, too. If, on the other hand, you score but you know that you won't play for another one or two games, it's difficult to keep your intensity levels high and your momentum going.

In addition, we had not had the hardest of pre-seasons, which meant that, as with Luiz Felipe Scolari, we began the season very well, scoring goals, winning games, because we were fresh. At that stage, André was full of confidence, and was playing youngsters, including Daniel Sturridge. Then we started flagging in the second and third months, losing important games against Manchester United, Arsenal and Liverpool (the latter two at home). There was even a point, in October/November, when we suffered three Premier League defeats in four games, and three defeats in a row, including a Champions League loss to Bayer Leverkusen, and a loss at home to Liverpool in the Carling Cup quarter-final, just a week after we'd lost to them at home in the league. In December, we suffered three consecutive 1–1 draws against Wigan, Tottenham and Fulham.

The senior players among us didn't know where we stood, so it was difficult to know what to say to the younger members of the team in terms of strategy and keeping our spirits up. We couldn't really say to them, 'Why are you doing this?' or 'Try to do that,' because we didn't have much communication with the manager and therefore didn't know what he wanted from us as a team.

The home loss to Liverpool was symbolic of the strategy at the time. André had been very keen to build up an attack from the back, starting with the goalkeeper, feeding to the central defender, and moving the ball up the pitch like that. I wasn't happy about it, because it's very difficult to do in the Premier League. Teams generally press high up the pitch. I felt it was better to kick it long, play the second ball and start from there, otherwise there was the risk of conceding a goal. I made my views known, but André was convinced we should do it his way. In the team meeting the evening before the Liverpool game, he said that he disagreed with me and that we should play his way. OK, that was fine. I was picked for the starting eleven, with Nando on the bench.

The game got to 1–1, and I was substituted in the eighty-fourth minute. In the eighty-seventh, we tried to start an attack from the back, lost the ball, Liverpool's Glen Johnson got hold of it, ran past several defenders – goal! Huge frustration on my part.

The next day, the manager called the senior players together – me, JT, Petr, Frank. He wanted to know what was going on, why we were not winning games, why this, why that. He seemed to be asking for our advice and to want our help. As ever, I spoke up, and at least tried to explain things from the strikers' point of view – he needed to stop rotating us; it would be better if he gave me, say, three games to show what I could do. 'If after that, you're not happy with me, fine, bye bye. Pick somebody else.' He seemed to listen to what I was saying. I also advised him to put on hold his philosophy of how to play, at least until we'd got a few wins under our belt and our confidence back. Again, he seemed to take on board my comments.

The next day, he called a full team meeting. We were all keen to hear what the manager would say.

'We have to stick to our philosophy, the way we are playing. I believe this is how we will win the Champions League,' he told us. He could not have been clearer. It was as if the conversation with Petr, Frank, JT and me had never happened. As far as he was concerned, it was business as usual. He wanted to continue to do things his way.

André then asked each player in turn if they believed we could win the Champions League. They all answered yes. When it came to my turn, I said, 'I'm sorry, coach, but I don't believe we can win.' I felt I knew André well enough as a person, given how far back we went, that he would understand me, and understand that I was not afraid to speak my mind and to be honest. I really felt comfortable enough with him to be able to do that. He was obviously disappointed.

'Ah, Didier, you have to believe,' he replied, and gave me all the reasons why.

'I'm sorry, André, but I don't believe.'

There wasn't a bad atmosphere after this exchange, but it was probably as disappointing for him as it was for me. For the next few days after that, it became quite amusing, because several players started teasing me whenever they spotted me. '*Believe*, Didier, *believe*!' they would say, laughing.

Then, in early December, Nicolas Anelka and our Brazilian centre back Alex asked to be transfer-listed, so they were banned from training with the first team. That was not good for us at all. In the eight years I'd been there, I had never seen that happen. But the manager's view was that he was there for the long run, those players were about to leave, and the owner was fine with what he'd done. Those who wanted to work with him could stay; those who wanted to leave could train with the reserves.

That meant we were down to two senior strikers, Fernando Torres and me. However, since it was clear that I was not part of the manager's future plans, other clubs were starting to make enquiries. Shortly after that, I got back from training one day, looked at my phone, and saw that I had a missed call from my agent. I called him straight back. I'd had an offer from a Chinese club, the same one that had made an offer for Nicolas Anelka. So I went to speak to the manager.

'You remember what you said about players who weren't happy?'

'Yes,' he replied.

'Well, I've got an offer.'

He realised that if he wasn't careful, he could be down to one experienced striker in a matter of days. I was asked to say nothing, and not to make any decision. I respected his request and decided to put any offers on hold.

At the start of January, I had to go to Africa for the Africa Cup of Nations. In the past, the tournament had often been an interruption to my season. This time, I had never been so happy to go.

By the time I came back at the end of February, after Ivory Coast had yet again lost in the final in a penalty shoot-out, this time to Zambia, I knew that communication between the manager and the players was at breaking point. He had fallen out with some, while others were demotivated. In the Champions League – last-sixteen first leg at Napoli – senior players, such as Frank Lampard, Ashley Cole and Michael Essien, were left on the bench, we lost 3–1, and Roman Abramovich questioned team selection for the first time.

Results were not good in the Premier League, either. We were no longer contenders for the title, having dropped out of the top four in mid-February. A loss at West Bromwich Albion on 4 March marked the end of the road for André. We were now four points adrift of fourth-placed Arsenal, a situation that we had never found ourselves in during all the years I had been at the club. The next day, to nobody's surprise, André was sacked.

He had really wanted to succeed, and he clearly has many talents as a manager. I like him very much as a person but, in my opinion, André's mistake was to think that it was going to be easy, that we just had to do things his way and we would win. Maybe that's what he'd done at Porto. But football is not like that. You cannot succeed on your own, it's impossible. The game is made up of individuals, many of whom have a lot of experience, so you have to all work together. You have to be able to listen to them and communicate with them. Otherwise, if you manage a team like Chelsea, you're heading for a fall.

Roberto Di Matteo, André's assistant, was appointed as caretaker manager, and immediately the team returned to form with a string of wins in the Premier League, FA Cup and Champions League. The result in the latter competition was particularly important because we managed to reverse the 3–1 defeat at Napoli with a fantastic 4–1 win in extra time, in which I scored the opening goal to set us on our way.

In the FA Cup, we notched up some satisfyingly big results, including a 5–2 quarter-final win against Leicester City and a 5–1 semi-final success against Tottenham Hotspur at Wembley. In the first of these games, Fernando Torres scored a pair of goals, his first since joining the club, which was a relief for everyone, especially for him, and was a sign that we were all getting our confidence and our team spirit back.

Roberto Di Matteo began his time as manager a bit tentatively. He wasn't communicating much with us, but the whole team had a meeting and John Terry remotivated us, telling us that it was important for us to take responsibility for what we did on the pitch, that we had to stick together and be strong again as a unit, as a team.

I addressed the gathering, too. 'I could have left in January,' I said, 'but I'm still here. Why? Because I believe we have a chance to win the Champions League. Maybe I'm wrong and we won't, but I will do *everything* to win it. I have been here for eight years now, and when they put me on the bench, I don't complain. So if I see a guy who *is* complaining because he's not playing, or something isn't happening for him, he will have a problem with me. If you're not happy because you're not playing, go and see the manager. But between us, the players, we want to see happy people, we want to enjoy our football, and let's try and win the Champions League.'

That's how we started to rebuild the team. It was a psychological thing more than anything else. John, Frank, Ashley, Petr, me, that core of senior players, we started to reclaim the leadership and to rebuild team morale. Before long, Roberto understood what was happening and began to speak to us and to communicate with the team.

He would call me, for example, and say, 'Didier, you can't play every game. I'm going to give this game to Nando,' or, 'You can rest for this game, but the next one is important. You need to be ready for that game.' I would then be able to prepare myself. I used to tell Roberto, 'All I want is for you to tell me, *before*. If I'm not playing, fine, but I don't want to come to the meeting, see the team sheet and then discover that my name is not on it. Then I get frustrated. I'm not like a seventeen-year-old who pulls a long face if he's not picked. No. Don't worry. Just say, "You're not in." You don't even have to *explain*; just say I'm not in, maybe because you want to try something different. But it's your decision, end of story.'

Communication – that's all I have ever asked of managers. It's so incredibly simple, but it's amazing how often it doesn't happen. Roberto Di Matteo is a smart guy, though, so he took on board my comments and those of some of the other senior players, and the results on the pitch spoke for themselves.

Our 5–1 FA Cup semi-final win against Tottenham Hotspur in mid-April was a clear example of that. I scored one of the best goals of my Chelsea career in that game, our opening one, just before half-time. Frank Lampard hit a long pass from deep inside our half. I controlled it and turned, while fighting off William Gallas's challenge, got a vital half yard ahead of him and fired the ball off my left foot right into the top of the net. Carlo Cudicini dived in vain to save it. It was a really important goal for me and for the team. It got us off the mark and freed us up to score many more.

In the final, against Liverpool a few weeks later, Ramires opened the score for us after only eleven minutes. I really, really wanted to score, so I was not relaxed and wasn't playing very well. At half-time, I told myself not to put so much pressure on myself, to try to forget about scoring but focus on helping the team to play. Then, seven minutes into the second half, Frank Lampard gave me the most perfect pass and I drilled it into the corner with my left foot for what turned out to be the winning goal in our 2–1 victory. Yet again, mine had been an all-important goal.

It was my eighth goal at Wembley for Chelsea and I had become the first player ever to score in four different FA Cup finals – I'm really proud of that record. Without Frank, though, it would not have been possible. He was involved in so many of the important goals of my career at Chelsea. Whatever people might think, that sort of success does not come about by accident. After training, we would often stay behind for five, ten or even twenty minutes, working in front of the goal, trying to put the ball in the net by developing a partnership where each of us instinctively knew where the other one was going to be, or what he was going to do next. Frank worked and worked, as did I, and we pushed each other constantly to become better and better players. Like me, he'd had to work really hard throughout all his career to reach the level he did, so we had similar mentalities and we instinctively understood each other. Our success hadn't come easily, and we both knew that talent was never enough; hard work could beat talent. That work ethic is one of the many reasons why I have so much respect for Frank, and why I feel honoured to have had such an amazing partnership with him at Chelsea.

When I scored our second goal at Wembley, I almost couldn't understand what was happening to me, I was so happy. Goal celebrations are usually instinctive, and on that occasion, my first thought was to thank God for enabling me to score, and to wonder *why* was I always scoring these important goals in finals? I will never get an answer, obviously, but it didn't matter. It was an incredible feeling. And for us to win a trophy, after the season we'd had, was almost unthinkable, given where we had been at the start of the year. The biggest game of our careers was coming up two weeks later, and we could not have had a better way of preparing ourselves than rekindling the feeling of winning a trophy, and knowing that we could win again.

14

ONE NIGHT IN MUNICH

WHERE to begin to describe the most incredible night in my football life? Maybe I have to wind back the clock to when we won against Benfica in the quarter-finals. We had managed a 1–0 away win in the first leg, and when the whistle went at the end of the return leg at Stamford Bridge, we had won 2–1, 3–1 on aggregate. I had been on the bench for most of that game, so I could have come away from the tie with a sense of frustration. Instead, my main feeling was one of elation that we were through to yet another semi-final – our sixth in nine years. I never take anything for granted, including the result of this game, so I was very happy. However, when I went back to the dressing room, although I could see that everyone was happy to have qualified, there didn't seem to be any great celebrations. So I started screaming and leaping about.

'Yeah, we're in the semi-final again!' I shouted, while everyone else just stared at me, no doubt thinking, 'Didier has really gone crazy this time! What's wrong with him?'

'When was the last time you got to a Champions League semi-final?' I asked of various younger players.

'Errr . . .'

'Yes, you don't remember, because you never have. So enjoy it! Be happy!'

Even Robbie Di Matteo was saying, 'Yeah, sometimes it's difficult to leave players out.' So I turned to him and repeated the question.

'My friend, when was the last time you were in the Champions League semi-final?'

'Yeah, never.'

'Yes, so relax, man, and enjoy it! Enjoy the moment!'

I'm a serious guy when I need to be; I work hard when I need to; but when I can, I like to have fun and to enjoy the moment – and this was just such a moment. Yet everyone was behaving as if it was normal to have reached that stage of the competition. But it wasn't normal. For me anyway, it was a really big deal. Plus, we would now play Barcelona, which would give us a chance to avenge our controversial loss to them in our previous semi-final in 2009.

The last part of the season, from February until May, is always the most important – that's when you win the trophies. This time, I did everything I could to make sure this was going to be *our* time, *our* moment. I made sure I prepared really well physically, but I also spoke to my team-mates to make sure they realised how important this period was going to be for us.

I remember saying to Juan Mata one day, 'Please, I need you to help me to win the Champions League.' His look of aston-ishment spoke volumes! 'Yes, because it's you; you need to help me, Juan. I've been here for eight years and I haven't won it, so maybe you're the one who is going to help me finally.'

He continued to stare at me in total surprise, unable to reply. 'And if we win the Champions League, my friend, I will give you a *nice* reward!' I burst out laughing, as did he, although he was obviously a bit confused. It's not that he needed any incentive in the game, but I think he realised that, although I was laughing, I was also deadly serious in my desire to win this one trophy that had eluded me and the club for so long.

The first leg of the semi-final was at Stamford Bridge. Barcelona had one of the best players in the world, Lionel Messi, plus some other pretty useful players, including Alexis Sánchez, Xavi and Cesc Fàbregas, to name but a few. The night before the game, we had our usual team meeting, studying their play, the way they built up an attack, one hundred passes, impossible to get possession. We knew how difficult it was going to be. Then, at the very end, Robbie Di Matteo did what he always did and put up a list of the opposing team's top scorers. Usually, the list would read something along the lines of Rooney – 22 goals; Van Persie – 15 and so on. When the Barcelona list went up, sure enough, in third place was Xavi on 14, in equal second place were Alexis Sánchez and Cesc Fàbregas on 15, but we all just laughed when the top scorer came up on the screen – Lionel Messi on ... 63 goals, 14 in the Champions League alone! But 63 that season? It was such a ridiculous figure that we looked at each other in disbelief and laughed – what else could we do? I even took a picture of the number because it was so outrageous.

Once the game started, Juan Mata, who normally touched the ball a lot, didn't get near it and I wasn't much better. Whenever I was on the ball, I'd look up and their goal seemed so far in the distance because they were putting so much pressure on us, closing us down constantly. The only way to get at them was to play the counter-attack, and as soon as we managed to get the ball, to use the pace of Ramires, with Lampard in support, to break away. That was the theory anyway. They had over 70 per cent of possession in that game, and many many big chances, including twice hitting the wood-work, and once having a Fàbregas shot cleared off the line by Ashley Cole. We, on the other hand, had one chance, and one chance only. It happened, not surprisingly, on a counter-attack, and exactly how we'd planned. Just before half-time, Messi lost the ball to Lampard, who lobbed a perfect pass out to Ramires on the left; he controlled it with his head, ran on, outpacing the defenders, then cut it back across the box to me and I was able to sweep it into the net with a strong left-foot shot. The whole thing happened so fast that Barcelona were caught out. I ran to the corner flag, as I often do, knelt down and saluted the fans. To be honest, I was too tired to go running round in celebration, and when we went in for half-time soon after that, everyone was panting and breathing heavily from all the running and defending we'd had to do. I am a striker, but in that game, I was playing like a midfielder, because they were pressing us so much.

In the dressing room, Juan Mata was moaning and moaning, and he complained to me that he wasn't getting a look-in on the ball. To me, that was the least of our worries.

'My friend,' I replied slowly, getting up close to him, 'today, don't worry if you don't touch the ball. Just run! Then, when you're tired, tell them, and they'll substitute you. It's not a problem. I hardly touched the ball, but I'm not complaining. It's the *result* that counts. OK?'

We adapted. We weren't the better team, but we won, 1–0. Mission accomplished.

Our next task was to go to the Nou Camp to play a very, very good Barcelona team. Same tactic as before, except we conceded a goal after thirty-five minutes, so we were back on level terms on aggregate. A couple of minutes later, we had a big set-back – JT got sent off for an off-the-ball incident when he kneed Alexis Sánchez.

It would have been easy to give up after Barcelona went 2–0 up with a goal from Iniesta that followed a perfect assist from Messi, but that never entered our minds. In the previous eight years, whenever we had played in Barcelona, we had almost always scored. Maybe that was why I had the confidence that we could certainly score that evening.

Moments before the half-time whistle, Lampard laid a ball on to Ramires who, out of nowhere, scooped it up over the head of Víctor Valdés, the Barcelona keeper, and scored. That was a vital goal because it meant we went in level at half-time on goals scored, ahead on away goals. Psychologically, that was obviously really important for us. The message in the dressing room was 'OK, we're down to ten men; we now have forty-five minutes to resist.' That was when players really stepped up to take responsibility. The manager was telling Branislav Ivanović to play centre back but José Bosingwa said, 'No, no, *I* will play centre back,' and carried on to say where he thought others could play. We were all really involved in the decision-making and in discussing what was going to be needed out there in the second half. 'I don't care,' I remember saying, '*I* can play left back if necessary. We don't need a striker. I'll play striker *and* left back, whatever it takes.' We completely reorganised ourselves, and in the second half we resisted and defended as if our lives depended on it.

Unfortunately, in my over-eagerness, I gave away a penalty to Cesc Fàbregas. Lionel Messi stepped up to take the spot kick. Surely this would nail their victory and allow them to book their flight to Munich for the final? Maybe the gods were looking down on us that evening, or maybe the fact that Messi had never actually scored against us preyed on his mind. In any event, he promptly sent his kick crashing against the crossbar. There are days when these things happen, and you just get a feeling.

We kept going, hoping that we might score, but focusing mainly on preventing them from doing so. By the eightieth minute, I could no longer run, and was substituted by Fernando Torres. The minutes ticked on towards the end. Suddenly, in stoppage time, Nando did to them what they had done to us in 2009 at Stamford Bridge. He scored, and in a way that has gone down as one of the most extraordinary goals in Chelsea's history. Completely against the run of play, he collected a long pass from deep inside our half, ran half the length of the pitch, with no one around him, and dribbled the ball calmly past Valdés and into the open goal. It was a completely crazy goal. We were deliriously happy, the fans went mad, and the entire team jumped on top of Nando in celebration of what he had just done. You never normally qualify like this, not after being one man down for almost an hour, that man being your talismanic captain, not when you are playing against possibly the best Barcelona team there has ever been.

Here we were, back in the final, against all expectation,

despite being once more dominated by our opponents – they'd had over 70 per cent of possession in this leg as well. But some results are inexplicable and incredible, and this was truly one of those. The celebrations went on long into the night!

I have talked already about winning the FA Cup against Liverpool two weeks after the Barcelona game. Then we had another two weeks to prepare for the final against Bayern Munich – in Munich. Usually, to be playing a home team in such a big game would be a handicap, and clearly the game was going to be very difficult for us, but strangely, I didn't let that worry me. I had played them twice, including once in their old stadium, and I had scored on both occasions. So although they were undoubtedly a strong team, I had a good feeling going into the final.

Unlike in Moscow four years earlier, when we had flown out two days early – too early in my opinion, because two days had felt like a week by the time we'd actually started the game – this time round, we simply flew out in the morning, the day before the game. That day, you could feel tension in the team because players weren't behaving as they normally do. There was less chat; we were more subdued and focused on what lay ahead.

At the team meeting, the evening before the game, the manager put on a video. We had been expecting the usual film of the opposition, which the manager would use to explain and prepare us for the game. That was not what we saw. In fact, it was a complete surprise. In it, everyone's wives, girl-friends, kids, were sending us messages of support, telling us how much they loved us, how they were thinking of us, and so on. This had obviously been recorded without our know-ledge in the previous couple of weeks, and seeing them on screen like that was really powerful and moving for us all. Some players got quite emotional; others joked about it, as a way of masking their feelings. No one was left untouched, though, by Robbie's clever idea, which was really special for all of us.

The tactics we decided to use for the final were similar to those against Barcelona. We knew they would have a lot of possession, and would press very high, making it difficult for us to have possession in their half. We therefore knew that we had to be very strong defensively and, as soon as we got the chance, we had to attack. But, we told ourselves, we knew how to defend against the very best, even when we'd been down to ten men, so we were not scared. We were also quite confident that we could score at least one goal because we'd done that in the past, too, against them. As a result, we went into the game in a very positive frame of mind.

The stadium was three-quarters red thanks to Bayern's sheer numbers of supporters. It was like playing an away game, except it was the biggest game of our careers so far. Other than Paolo Ferreira and José Bosingwa, who had won with Porto, none of our squad had ever won a Champions League trophy, and eight of us had been in the losing 2008 final against Manchester United, so the stakes were certainly high.

As John Terry was suspended, Frank Lampard wore the captain's armband, and from the very start we found ourselves under constant pressure defensively. Plus, they were closing us down whenever we tried to build any sort of attack. We kept trying, but we couldn't get past them. In the second half, the score remained 0–0, and we knew that, statistically, in these sorts of games, whoever scored first almost always won the game.

We were trying to win the ball higher up the field than in the first half, instead of always being pressed back, but that was difficult because, not only were we missing JT, but both David Luiz and Gary Cahill were playing not fully fit. Ryan Bertrand on the left wing was young and relatively inexperienced at the time, and in danger of being overawed by the situation. The previous day, when he'd seen his name go up on the team sheet, he'd just sat there for a good ten minutes, staring straight ahead of him, to the extent that I'd actually slapped him on the shoulder, almost to wake him from his trance-like state and encourage him. 'Come on, Ryan, you have to eat something to stay strong, because tomorrow you're going to run a lot!'

And then, in the eighty-third minute, they scored. A Thomas Müller header off a Toni Kroos pass. Unmarked. Not the best header, but simple. For me, that was it. Game over. When Chelsea score at that stage, it's over for the other team, so I was really worried it would be the same here. The end of our dream, once again.

As I replaced the ball on the centre spot for the re-start, I was just saying, 'No, no, no!' but Juan Mata, all of 24 years old, was the one to urge me on.

'No, Didier,' he said, 'you have to believe, you have to believe!'

Off came Salomon Kalou, on came Fernando Torres. Three minutes from the end, Nando earned us a corner. Juan Mata took it. A mass of players were in the box. I heard David Luiz telling Bastian Schweinsteiger, 'Just watch, we're going to score now.'

The ball soared high towards us, I ran the width of the box, ghosted in on the inside post, outfoxed my marker, and, just as my uncle had taught me to do all those years ago, timed my run and my jump to perfection. The ball fizzed off my head and straight into the net, past the flailing hands of Manuel Neuer.

All those months ago, I'd asked Juan to help me to win the Champions League. Now he had saved us, he'd put us right back in with a chance with his superb corner kick. As I ran to the touch line and sank to my knees to celebrate, I was in a complete trance. I'd been speaking to God for many minutes now, begging him, 'If you really exist, show me, show me!' So when I scored, all I could do was thank him over and over again, raising both index fingers up to the heavens, as a way to say, 'Why, why, why? Why had he shown me?' I had asked – and I had received. It was unimaginable, unhoped for, and completely inexplicable.

Extra time was extremely hard for all of us. We were all exhausted. I couldn't really run and was starting to cramp. I was trying to defend but was no longer in full control of my body. In one defensive action in the box, I clipped the heel of Franck Ribéry as I was trying to make a play for the ball from behind. One moment of clumsiness – penalty. I was in disbelief. 'Oh my God! What have you done! Why does it always happen to me, why? I did it in Barcelona, I have done it here now.' If they score and win from there, I told myself, there is absolutely no way I can ever go back to London.

Then we saw who was taking the penalty – Arjen Robben.

Ex-Chelsea team-mate, a good friend of mine, and of Frank Lampard's, and an all-round good guy. So we went up to him, and started putting psychological pressure on him. 'Arjen, you're a Chelsea player, you can't do this! Don't do it! Anyway, we'll know where you're going to shoot,' and so on. We got inside his head, definitely, because his kick was weak – definitely weaker than it would normally have been – and Petr saved it. Petr had, as always, done a huge amount of preparation and work with the goalkeeping coach to try to identify where the players were likely to put the ball, from the way they ran up or took their first steps, from their body language. Not for the last time that crazy evening, his work paid off.

The dreaded penalty shoot-out arrived. We know before-hand more or less who the penalty-takers are going to be, but there is always some pitch-side discussion, partly to do with who is left to take them, after substitutions have been made, and who feels comfortable on the day. So we all gathered around Robbie and helped him to draw up the list. I always put myself either first or last.

'Frank first,' I said. But Juan Mata wanted to take the first. 'No, no, let Frank take it first, then you can go second or third, up to you, but . . .'

'No, no, I want to be first,' he insisted.

'OK, you go first then.'

Frank Lampard went down as number three. 'You put your best ones at numbers one, three and five,' I said. 'So if you miss the second one, you still have a good taker for the third; and if you miss the fourth, you've got a good one for the all-important fifth.' It's a very good strategy that has been shown to work. The order was finally agreed, and we lined up on the pitch for the start. The whole stadium seemed to be a sea of red, although our own fans were doing their best to encourage us by chanting as loudly as they could. John Terry came down pitch-side to be with all the coaching staff and subs. They say it's always worse for those who are watching, and I can't imagine how difficult it must have been for him not to be able to play a part in this shoot-out as a result of one moment of madness in the semi-final.

Bayern went first, their captain Philipp Lahm scoring with a hard, low shot to Petr Čech's left. Juan Mata then stepped up. He hit the ball well, but it was up the middle, and Manuel Neuer saved it. 'Oh no, not again!' I thought. Their centre forward Mario Gómez made no mistake with his shot, straight down to Petr's left. David Luiz took a very long run-up from well outside the box, and sent his ball safely into the top right-hand corner. Their goalkeeper then stepped up. It's unusual, but not unheard of for goalkeepers to take penalties. Maybe it was a psychological ploy to show Petr that he could outplay him both with his hands and his feet. His shot was not the best, but it went in nonetheless, just getting past Petr, who had guessed correctly and dived to his right. Frank Lampard, our number three, and a rock, scored with a no-nonsense hard shot, blasted upwards to Neuer's right – 3–2 to Bayern Munich.

So far, they were shooting well, no doubt about it. But we were not giving up. We were constantly encouraging each other: 'Choose a side, then shoot strong,' 'Don't hit the ball low without power,' 'If you miss, you miss, but at least go for it.' We were as united and supportive of each other as it was possible to be. There was also an extraordinary focus among us.

As the shoot-out progressed, some of us, myself included, sank to our knees and began to pray, looking up to the heavens for guidance and inspiration. It was a surreal moment, where nothing else was registering, and it will stay with me until my dying day.

It was now the turn of their number four taker, Ivica Olić. He had come on during extra time in place of Franck Ribéry, but he hadn't really featured much. I suspect he didn't feel completely confident because when he took his penalty, it just wasn't the strongest it could have been. Petr dived to his left, saved it, and with that, put us right back on equal terms. Game on!

Next up, Ashley Cole. He was one of our best penalty-takers. Sure enough, he looked almost relaxed as he calmly sent the ball flying easily past the goalkeeper to the right – 3–3. Massive pressure now on Bayern, and on Bastian Schweinsteiger, their fifth taker. All I could think at that stage was, 'If he misses, it's down to me! If this guy misses, it's *all* down to me!'

He placed the ball, took a few steps back, then a few steps towards the ball, stopped briefly (did he change his mind about which way to send it?) shot . . . and the ball ricocheted off Petr's left post. He'd missed! A split second afterwards, everyone started jumping around like crazy – except me. I knew now we would win, but I *had* to stay quiet. 'Calm, calm,' I told myself. 'Quiet, quiet.' I heard someone say, 'Come on, Didier, come on.' As I walked up to place the ball, I glanced up at the goal. It suddenly seemed huge. I could see Neuer jumping around, holding the bar, doing all the usual tricks to try to put me off – not in a bad way, but just to try to get inside my head, to show me who was boss. I put the ball down, I pulled up my socks, I stared down at the ball. I wasn't nervous, I was the opposite. It may sound surprising, but I was really confident, really sure of myself. 'Wow, this is really something,' I clearly remember thinking, almost like an out-of-body experience.

I then decided that, because Neuer had been onto every ball, I would change my run from my usual longer one to a very short one. That way, he wouldn't have time to read my run-up. I even, for a brief moment, contemplated doing something really crazy like a Panenka-type penalty, where you pretend to shoot hard, but then shoot slowly so that the ball is chipped in high up above the keeper. It's very high risk – Messi scored one such in 2015 – but I was thinking that for such an important moment, maybe I should do something unforgettable. I quickly came to my senses – fortunately, probably! Instead, I told myself something that I have been telling myself since I was a young boy, 'You love being in this position. If you score, we win. If you miss, you miss. But you love that responsibility.' It's true, I loved it, and although I sometimes missed, I scored much more often than not. It's more difficult for a goalkeeper to save than for the player to score, so the odds were definitely in my favour. Plus, I just felt the script had been *written*. When it's yours, it's yours, nothing anyone can do. On another day, I might have been stressed. On this day, I felt strangely calm. At peace.

I kept my eyes down, avoided looking up at the goal, and just glanced up briefly at the referee, who promptly blew his whistle. I took my two steps, pretended I was really going for it, then stopped very briefly. In the space of a millisecond, I saw the goalkeeper begin to move to his left, and I shot to his right. I didn't even shoot, in fact – I placed the ball. And I had secured the winning penalty.

'Oh my God! Oh my God! Oh my God!' ten times, twenty times, those were the only words going round inside my head in those first few seconds after I scored. My first instinct was to run straight towards Petr Čech. He was the one who had actually won the trophy for us, saving all those penalties, but particularly the last one, and I wanted to acknowledge that first and foremost. I just had time to embrace him before we were immediately submerged – literally – by the entire team, squad, whoever. I don't know, but I could feel body after body landing on top of me, hitting me, smothering me. As soon as I managed to extract myself, I saw Florent Malouda, who had come on late in the game. I gave him such a huge hug because the two of us had shared such an extraordinary and long journey together, right from our days at Guingamp, in what now felt like another life. It was so special for me to be able to share this ultimate moment of success with him.

Then I ran to the other side of the pitch to where all the incredible Chelsea fans were, to share the best day of my footballing life with them, all the better for having waited so long for it. They deserved this trophy so much and it was amazing to be able to play a part in winning it for them. It was unreal and strange to be able to tell myself, 'Oh God, so *this* is how it feels to win it! I have always wondered, but now I know!'

I didn't want to leave the pitch. JT, Frank, Petr and I found ourselves together at one stage, and I thanked them for what they had done, and told them it was an honour for me to have played with them. We were all gabbling away, we were just so happy, we never wanted it to end. We were aware, though, of how devastated the Bayern Munich players were. Several were in tears. They were just on the pitch, empty, traumatised, and some of us tried to comfort them, even though there is nothing much that can be said at a time like this. Still, I thought it was important to show that I understood – after all, I had been in that position four years earlier.

The trophy ceremony whizzed by in a blur, to be honest, and then we were back in the dressing room, passing the Cup around, admiring it, the feeling slowly sinking in that it really was ours. We were there for hours and hours, just soaking in the feeling of what it felt like to have won. There was champagne, there was dancing, there was singing, there were speeches, from the manager down to every player. The owner didn't say much, but it was clear that he was incredibly happy and grateful to us all.

At one stage, draped in the flag of the Ivory Coast and clutching the enormous, beautiful trophy, I stood up and began to address it directly. The entire room fell silent. The owner, the manager, the players, all looked on, as I spoke. 'Why? Why have you avoided us for such a long time?' I began, before talking about Barcelona in 2009, Moscow in 2008, and everything we'd had to do in this match in order, finally, to be able to claim this trophy as our own. Some of those who witnessed my speech told me afterwards that it almost felt like a religious experience. For me, it was important to show how much winning this Cup meant to me after all those previous, terrible experiences. It was my way of making my peace with the Cup.

The team did not leave the dressing room until well after midnight, and the journey back to our hotel, on the bus, was mad. We were singing, going crazy. I kept looking back at that beautiful stadium we were leaving behind, now lit up all in blue, and wondering at how extraordinary life could be.

My phone, needless to say, was on fire, and when we reached the hotel, we met up with all our families and friends. My wife and kids were there, of course, and I'd invited my entire family – a large one, it's fair to say, by the time you count everyone – as well as many friends and all sorts of special people in my life, including Marc Westerloppe from Le Mans and other former coaches. It was their day as well. I wanted them to see their kid, this boy whom they had encouraged and stood by for all those years, and I wanted to share my happiness with all these people. My wife told me that she couldn't even watch my penalty because she'd been so stressed, and that my son Isaac had been in tears when they had scored. It was all unreal. Those last ten minutes of the game, the extra time, the penalties – it was all like a movie. And like the best movies, it had had a happy ending!

Eventually, the kids got tired and went to bed, while the adults continued celebrating on the hotel's roof-top terrace. At one point, we threw Robbie into the pool – well, he deserved it, we thought! I did not sleep at all that night. None of us did. It was a really happy, happy night. I looked out from that hotel roof-top and surveyed the whole of the city beneath us. We had put the entire city to bed, partied into the night, and we were still there when people began to get up and the sun peeped over the horizon for the start of another day. For that one night, we truly felt like the kings of the city. I felt so good, so good, and I made sure I enjoyed the moment, which went by far too fast, and recorded it in my long-term memory for ever.

By eight o'clock in the morning, we were back on the coach and heading towards our plane. Once we had taken off, David Luiz took the air stewards' microphone and led the singing – no chance to sleep. At Heathrow, fans greeted us, more than we could ever have imagined.

The parade through the streets of Chelsea that day was even more crazy and emotional. We paraded the FA Cup as well as the Champions League trophy, and thousands of fans lined the route. Everyone was singing, celebrating, enjoying this moment. For me, though, it was bittersweet, because it was my last celebration. I knew – and everyone else suspected – that I was leaving, so it was a very intense, emotionally charged parade. One player took the mike at one stage to sing, 'We want you to stay, we want you to stay-ay-ay, Didier Drogba, we want you to stay,' to the tune of that well-known football chant. I was choking up, but trying not to show it.

After the parade, we were taken back to our starting point, a school's carpark, and in that school's gym I gathered all the team around me.

'I'm really happy to have done this with you,' I said, 'and you have given me the best present I could ever have asked for. I wanted to tell you that I'm definitely leaving . . . and . . .' I couldn't finish. I was in tears. I was *so* sad and emotional, but I had decided after we won the Champions League that it was time for me to go. My goodbye was a really difficult moment. I had developed a huge bond with all the players and with some in particular – Salomon Kalou, José Bosingwa,

Flo, Frank, Petr and others. That bond was special and deep, so it was a wrench to leave them.

When I returned home, my wife was really sad, too, as were the kids. Then I got a call – come out, come out, let's spend the evening together, let's celebrate. So that's what we did. We went out as a group of players with our wives and girl-friends, and that really helped to lift my mood.

But those goodbyes encapsulate the story of my life. From as young as I can remember, every time I start to feel good somewhere, I go. It happened when I was a kid, it happened in Le Mans, Guingamp, Marseille, and now here. It never gets any easier. I just have to accept that's how it is.

15

ADVENTURES IN CHINA AND TURKEY, 2012–2014

WHEN we finally won the Champions League, I was 34, my contract was up for renewal and it felt like the right time to seek new adventures. During the season, we had been trying to come to an agreement on the best way to stay together, given that, as is normal with many top clubs, Chelsea only offer one-year contracts to players over the age of 30. I wanted a plan for the next couple of years because I still felt I had a lot of top-level football in me.

I knew I could never move to another English club. I owed too much to Chelsea, my blood was blue through and through, so the prospect of playing for anyone else in England was unthinkable. A lot of clubs abroad were trying to sign me but I only made my decision after the final in Munich – and if we'd lost, I would have stayed at Chelsea to try again.

I also wanted a new challenge. After eight years of stability, it felt right to be setting off into the unknown again. I had stayed in touch with Nicolas Anelka when he moved to China to play for Shanghai Shenhua, and he seemed to be enjoying the experience. They got in touch and in the end, we came to an agreement, soon after the end of the season. On 19 June 2012, I announced that I had signed a two-and-a-half-year contract with them, and would be starting in July, halfway through their season, which ended in November.

On Chelsea's pre-season tour to Hong Kong and Malaysia the previous summer, we had been astonished by the fervour and passion for football in Asia. The fans clearly loved the club, and me too, and this had helped me to make up my mind. Obviously, the terms being offered by Shanghai were good, but I mainly wanted to experience new things, explore a part of the world I did not know, and live a bit of an adventure.

Soon after signing the contract we were on our way and as my family and I entered the airport's arrivals hall, we were hit by a wall of sound and a sea of people. It was beyond anything I had imagined. It was the sort of welcome normally reserved for rock stars. People were screaming, crying, pushing, shoving, having to be held back by security guards. Outside, it was the same – total hysteria and madness, fans everywhere, chanting my name, waving the Shanghai Shenhua flag, trying to get a picture of me before we were ushered into the safety of a waiting car and driven to our hotel.

It was a great welcome, and an encouraging start to my time with the club. For the first few weeks, I stayed in a lovely hotel. Then I moved to a beautiful apartment that looked out over the Yangtze river and had amazing views.

To be honest, I knew very little about China or Shanghai before going there. I didn't know, for example, that Shanghai is the largest city by population and, with 24 million inhabitants, it has the same population as the whole of Ivory Coast, which was quite a thought-provoking statistic!

My family stayed with me during the school holidays. Fairly soon, it became obvious that, as we had suspected, they could not stay with me permanently. They were too settled in England. The children loved their schools and had lots of friends, and my wife and I felt it was important for them to maintain that stability. Remembering my own lack of stability as a kid, I did not want that sort of nomadic life for my children. We therefore decided that the family would stay in England, and I would return in November, at the end of the season, and stay until the new one began in February. This gave me almost three months with them. I would also fly home for a brief trip in September, during the international break, and they would come to stay with me in the school holidays, such as Easter, whenever possible.

In the end, it meant I would actually see them quite a lot, even though I'm not denying it was sometimes hard to have to Skype in order to keep in touch with my children. This was complicated by the time difference. I had to get up at four or five in the morning in order to speak to them during what was the evening in England. Luckily, our Argentinian manager, Sergio Batista, had the same problems with his family back in Argentina, and as there were several foreign players in the team, he shifted training times to late afternoon. This meant we could wake up very early, speak to our families, then go back to sleep until lunchtime if necessary.

My first game – I went on as sub in the second half – was away to Guangzhou R&F. One of the things I had to get used to very fast was the travel, especially the huge distances between games. Guangzhou was a case in point. Its old name was Canton, and, being in the south of the country, it was technically not as far from Shanghai as some of the other cities we would have to play against, but it was still a thousand miles away! To drive would have taken about sixteen hours, so obviously we flew, and the flight took 'only' two and a half hours. It was like flying to Madrid to play a league game.

It was also a shock to discover that I had never heard of most of the cities we went to, yet they all had populations in the millions. Guangzhou, for example, had 14 million inhabitants! Changchun, the northernmost city we had to play against, 1,250 miles away, had a population of 7½ million, not much less than London's. Yet I had never heard of it. It was quite humbling to realise how little I knew about the country, and it was exciting to find out.

Communication was not really a problem because translators were assigned to foreign players. They accompanied us anywhere we needed to go and were always there at the club to help us. A few of the Chinese players spoke a little English, and our goalkeeper spoke the language well, but most of the team spoke no English at all. What I loved about them was that they really wanted to learn, not just the language, but obviously about football as well. They would look at Nico and me, for example, and just stare in wide-eyed amazement at some of our moves, what we did in practice, how we played within a team. Many of the players were young, so one of my aims when I went there was to help them to improve and to become more confident. They were super keen and hard-working and I wanted them to be proud of what they were achieving.

The first game in which I was in the starting eleven was in

early August against Hangzhou (population 'only' 2½ million) Greentown. I will always remember that game because it taught me a lot about the Chinese mind-set. One of our defenders, a Chinese player, had made the error that allowed the opposition to open the scoring. He'd lost the ball, and they had scored from the counter-attack. I could see that he was really down. He was devastated by his mistake. Five minutes later, I scored a vital equaliser. So I ran straight up to him, and although I didn't speak a word of Chinese and he barely spoke any English, I tapped him on the back, saying, 'It's OK, it's OK,' to make him understand that it was fine, he could relax. I went on to net another goal and we gained a good 5–1 victory.

The next day, although we had the day off, I went down to the training ground, just to have some treatments and see to a few things, and who did I see on the pitch, working away on his own? The defender whose error had led to the opposition's goal the day before. I could see him practising the action, trying to perfect a move, presumably so that he would never again make that mistake. I went up to him, accompanied by the interpreter.

'My friend,' I said, 'what happened?' The player answered at length.

'He said that he had made a mistake,' the interpreter translated, 'that it was his fault, that he was ashamed of this, and that you had saved him.' I was stunned. He was almost saying that I had saved his honour.

'No, no,' I reassured him, 'that's what team-mates are there for. You make a mistake, I correct it if I can. If I make a mistake, I hope that you'll do the same for me, but that's what it means to be part of a team.'

It was quite an emotional, intense moment, and one that

taught me a lot about the way the Chinese people think. Also, I understood that they had a lot of respect for others, as well as passion for the sport. In any event, our little exchange had been an eye-opener.

From the moment I arrived in Shanghai, I met a lot of people and made some lovely friends. I was invited to events and restaurants, and everyone was extremely kind and welcoming to me. I wanted to experience life there to the full, to learn about the food and the culture, so I was happy to go out. People were incredibly generous, always giving me gifts. It was mad and sometimes it was too much for me. I could see how much respect there was in their culture, and, being a different colour and about a metre taller than most people, I certainly stood out, which meant that I never went anywhere unnoticed and without a great deal of fuss being made of me.

I got to know an Ivorian who had been living in Shanghai for a number of years and who spoke Mandarin and Shanghainese, the local dialect, extremely well. He helped me a lot to under-stand the culture and the customs, and early on he explained to me that I had acquired an almost god-like status. Actually, it was almost embarrassing because he told me I was considered like a reincarnation of an ancient god. That was ridiculous, and it would have been funny if it hadn't been slightly disturbing.

My Ivorian friend told me that even those whom I now considered friends were calling me – in Chinese – 'The Almighty'! When my friend told them that in French the word is '*Le tout-puissant*', they switched to that. I'd meet up with them, and they would greet me by saying, in their Chinese accent, 'Aaah, Le Tout-Puissant, how are you?' I used to laugh because it was nice, but I certainly didn't take it seriously.

For the first few months, my experience of football in Shanghai was a very positive one. Then, towards the end of the season, because of a financial dispute between the club's shareholders, we started to be paid late – foreign players and, worse, Chinese players who needed their salary much more than I did. Eventually, the money would arrive, just in time.

The day came, though, when our salaries were over two weeks late, with no sign of payment. There was a game the next day. So I went to the training ground and told the manager I was not going to play, not for myself, but to make a protest on behalf of the others who needed the money. I wanted to make sure my team-mates got paid.

The next day, I played, of course, not because I cared about getting paid, but to make sure my team-mates did. I did not want to let them down. That time, at least, they got the money they were owed.

Just before we were about to go home at the end of the season, Nicolas Anelka and other players warned me that it didn't look as if we were going to get paid on time during our time away. I went home, and, as they had predicted, we didn't get paid in November, or December, despite letters and emails from me and my agent.

On a more enjoyable note, while I was back home in London I organised a dinner for my former Chelsea team-mates. In the February before, I had jokingly said to Juan Mata, 'help me win the Champions League and I will give you a present.'

While I was in China, I had thought about our achievement and thought it would be nice for us all to have something to commemorate it. I am a big fan of basketball and in the USA when the team wins a championship they all receive a ring to celebrate, so I came up with the idea of doing the same for my team-mates. In December, when I went back to London, I organised a small dinner for all my former Chelsea team-mates with whom I'd won the Champions League the previous May.

It was held at a hotel near the ground and was very low key. They thought it was just for us to catch up and I surprised them by giving them each the ring that I'd had specially made by a jewellery designer – each with the date of the Champions League final and all separately engraved with each player's name. I got watches for the back-room staff, again engraved with the date of the Champions League final. I had wanted to host this dinner to show how important the team was to me and for us to have something really special to remember what we had achieved.

January arrived, and I went to the Africa Cup of Nations in South Africa. It was also transfer market time. I realised that if I went back to China in February I would have lost out on any opportunity to move to another club in the January transfer window and this was the real problem for me, not the financial one.

So I resigned from the club – as did Nico – and very soon after got some offers. I could have signed for Juventus, who wanted me to go there on loan only, because they were worried about FIFA releasing me from my obligations with Shanghai.

At the same time, I had also got an offer from Turkish club Galatasaray. They even came to see me in South Africa, and I was keen to go there because it would be an opportunity for me to get back into Champions League football, and to play for a top club in another country. So at the end of that month, I signed a one-and-a-half-year contract with them to start as soon as the Africa Cup of Nations was over. Shanghai disputed the deal but, in the end, FIFA granted me a temporary licence to play and everything was sorted out.

I was really happy to be joining Galatasaray. They were a strong team and the manager, Fatih Terim, nicknamed 'Emperor', was recognised as among the best in the world, and the only one to have won a European trophy with a Turkish team. A former Galatasaray player, he had huge charisma, was in his third term as manager of the club and, after leaving the following September, he was appointed national manager. Wesley Sneijder was signing from Inter at the same time as I joined, which clinched it for me, and my friend and Ivorian brother Emmanuel Eboué was already there and enjoying it. In addition, the stadium where they play is huge, modern and, with a capacity of more than 50,000, is one of the best in Europe.

As in China, my arrival at the airport in Istanbul was crazy. There must have been thousands of fans waiting for me. The Turks are known for their passion about football, and I certainly saw it for myself the moment I stepped off the plane.

The language barrier was not so severe as in China. Although many of the players were Turkish, as was the manager, most of them spoke enough English to be able to make it the language of communication between us all, and that helped me to settle straight in.

I initially lived in a hotel, as is almost always the case when footballers change clubs, but in May, I moved into a beautiful house on the European side of the Bosphorus, just five to ten minutes from the city centre. I chose it because it had a pool and I wanted to enjoy the outdoors and the good weather. I also wanted to live in a place where my kids would be happy to come and stay.

For my first game, in mid-February, I came on in the second half. We were drawing 0–0 away against Akhisar Belediyespor, and the manager asked me if I was ready. 'Yes, I think so.' So I warmed up and went on. First cross, header, goal! Simple as that. I had scored, not quite on my first touch of the ball, maybe on my third. But once again, I had scored on my debut game – I think I have almost always done that, and I wanted to try to continue that record. I will never forget the reaction of the fans – total madness broke out. I have seen and heard some amazing fans in my time, truly, but these fans were absolutely crazy.

When I joined the club, I made a deal with myself that I wouldn't go out for dinner with my team-mates until I'd scored my first goal. Well, I didn't have long to wait! From that day on, the media, the fans, everyone was behind me, welcoming me, and that felt great. The fans waved banners and during games they would sing, 'We have Drogba, you don't.'

One of the big pleasures that season was playing once again in the Champions League. We had managed to beat Schalke in the last sixteen and now found ourselves in the quarter-finals for only the second time in our history. There, we were drawn against none other than Real Madrid, managed by none other than Mr José Mourinho. Before the first leg, in Madrid, José and I exchanged text messages, which we often did anyway. Nothing very interesting, just wishing each other luck for the game, but José's texts always have a little something extra in them, just in the way he phrases them, because he knows I want to win, and that a game is a game. It's all good-natured teasing, and he always

...it makes me laugh every time and shows that we ... lost that connection that we always had at Chelsea. For ... it's a good feeling to remain in close touch with him.

We lost that away leg 3–0. The return leg, in early April, was going to be a huge game, and we hadn't given up hope of winning. Or at least, I hadn't. At half-time, we were trailing 1–0, and the manager wanted me to come off, so that I could save my energies for an important game that weekend. He sent his assistant to tell me what had been decided.

'Come on, you can't do that!' I protested. 'We can still win the game, we can still qualify. If you make this change, it shows that you don't believe we can still do this. But I believe!'

In the end, I stayed on. In the second half, we equalised and scored again, 2–1, and I scored our third. We needed one more goal to level the scores on aggregate, although they had an away goal. I managed to score, but sadly I was offside, and Ronaldo killed the game by scoring in the last few minutes. We were out of the competition, but it was one of Galatasaray's best home games for years – and it had been against Real Madrid.

After the final whistle, José came onto the pitch and said, 'We were scared, we were really scared, you know!' That game against Real was probably the highlight of my first five months there.

Everyone told me one of the other highlights would be the Galatasaray–Fenerbahçe derby in mid-May. Galatasaray is based on the European side of Istanbul, Fenerbahçe on the Asian side, and the two clubs have been deadly rivals for over a hundred years. Fights occur regularly between fans. I had been told that to become a real Galatasaray player, you had to score against Fenerbahçe. I'd also been warned that derbies against them took on a dimension not known anywhere else, certainly not in England, despite the great Liverpool–Everton and Arsenal–Tottenham rivalries. 'You'll see, Fenerbahçe have crazy fans, blah blah, the atmosphere is crazy, blah blah.'

After that build-up, I was a bit disappointed, to be honest, By then we had already won the league, which for us was a really big deal, so when we went there (it was an away game), the atmosphere was actually a bit subdued. What was even more disappointing was to hear some racist chanting by the home fans directed at Emmanuel Eboué and me, and I'm not sure anything was done about it, although I do know that the events were considered a low point in our rival club's history.

After a good pre-season, in early August 2013 we won the Emirates Cup at Arsenal, in which I increased my goal tally against the Gunners by two. This also meant that I had scored 15 times in 15 games against them which was a good statistic! Then, in mid-August, we had to play Fenerbahçe again, in the Turkish Super Cup, which pits the winners of the league against the winners of the Turkish Cup. This time the atmosphere was much more representative of derbies between the two clubs. At 0–0 after full time, we went into extra time. As has happened so often before, I scored the vital goal, in this case the single goal that gave us the Cup, against our biggest rivals. I had fulfilled my mission. I was now a fully fledged Galatasaray player! Immediately, the passion of the fans exploded. It was not like anything I had ever seen before. Their club is a religion for them, and support for it runs down from one generation to the next with a fervour that is difficult to understand.

The rivalry is so intense and the expectations so high for each club that when we found ourselves a few weeks into the

to Fenerbahçe, our manager was sacked.
being second, only a few points off the
ter rival – is almost like losing the league, so
why the manager had to go. It's crazy, because
se long, there's time to come back; but no, it seemed
that he had to go. In his place came Roberto Mancini, who
had been sacked from Manchester City the previous summer.

We won our first twelve home games with Roberto, and
although we went on to finish second in the league that season
– which naturally cost Roberto his job – we did win the Turkish
Cup and qualified for the knock-out stages of the Champions
League, which was a big achievement because we had both
Juventus and Real Madrid in our group.

Real, now managed by Carlo Ancelotti, beat us easily in
both games, but in the first leg against Juventus, in Turin, we
held them to a 2–2 draw, a really impressive and important
result for us. The return leg was in early December. The night
before, we were in the team hotel in Istanbul, and I remember
looking out and realising that the rain that had been falling
earlier had turned to snow.

The next day, after a lot of work had been done by the
ground staff to clear the pitch, we started the game, but not
long afterwards, a huge snow and hail storm descended on
the whole city. In the space of a few minutes, the entire pitch
was covered, the lines invisible, and the players couldn't run
because of the stinging snow and hailstones getting in our
eyes. I've rarely seen hailstones so big – the size of melon
balls – and never have I seen snow falling so thick and fast.
Within five minutes you couldn't see any grass on the pitch.
The game was abandoned, because it was too dangerous to

keep playing, and we had to wait until the next day in the hope that we could continue the tie. If it was abandoned altogether, at 0–0, then as things stood in the table, Juventus would qualify, along with Real Madrid. So we were really hoping that we could play the next day and get the win we needed to go through instead of Juve.

Again, the ground staff worked tirelessly to clear the snow and the game did go ahead. It was a freezing cold Wednesday afternoon, but in a clear example of how dedicated our fans were, the stadium was full to the brim. It was actually still snowing – though lightly – for much of the game, and the pitch was in a disastrous condition because of the weather and the snow-clearing efforts of the ground staff. In fact, it was so bad that it was almost impossible to play. But we had no choice, and we pushed and pushed and pushed, and, with just five minutes left of full time, I flicked a header that Wesley Sneijder seized upon to score. We had scored against all odds, and our 1–0 victory sent us through to the last sixteen of the competition, ahead of mighty Juventus.

For us, it was a fantastic achievement, and we looked forward to seeing who we would play in the round of sixteen. The draw was made – we would be playing Chelsea! Now managed by José Mourinho. As an added subplot, when our manager Roberto Mancini had left Inter Milan in 2008, José had succeeded him, before going to Real and then back to Chelsea, so for the media, there was plenty to write about. We had two months to go until the tie but soon it was the only thing people talked about to me.

The first leg was in Istanbul. Chelsea started well and Fernando Torres scored in the ninth minute. José's team knew what to do. Not only did they block everything, they were also blocking me. I had to try to find a way through, so I stopped playing striker, moved around a lot, and tried to create space for my team-mates. In the end, we managed to equalise in the second half, but we knew the return leg at Stamford Bridge would be very difficult.

The return to southwest London was strange for me. It came at a time when I was not playing well and not scoring. Then, the day before the game, we went for a training session at Stamford Bridge and suddenly, boom, boom, boom, everything came together, and I could do no wrong. All my team-mates noticed. 'Wow, Didier, you're on fire!' They assumed it was because of the importance of the game, but as much as anything, it was actually because all my instincts, my sense of space, the dimensions of the pitch, the goalmouth, all these things came back to me. Even with my eyes shut, I knew where that goalmouth was, I knew where to shoot, I knew what to do. I knew that stadium like the back of my hand. It was like returning to your home when you've been away. Even in the dark, you remember where everything is, where the light switches are, how many steps are on the stairs, and which doors creak when they open. That's when I realised how much I missed the place.

Not surprisingly, I did not have a good game. It was too emotional for me, too intense. To come back, to hear the fans, to see the sea of blue both on and off the pitch, it was impossible to block out my feelings and to play as if this team meant nothing to me. We soon conceded a goal, and if you are chasing the score at Stamford Bridge, it's a really difficult task.

The 2–0 win for Chelsea was not a surprise, even though we were obviously disappointed not to be going any further. I know myself well enough, however, to understand why it had been so tough playing Chelsea. It was the same thing when I had played against Marseille a few years before. Some players can manage to detach themselves emotionally when they go back to their old clubs. I can't, especially when the club is where I spent eight amazing, successful years.

16

RETURN TO CHELSEA, 2014–2015

My contract with Galatasaray ran out at the end of the 2013–14 season and they wanted me to stay, but I'd had an offer from Juventus. Their manager, Antonio Conte, really wanted me, and I had always been interested in playing in the Italian league, but I was hesitating because I was happy at Galatasaray and wasn't sure whether to stay or leave. In the event, Conte left the club by mutual consent in July 2014. It would have been an electric attack, though, playing with Tévez upfront. Plus Juventus are a big, big club with a long history and it would have been an honour to represent *La Vieille Dame*, as the club is affectionately known.

While José had been away from Chelsea, we had stayed in touch regularly and our friendship had continued. After I, too, had left, and he was still at Real Madrid, he told me, 'You have to go back to Chelsea one day. This is your club, you belong there.' He even said, 'If I go back, I cannot go back without you, so you have to find a way back.' During the summer of

2013, when he was back at Chelsea, he had tried to sign me, but Galatasaray had said no because I had only joined them that January.

So when I told him that I had this opportunity to go to Juve, he said, 'No, you have to wait, you have to wait.' And the great thing was Roman Abramovich wanted me to come back too, so in late July, Chelsea offered me a one-year contract. José declared that he'd signed me not for emotional reasons but because I was still one of the best strikers in Europe. That was really good for me to hear. As for me, it had been an easy decision to make – Chelsea was my home, and I had a special relationship with José, so I couldn't turn down an opportunity to work with him again. Simple as that.

The first time I returned to Stamford Bridge, it felt like I'd never been away. Despite there being a lot of new faces since 2012, it was still the same shirt, the same badge, the same stadium – and of course the same fans. And John Terry and Petr Čech were still there. I was very grateful to Oscar for returning the number 11 shirt to me, which he'd worn after I left. That was a really generous gesture. He needn't have done it but it was a great way for me to return to Chelsea.

One of the players I was pleased to find there was Eden Hazard. Back in the summer of 2012, just as I was leaving Chelsea, I'd persuaded him to sign for the club. He said at the time that he wasn't sure what to do because he wanted to play Champions League. We had finished sixth in the Premier League that season and clubs such as Manchester United and Real Madrid were also interested in him. But after we won the Champions League, I got Gervinho to call Eden and I persuaded him that Chelsea would be the right place for him.

He told me afterwards that he was amazed I had made that call and that it had been a big reason why he'd come to Chelsea.

It was strange, though, to have José back as the manager. He had actually left in 2007, and so many things had happened since I had last played for him. It was interesting because he had changed in the way he spoke to his team. In 2004, when we had both arrived, he was more direct, more abrupt with us. Now, it seemed to me he had mellowed! He had adapted in the way he delivered his message to us. Maybe this was because there were some young players in the squad this time round, compared to 2004 when we were a bit older and more thick-skinned. You can't talk to young players in the same way that you talk to experienced ones, so I think he had become more careful in the way he spoke.

What hadn't changed was his attention to detail. In 2004, a whole team had been dedicated to gathering information on the opposition, doing all the video analysis, watching the games. Before every game, José would give us a thick file containing all these detailed notes, which we would study. The team meeting the day before would simply be a reminder of that information. By doing all the work in advance, they gave us the tools to win. That is still how it works. In addition, José knows every single player, from every single league – and not just the English league, but foreign leagues as well. So when we go on the pitch, we too know everything about our opponents. Nowadays, of course, all the top teams have this attention to detail, but back in 2004, apart from the very top teams, it was rare.

What had also changed since my early years with Chelsea was the way of playing. In the past, it had been more focused on efficiency, directness. We made use of the fact that we were a very physical, powerful squad, good on the counter-attack. We were strong on defending, on holding the ball, and then, whenever there was a half-chance of a goal, we'd go for it. Now, again maybe because of the players in the squad, we were passing more, playing more possession football, playing less directly and if necessary with a slower build-up compared with José's first time in charge.

The tactics were obviously working because right from the start of the season we were dominant in the Premier League and remained unbeaten in all competitions right the way through until early December when we lost away to Newcastle.

Frustratingly, I had twisted my ankle in a pre-season friendly just before the start of the season, and it had taken me a while to get fit. So it wasn't until late October that the manager was able to use me, when Diego Costa got injured. I was so happy to be playing again that in the first three games I played, I scored in each one.

The first game was at home to Maribor, in the Champions League, where I converted a penalty, contributing to a fantastic 6–0 win, our biggest ever in that competition.

My second goal was away to Manchester United. The last time I had scored at Old Trafford, my goal had won us a Premier League title, so it was a big moment for me this time when, with the score still at 0–0 after fifty-three minutes, I leapt up to head the ball in from a corner. That was a good feeling! Our strong defending kept Manchester United from getting back into the game, and it looked as if we would be returning to London with a win, until Robin van Persie equalised with his left foot in the final minute of stoppage time. That was really disappointing, even though the draw still left us well clear of second-placed Southampton.

In contrast to playing at Old Trafford, my third goal came two days later, on a wet and windy Tuesday evening, on a muddy, sodden pitch in Shrewsbury. To be honest, I had just about heard of it when we set off for our Capital One Cup fourth-round tie. Shrewsbury Town, in the Sky Bet League Two, had to put up a couple of temporary stands to accommodate the extra spectators expected that evening. It was a difficult game for us, partly because the conditions were terrible and partly because the opposition were probably fired up by adrenaline at the thought of playing Chelsea. They held us to 0–0 until half-time – I had a goal disallowed just before the interval – but in the forty-eighth minute, I scored my third goal in three games, after being sent through by Mohamed Salah's pass. Their seventy-seventh-minute equaliser shook us awake, and we put more and more pressure on them, until one of their young defenders headed in an own goal, under pressure from me.

Those three games took place in the space of six days and although that pace might have exhausted players who are younger than I am, I was using those games to improve my fitness. I have always loved playing frequently rather than once a week because it allows me to get into a rhythm and it raises my level. Plus, I still have my two physical trainers, Stéphane Renaud and Mathieu Brodbeck, who have been with me throughout my career. So although two days after a game, I'm destroyed and my muscles are really stiff, they work very hard with me, with stretches, massages and specific exercises, and I am able to recover much faster than if they were not around.

In January, I was honoured to receive the Tribute Award from the Football Writers' Association at a gala dinner at the Savoy Hotel. The award is given to someone who has made a big contribution to the game, and I joked, in my acceptance speech, that I would never have believed in 2004, when the press were criticising me so much, that one day the same press would host a dinner in my honour to give me this award. For this reason, the award meant a lot to me. I was really touched that both Petr Čech and Thierry Henry spoke kindly about me – two people for whom I have huge respect. José Mourinho wrote a really nice piece about me in the programme for the evening. He said so many things that humbled me because really he was the one I wanted to pay tribute to. José is someone who has transformed so many good players into winning players. He has done that in all the clubs he has managed, and even after he left Chelsea in 2007, our winning mentality stayed there. He's also someone who made me believe in myself, in my ability, even when I came back to Chelsea second time round. He told me that it didn't matter if I sometimes lost the odd ball, I just needed that one good ball, that one good pass, and I would still score. Even though the team was younger than when I joined in 2004, I thought, 'I'm going to show him that I can do it.' José always brought out that feeling in me. That's why we had a unique relationship.

The first day of March brought us our first trophy – the Capital One Cup – since José Mourinho's return to Chelsea, and the first for the club since 2013. For all of us, including the manager, it felt as if the club had waited far longer than that. Our 2–0 victory over Tottenham wasn't necessarily the best game of football, but as José said at the time, 'Finals are not to play, they are to win.' I came on in stoppage time, and for me, to be winning this Cup was special. This trophy was the first I had ever won in football when Chelsea won it back in 2004 during my first season; and when I left in 2012, I could never have imagined being in a position of winning another trophy with Chelsea. So for both those reasons, I celebrated long and hard after the final whistle went. John Terry, Petr Čech and I were the only ones who had been part of that 2004 team, and for some of the younger players, this was their first taste of winning with Chelsea.

We felt really positive for the rest of the season, despite a shock exit in the fourth round of the FA Cup at the hands of Bradford City, a game in which I'd played. Somehow we failed to win, even though we were 2–0 up after thirty-eight minutes. José said afterwards that he was ashamed to have lost – with no disrespect to our opponents – and the same could be said of the rest of us.

When we then lost in the Champions League round of sixteen to Paris Saint-Germain in mid-March, we were really disappointed because we thought we had a fantastic chance to go much further in the competition. On top of that, our opponents had had to play most of the tie with ten men after Zlatan Ibrahimović had been sent off after thirty minutes for a bad, late challenge on Oscar. I had come on for Ramires after ninety minutes with the teams on 1–1. The game had gone into extra time and although it ended 2–2, we never managed to create the breakthrough to give us victory and PSG eventually went through on the away goals rule. It was a night of drama and tension, and ultimately for us a lot of frustration.

At least the Premier League was going well for us. Very well, in fact. By mid-April, although we never assumed the title was ours, we had been at the top of the table since the very start of the season, and an important 1–0 win against Manchester United gave us a ten-point lead over second-placed Arsenal.

Our next game was against our London rivals, at the Emirates. If we beat them, we needed just one more win from the next five games to secure the title. With the following game being against Leicester City, we were hopeful we could secure the title in our away game in the Midlands, which would have been great.

We really wanted to win, to show that we were the best team in England, so the 0–0 draw against Arsenal was very disappointing. Roman Abramovich came into the dressing room afterwards to hug all the players and encourage us for the remaining games, so that made a big difference to the way we viewed the result.

Still, we would have preferred to have almost sewn up the title. Instead, after that Sunday game, we travelled up to Leicester on the Monday, two days before our midweek encounter. It was the first time that season that we had gone so early to an away game. Normally, we went up the day before but because it was potentially the most important week of the season for us, I think the manager decided we should be spending more time together before the game.

Leicester City needed the points to avoid relegation – they had won their last four games to move out of the relegation zone for the first time since November, but they were far from safe – so there was a lot at stake for both teams. It's always difficult to play away even in normal times, but at this stage of the season, we knew it was going to be even harder.

Our team preparation, however, was no more intense than usual. People might be surprised to read the following information on the build-up to the game, but, with José, we have quite a lot of freedom in what we do when we gather as a team before a game. We have to respect a few specific times, such as lunchtimes and team meetings, but otherwise, it's all very easy going. Even training is not heavy.

We arrived early on Monday evening and had a relaxed dinner. Then some of us watched TV or films. We could basically do whatever we liked with our time. The next morning, breakfast was optional. It always is, and some players prefer to sleep in and have lunch at about 12.30–1 p.m. We travel everywhere with our own chef who knows what we all want, so there is no specific set menu that we have to eat. Again, some people might be surprised that our diet is not more regimented but we are all adults, so we are trusted to make the right dietary decisions based on what is on offer. There's a lot of choice, including chicken, pasta, rice, paella, but always foods high in carbs.

There had actually been a very light training session on the Tuesday morning before lunch, but it was only about thirty minutes long, and we were walking and laughing a lot and doing some fun drills, so we didn't exactly build up a sweat. At one point, for example, we played a game: eight or nine of us stand in a circle, two in the middle, everyone has to touch the ball and the ones in the middle change. It's all done in a good atmosphere, and the aim is really to keep the body moving.

After lunch, the afternoon was free. Before dinner, we had the team meeting. José showed us Leicester's games and tactics, how he wanted us to defend, how they attacked and defended. They had actually changed their system about a month before – with success, given their recent run – so he showed us both their new system and their old one. The good thing with José is that these meetings are not long, ten to fifteen minutes at most, because he and his team have done all the work in advance. They have worked out exactly what they want to say to us, and we have already been given a lot of information on the opposition. The team sheet goes up on the morning of the game, by which time everyone is very clear about what we each have to do.

I remember that during dinner that evening, Eden Hazard spotted a ball in the corner of the room and wanted us all to play a game involving headers at table. 'No, come on, we're having dinner now!' 'OK, fine,' he reluctantly agreed. As soon as dinner was finished, though, off he went to collect the ball and we started playing this game.

There were six of us sitting at a rectangular table, three on each side. At one end, he put a bin on the ground. Starting with the two sitting farthest away from this bin, we then had to head the ball to each other, the ball crossing the table each time, until the final player had to head it into the bin. Well, that was the theory. The first time round, Eden was supposed to be the final player, but he missed, which resulted in a lot of laughing and cheering, including from the manager. He then had to go and sit farthest away, opposite Juan Cuadrado and we all moved up. I was in the middle, opposite JT, and Jon Obi Mikel and Thibaut Courtois were now nearest the bin. We started again, heading the ball from one player to the next, down the table, until John Obi Mikel managed to head it neatly into the bin, to great cheering and applause from everyone else in the rooms. Actually, someone filmed the whole thing and I put it on social media where it went viral. It still makes me laugh when I watch it.

I usually have a massage just before going to bed because it helps me get to sleep. The next morning, the day of the game, we went for a short walk together just before lunch, and in the afternoon, some of us, including me, played ping pong, before going up to our rooms to relax. We always have our own rooms, rather than sharing, because this helps us to rest.

The coach trip to Leicester City's stadium took longer than the forty-five minutes we had expected, so by the time we got there, we were actually late, and our routine was disrupted. We had to get ready quickly to go out for a warm-up, and everything was a rush. That might explain why the first half was very difficult for us, although to be fair to our opponents, they played well. They pushed us and were everywhere. They were the better team for the first half, and deserved the goal they scored moments before the half-time whistle sounded.

Now that we were 1–0 down, we were suddenly facing the possibility that our plan to win tonight might fail. The last thing we wanted was to run the risk of the Premier League title having to be decided in the last one or two games. The manager's half-time team talk was to the point! He said that some players were not performing at the level we should perform in order to be champions, and that the defenders were suffering. Some of us – the attacking players – were putting the defence, and therefore the team, in danger. It was true.

This sort of message can either break a player, who then cannot perform in the second half, or it can make him take responsibility to help the team. In my case, I knew what I had to do. I had to take the pressure off the defence, attack more and move more. Sure enough, within three minutes of the start of the second half, I scored. Branislav Ivanović ran down the wing, passed to me and I blasted the ball in from nine yards out. Yet again, I had stepped up and scored a much-needed goal that changed the balance of play in a game. It's a great feeling every time, and it never gets any less powerful.

It was my first goal for Chelsea since the start of the year – I was not the first-choice striker and wasn't starting regularly – so I had waited a long time for it. In this type of game, what is important is not the third or fourth goal; it's this sort of psychologically important goal. From that moment on, we were dominant. I missed a couple more good chances, but JT and Ramires made sure of victory and the 3–1 final score was a fair reflection of the game.

On the way back to London that evening, the atmosphere was very happy, very chilled and relaxed. No great celebration – it was far too early for that – but we all definitely had the feeling that the title would now be ours. Our next game was at home against Crystal Palace, and knowing that we could, and hopefully would, secure the title at home was very exciting.

I never had any doubt in my mind that we would win against Palace, even though they are always an awkward team to play. The way I approached the game was different, I think, from those players who were trying to win the league for the first time. For me, it was not about my own individual performance; it was about the collective performance, and making sure we got the points. But I knew what it felt like for the younger players because I used to be like that. The first time, you always think it's going to be fantastic, you're going to win 8–0, you're going to score lots of goals and you're going to be best player, the hero on the day. It's rarely like that. Eventually, I had realised the need to change my approach. Once I understood the importance of helping the team *as a whole*, that it wasn't about *me*, and that I did not need to score or be the best, I stopped putting pressure on myself and it freed me up to play better. If I gave everything for the team, something surely would come back to me. Maybe it's my personality but that's what I think.

Normally, a striker doesn't defend. Strikers don't drop back too much, and although they sometimes create assists, they really just stay up there to score goals. I'm a striker, but I'm also a team player. If the team is losing 3–0 and a traditional striker scores one goal so that the team loses 3–1, he's happy. He'll think he's done his job and it's the others who haven't done theirs. For me, if I give the assist and we win 1–0, I'm very happy, much happier than if I score and we still lose 2–1, because for me, my goal doesn't count. I want *important* goals, like the equaliser against Leicester City.

I have regularly seen other strikers who don't have that attitude, and play for their own glory, their own success. Sometimes, young players with this approach played for Chelsea, and when they moved on to different teams, I would have a word with them. 'You know, the best way for you to receive is to give back. If you want your midfielder to give you the ball every time, sometimes you have to say, "This is for you," and give him the opportunity to score or to shine.'

If you don't create a good atmosphere in the team, nothing good can happen. Sometimes you have to act for the greater good.

The same goes for life outside football, and for me, the two are related. Football is a reflection of the way you live in society, of the way you are as a person. It's impossible to put football on one side and life on the other; to be one way on the pitch, and completely different in life. Football entails actions – running after a ball, kicking it to someone, and so on – and life is also about actions. Nobody is perfect, certainly not me, but I'm very aware of my shortcomings and of trying to improve. I try to be the best I can, and to act, wherever possible, for the greater good.

The morning of the Crystal Palace game arrived. The routine with home games is always the same. We stay the previous evening at a hotel in Chelsea Harbour, about five minutes from the ground. Earlier that day, having already been given the detailed information regarding our opponents, we have had a team meeting at the training ground during which we have had the ten-minute video and instructions summarising everything about our opponents. This means that when we get to the hotel, everything has been said and there is nothing more to do before the game. We are basically there to relax. The next morning, there is a quick meeting about our set pieces, such as corners, how we should defend, who is marking whom, and that's it. All done.

Crystal Palace have some very good players, and although we tried to tell ourselves it was like any other league game and we just needed three points – rather than thinking 'three points for the title' – we were tired after the long season and were taken a bit by surprise when they started very well. They had nothing to lose because their position in the table was safe, so I started thinking it was going to be tougher than we'd expected.

We were awarded a penalty just before half-time and, to be honest, it came at a good point. When I saw that Eden Hazard was going to take it, though, I was concerned because he'd not trained for two days after getting a big kick on the leg during the Leicester game, and from the start he'd been telling me that he wasn't feeling too good on the pitch. So I was a bit worried that he would miss it. He sent his shot down the middle – which is what often happens when a player doesn't know where else to put the ball – and the keeper saved it. I had that split-second heart-stopping moment when I thought, 'Oh no, he's missed,' before, luckily, the ball bounced off their keeper and straight back to Eden, who then nodded it safely into the back of the net.

Normally, Eden is a safe penalty-taker. He stays cool and rarely fails to score, so it was unlike him to face such a situation. At the start of the season, we decide who is going to be our first, second or third penalty-taker, and he is always on that list. When I take a penalty, I always have a little 5 per cent element of stress, which I accept, because it's all part of my job. Maybe Eden feels it, too, but it doesn't show.

For me, when I take a penalty, I often decide at the last minute where I'm going to kick the ball. The ones I've missed have usually been because I've chosen the side in advance and the keeper has anticipated correctly, probably because he has been able to read my body language. Keepers watch videos of possible penalty-takers to try to detect their body language, so they know how to react if they see, for example, a player's left arm go up, or the upper body move slightly one way rather than the other. The kickers therefore have to try to keep one step ahead of them. In just a couple of cases have I shot badly or missed the target completely – such as the penalty with Ivory Coast in the 2012 Africa Cup of Nations final – and that, I have to accept, sometimes just happens. That one was disappointing but I don't let it affect me, and I don't think about it the next time I take a penalty.

In fact, I try to do three things when I take a penalty: focus on my body during my run, making sure that I stay strong when I kick the ball; watch the ball; and at the same time, have in my peripheral vision a perception of the goal and of the goalkeeper. That strategy was explained to me when I was at Guingamp, and was already 23, 24 years old, although actually I had already been doing it instinctively to some extent. But penalty-taking is something that all players can train for and improve, at all stages of their career.

Maybe the header-into-bin game earlier in the week had helped Eden after all! In any case, he was very relieved when he managed to score off the rebound, and he ran down the pitch, grinning away, wiping his forehead with his hand in a clear gesture of relief. He wasn't the only one who felt like doing that!

The second half was an exercise in keeping calm. We were focused on not dropping the points rather than on taking the lead and attacking. We knew that Crystal Palace were certainly capable of scoring, so we were definitely nervous during the second forty-five minutes.

When the final whistle went, we erupted into celebrations.

It was our first league title since 2010. JT was on his knees, because for him, and for other players who had been there since then, five years is a long time to go without a title. Even the owner, who is usually restrained in his reactions, was so happy that he punched the air in celebration.

For me, it was a case of goal achieved! When I re-signed, I said that I had come back to win the league, and that's exactly what I had done, so it was a great feeling. Funnily enough, this season, I had won exactly the same trophies as I had won in my first season for the club all the way back in 2004–05, so maybe it was all meant to be – as so often in life, I am convinced.

This year, though, we had won the league in an incredible way. We had led the Premier League from day one, and spent a record-breaking 274 days at the top of the table. No other club has done that. But we had a fantastic team, including a few older players, such as JT, Petr and me, who brought a lot of experience, and newer, younger players, such as Cesc Fàbregas, Eden Hazard and Diego Costa, who had a lot of talent and experience as well.

Eden made the best move of his career when he came to Chelsea. He now has a winning mentality, because at Chelsea, that is what everyone has. Then, once you have developed the habit of winning, and the team is good, you know how to keep doing it. I learned how to win a trophy when I came to Chelsea, and I now know how a team can be motivated, and how there are certain moments in a season when a manager and certain key players have to lift the team and bring a positive atmosphere. I did a lot of that during the season – motivating the players, trying to have an influence in the dressing room. I know about scoring the important goals, the ones that bring

21st May 2008, Champions League final against Manchester United in Moscow. A nightmare evening – as I always say it wasn't meant to be.

My partner in crime! This man always has my back.

25th November 2009, Champions League game v Porto, with close friend, Nicolas Anelka, who scored.

9th May 2010, scoring Chelsea's fifth goal in the 8–0 win against Wigan that secured our Premier League title.

May 2010, with JT, Frank and Petr, on our victory parade through the streets of south west London, showing off our Premier League and FA Cup trophies.

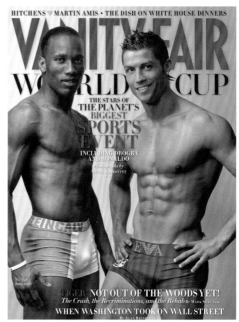

May 2010, with my second Golden Boot award, the first was in 2007.

It's always a pleasure to be featured on the cover of magazines, especially as in the case of *Vanity Fair*, the photographer was Annie Leibovitz.

February 2012, Africa Cup of Nations. Back row, l-r: Kolo Touré, Gervinho, Sol Bamba, Yaya Touré, Salomon Kalou. Front row, l-r: Boubacar Barry, Siaka Tiene, Didier Zokora, me, Jean-Jacques Gosso, Cheik Tiote. One of the best Ivory Coast teams I played for. We lost the tournament without conceding a goal.

19th May 2012, Champions League final, Munich, v Bayern Munich. I pray during the penalty shoot-out. With me, from l-r: Gary Cahill, Ashley Cole, Fernando Torres, Florent Malouda, John Obi Mikel.

With my brothers after the final in Munich. Yes, we finally did it!!

20th May 2012. Celebrating in the pool until the early hours – The night we owned Munich.

Proud of my family, proud of winning the Champions League. I feel very lucky.

Happy days at training session in Shanghai, October 2012.

August 2013, holding the Turkish Super Cup with Wesley Sneijder, after scoring a 99th minute winner against Fenerbahce.

24th May 2015, leading Chelsea out as captain with Isaac, Iman and Keyran, for my last ever match. Petr Cech and John Terry, behind me, were the only others still there who were with me when I joined Chelsea in 2004.

May 2012, surrounded by the silverware I have won in my time with Chelsea. L-r: FA Cup, Football League Cup, Champions League trophy, FA Community Shield, and Premier League cup.

Happy with my first season in Montreal scoring 12 goals in 14 games.

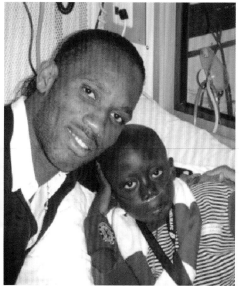

Above left: With my young friend Nobel in 2009. He inspired me to create the Didier Drogba Foundation.

Above right: March 2012, speaking at one of my Foundation's fundraising dinners in London.

Middle: One of the most emotional moments of the foundation's work: organising a Christmas party for kids.

Right: The most beautiful and important goal of my career: the clinic in Abidjan.

One of the proudest moments of my life: meeting Nelson Mandela in 2009.

With my beautiful wife, Lalla, at a fundraising dinner.

you the points and win you the trophies, and wherever I play, I always try to pass on that knowledge and experience. Eden has now learned that, and this will make him a vital player for Chelsea.

Diego, of course, was already a great player before he came to Chelsea – strong, physical and technically very good. But those of us who know the English league well were able to facilitate things for him a little by providing information about it, and about certain defenders. I could tell him, for example, how these individual players moved, tackled, played, and even if it only sometimes gave him an advantage and made the difference between scoring and not scoring, it was all helping him to adjust to English football. He certainly adjusted very fast and, considering he was injured for part of it, this allowed him to have a really good first season.

Winning that title felt fantastic not only for the team but for all our amazing fans. Although the actual Premier League trophy was not going to be presented until our last game three weeks later, we stayed out on the pitch for a long time that afternoon because we wanted to share our happiness with them. I love the understanding we have with them, the passion we all share for this club. It had been a long wait for them as well, so they were as happy as we were, I think.

Eventually, we went back to the dressing room to celebrate, which involved having fun with everyone, spraying champagne over a lot of people, singing very loudly (and not always very well) and dancing a lot. I believe in hard work, but I also believe in having fun when it's the right time to do it. And this was definitely the right time.

This celebration went on for a long time. We knew the

biggest one would come after our final game, so eventually I went home later that afternoon to enjoy some precious time with my family. At home I could fully relax for the first time in many weeks, knowing there was nothing left to prepare for, and nothing left to prove. In the evening, I went back up to London with a few players, including JT, to have more fun and more enjoyment of our victory. The last time we had won the trophy, in 2010, it had gone down to the final day of the season. This time, I won't say it felt easy, but it was definitely less intense. We had won it in a way that was rare, and that we were unlikely to repeat many more times. We were very aware of our achievement and we made sure we celebrated in a suitable manner!

17

AN ELEPHANT IN THE ROOM

I HAD two passports, one French and one Ivorian. I grew up in France and could have represented either country, at national level. Several factors influenced my choice. The first was that, having never been part of their youth system because I had never been in one place for long enough, I had never been selected for junior French teams at any age level. Secondly, Thierry Henry, David Trézéguet and Nicolas Anelka, among others, were already well-established members of the national team, and in my early twenties, I was not the player I later became, so I had no chance of being considered. Finally, my uncle had played for the Ivorian national team, and although I had grown up a long way from my country of birth, I always felt an undeniable pull, and I really wanted to continue the family tradition and pull on the jersey for 'The Elephants', as our team is nicknamed. Even when I was young, I used to get goosebumps whenever I heard our national anthem. For me, my link to my country ran very deep, even though, by the time I was finally called up, I had not lived there for many years.

The phone call asking me to join the team at a meeting near Roissy airport, on the outskirts of Paris, came in August 2002. I was 24, and had just started my first full season at Guingamp. That was my first chance to meet my future team-mates and I was intimidated by some of the established players, some of whom had won big European competitions with clubs such as Inter Milan, Marseille and Feyenoord. And there was me, in my corner, just starting in a small club in Brittany. We had a new manager, though, Robert Nouzaret, a Frenchman who had spotted me when I had been at Le Mans and he had been the manager of Bastia, the Corsican Ligue 1 club. We also had a new Federation president, Jacques Anouma, who wanted to shake things up a bit, instil a bit of order and discipline into the team, and who had big ambitions for us. He felt that, with the players at his disposal, we should be aiming to qualify for the 2004 Africa Cup of Nations as well as, for the first time in our history, the 2006 World Cup. He was right. There was no reason why we should not do a lot better than we had done up until then, and it was exciting to feel part of a new team and one that wanted to go places.

Two weeks after that meeting, Jacques Santini, the manager of the French national team, called my agent – was Didier still free to play for France? To get that call was incredible and not something I had been expecting. 'Sorry, you're too late,' my agent informed him. That said, I'm glad the timing worked out that way, because it was the right decision I made, and I would not have changed it for the world.

Our first game, a qualifier against South Africa for the 2004

Africa Cup of Nations, was played in early September 2002 in Abidjan, the capital. That was our last chance to qualify, and sadly it ended in a 0–0 draw. Although it was disappointing, we knew we had a good new team coming through and that our results would start to improve. The result is therefore not what I remember about that day. Instead, what is seared in my memory for ever is the excitement of walking out into the cauldron of heat that was our national stadium, the Stade Félix Houphouët-Boigny. The atmosphere was extraordinary and bore no resemblance to anything I had ever experienced. It felt like the spectators had been taking part in a show all day. From about ten o'clock that morning, the stadium had been full to bursting. Popular artists and musicians had been performing, and everyone had been joining in. Music, dancing, drinking and fun had therefore been going on for several hours by the time we stepped onto the pitch halfway through the afternoon. We could feel a carnival atmosphere all around us and that definitely added to the excitement of playing for our country. I soon learned that this pre-match atmosphere was the norm for every game!

What also hit me that afternoon was the stifling heat. I will never forget that, either. I felt as if I had walked into a sauna. By the end of the warm-up, with no shade to shelter in and the temperature up around 40°C and very humid, I felt like I was suffocating and half dead. I could feel the heat from the ground sizzling through my boots, overheating my feet. How on earth was I going to be able to run for ninety minutes?

When the national anthem was played, the entire stadium sang it, all together, proudly and loudly, and I felt the hairs stand up on the back of my neck. I can still feel the emotions of that moment whenever I think back to that day. In one fell swoop it reconnected me to the country I had left behind all those years ago and to which I had always felt so drawn.

Ten days later, civil war broke out in Ivory Coast. I thought my return to my country would be simple, but suddenly everything became complicated. For those of us who lived abroad, watching the war from thousands of miles away was difficult. At least I knew that family members in Ivory Coast were not in any physical danger, but it was still shocking to see the country so divided.

Fighting continued into January 2003 when an unstable ceasefire was signed, but for the next couple of years, there were regular outbreaks of fighting between rebel and government forces, despite the presence of French and UN peace-keeping troops.

During that time, as we began our campaigns to qualify for the 2006 Africa Cup of Nations and the 2006 World Cup, we continued to rebuild our national team, and I was scoring in almost every game – not just one goal, but often two or even three. My presence in the team was becoming more important, not just as a player but also as someone who was prepared to speak up on behalf of others. My experience at Marseille and, from 2004, at Chelsea, taught me how to respect the older, senior players, but also how to speak up whenever necessary. In 2005, when it was time to change the captaincy, I was asked to take on the role. For me, that was a fantastic honour and a challenge that I was really happy to accept.

In September 2005, the country was again on the brink of another full-blown civil war. At the same time, people were uniting behind our team, hoping we would qualify our country for the World Cup in 2006, something we had never achieved before. We were in a good position by September 2005, leading our group, but we badly needed at least a draw against Cameroon to keep our chances alive. A win would have given us automatic qualification and was what everyone was fervently hoping for.

Cameroon were, and are, our main rivals in Africa. Whenever the two countries play, that sense of rivalry and importance means the games have extra tension. They are nicknamed 'The Lions', we are 'The Elephants'.

The game on 4 September 2005 was a huge one for both teams. I could think of little else in the weeks leading up to it, as pressure built on the entire team to deliver the wished-for result. The problem in Africa is that 'a result' does not mean a draw; it means a 3–0 or 4–0 win, something the people can really celebrate. Everyone, from the media to the public and even the management, was talking of nothing else. No one would entertain the idea of anything other than a clear-cut win. I had this Chelsea mentality where, OK, a win would be ideal, but a point is a point, and you still maintain your lead. But for a country that was in such a bad state, I knew that a win would help to provide a unifying moment of national joy. So there was a lot of pressure on us in this game.

I was really moved when Roman Abramovich decided to come with José Mourinho to watch the game. They flew out on the former's private jet and, as he had never before set foot on the African continent, I think he found the whole experience unforgettable! The fact that they had taken the trouble and time to attend meant so much to me, because it showed how much they valued their relationship with me, and gave me another reason for wanting the victory really badly.

In the event, I played as if I was in another zone. It remains one of my best international performances. It's just a shame that the result did not go the right way.

The opposition scored the first goal, but I equalised. Then, just before the end of the first half, they went ahead again. I refused to give up because I was so determined to qualify. In the dressing room, I was urging all the team on. 'We're going to come back. We're going to score, and then we have to keep the game at 2–2. Because one point is good, it's enough.'

Sure enough, ten minutes into the second half, we got a free kick and I took one of the best free kicks of my career to equalise again – 2–2. 'We have to stay calm, keep the ball, keep possession,' I insisted. Instead, the team kept attacking and attacking. It made for a dramatic game and spectators fainted as the team diced with danger. Ambulances took them to hospital. And then, in the last minute, we gave away a foul. Free kick. Goal – 3–2 win for them. Everyone was absolutely devastated, the team and all the supporters. This was the first home defeat for the national team in the last ten years. It took a long time for us to leave the stadium.

That result meant that qualification hinged on the last round of games a month later. We were due to play Sudan, away, and we had to win – which we expected to. But Cameroon were due to play Egypt, in Cairo, on the same day and at exactly the same time, and if they won, they would finish ahead of us in the table and qualify for the World Cup.

Normally, Cameroon would have expected to beat Egypt,

but the day before the game, I got a call from Mido, the Egyptian striker with whom I had played at Marseille.

'My brother, win your game,' he said, 'because Egypt always creates problems for Cameroon.'

'Yeah, yeah,' I replied. I was really down, because the result of the group was out of our hands. 'We're going to beat Sudan, but I'm not sure Cameroon will lose or draw.'

'No, it's OK, we'll take care of them,' he continued, staying positive.

For us, the game was not a difficult one and we soon went ahead. Our bench was in permanent phone contact with one of our physios, who had had to go back to France because he'd lost his passport. He was able to relay all developments in the other game because it was on television.

Late in the second half, we were leading 3–1 (which ended up being the final score), while the other game stood at 1–1, after Egypt equalised in the eightieth minute. I was so tense by then that my legs refused to carry me. I couldn't run. I was rooted to the spot.

'Run, run!' shouted the coaches from the dugout.

'What's the score? What's the score?'

'Forget it, it's OK, just keep running!'

'I can't, I'm drained, just tell me the score!'

'No, no, just play!'

But I was so convinced we were not now going to qualify for the World Cup because of what was happening in Cairo that I couldn't move or do a thing.

Finally, the whistle went. Our game was over. Surprisingly, theirs still had a couple of minutes left to go until the ninety minutes were up, followed by time added-on. Strange, given that we had kicked off at the same time. But this is Africa, and I'm not sure what happened in their second half to delay things so much. When the additional time was flashed up, we were told via the phone that the referee had given five extra minutes. Five! Their score at this stage remained 1–1 and although there were still those additional minutes left to play, all our team started leaping about as if we'd already qualified. I was the opposite. 'No, no, no, wait. It's not finished!' Adrenaline was suddenly coursing through me, and my heart was beating so fast it felt as if it would leap out of my body. We were all huddled around this phone, speaking to our physio, wanting second-by-second commentary on what was happening in Cairo.

I just knew. I had this premonition – they're going to give a penalty, Cameroon are going to get a penalty. The next thing I knew, the referee had given a penalty!

When I look at replays, it was never a penalty in my opinion – at best, it was a very soft one. Maybe the pressure of the occasion and the crowd got to the referee and influenced his decision. In any event, here we were, the other game was in the ninety-fifth minute, seconds from the end, and we were at the mercy of one kick – one kick that would decide our fate.

I felt sick. My team-mates were in shock. We all linked arms in a circle, as if to support our slender hope that we might still get through. We were so emotional. 'Everyone, let's pray! Didier, come on, let's pray,' urged Ahmed Ouattara, a former player who was working with the team at that time. Several of us, myself included, immediately got down on our knees, fervently sending prayers to the heavens, in a desperate bid to be heard. Those few seconds while we waited for the outcome of the penalty were excruciating and seemed to drag on for ever. Then, out of nowhere, we heard shouting down the phone. It took a few seconds for the news from Cairo, via Paris, to sink in – the penalty had hit the post! It had missed! We were through!

Kolo Touré and I still didn't want to believe. 'Ssshhh!' we begged, trying to calm things down. Some were already leaping around, while others continued to pray. 'It's not finished, it's not finished.' Fortunately, within seconds, it really was all over. Then I gave in completely to my elation and started running around the pitch like a madman, hugging everyone, especially our new manager, Henri Michel, who had made our dream come true. I was in total disbelief and was soon crying tears of both joy and relief, along with most of my team-mates. We got down on our knees and thanked God, before eventually, after lengthy on-pitch celebrations, carrying Henri Michel off the pitch in triumph.

Back in the dressing room, the celebrations continued. It was packed with people who had all come to congratulate us for what we had achieved, our first-ever World Cup qualification. This was an historic moment of united joy at a time of great national difficulty.

Suddenly, among the cheering and happiness, I noticed that we were being filmed by the Ivory Coast national television, Radio Télévision Ivoirienne. 'Give me the mike,' I asked the cameraman, who duly handed one over. We had always said that if we managed to qualify, it would be for the people, a way to ask them to bring peace back to Ivory Coast, and here was our opportunity.

Spontaneously, with no forethought or prepared speech, I asked all my team-mates to gather round me. 'Ssshhh, guys, listen, listen,' I asked. The dressing room fell completely silent. You could have heard a pin drop and everyone looked at me as I issued an impassioned plea to my fellow countrymen.

'My fellow Ivorians, from the north and from the south, from the centre and from the west, we have proved to you today that the Ivory Coast can cohabit and can play together for the same objective: to qualify for the World Cup. We had promised you that this would unite the population. We ask you now,' I continued, gesturing for everyone around me to get down on their knees, 'we ask you now: the only country in Africa that has all these riches *cannot* sink into a war in this way. Please, lay down your arms. Organise elections. And everything will turn out for the best!'

I had no idea if my plea would be heard, either that day, or in the future. I had no idea how many people would see or hear my words, or if any of them would listen. All I knew was that it had come from deep within my heart and was completely instinctive. It came from the love I had for my country and my sorrow at the state it was in.

The next day, we flew back to Abidjan. On the plane, I was so drained by the previous twenty-four hours that I sat there in a state of profound emotion, thinking of everything that had happened to me over the last five years and remembering how far I had come since I had left my country as a five-year-old boy. I thought about my family, the love I had for them, and in particular I thought of my father's mother, my beloved grandmother Zehe, who had sadly passed away. I ached at the thought that she was not alive to share this moment with me and to be proud of me. I had worked so hard to get where I was. During the flight I was really affected by all these thoughts, swirling around my head, and I began to cry.

By the time we landed at Abidjan, the crowds waiting for us were huge and the scenes of celebration were crazy. My parents were among the first to hug me and welcome me, and my reunion with them was very emotional, even though I had seen them just a few days before. I could tell they were really proud of me, not so much because of our qualification – that was almost secondary – but for the message I had sent out for peace. I later found out that my plea was played every single day on the main television and radio news bulletins for weeks afterwards. I had never expected to have this kind of impact, but obviously, by the end, it had become a loud and powerful message.

On the way into town, the scenes were as mad as at the airport. This was more craziness than I had ever seen. There were people as far as the eye could see, perched on buildings, sitting in trees, waiting for hours in the searing heat, waving flags, blaring horns, cheering and crying with joy, their arms outstretched towards our open-topped bus as it inched its way along the streets to the president's residence. Complete madness. Our country had qualified for the World Cup, and it seemed that, at least for the time being, bitterness between people was being suspended. There was still a long way to go until real peace was achieved, but it was a start.

18

WORLD CUPS AND OTHER CHALLENGES

WHAT I wanted most was to win something with our team. With players such as Kolo and Yaya Touré, Emmanuel Eboué and Arouna Koné, we had a great team, so we went to the 2006 Africa Cup of Nations in January full of confidence that we could do well. Our group included the hosts, Egypt, as well as Morocco and Libya, and after two wins from three games, we were able to progress to the quarter-finals. There, we were drawn to meet Cameroon, our long-standing rivals and among the strongest teams in the competition, along with Egypt and us.

The game, in Cairo, was high in drama. It was 0–0 at full time, and we opened the scoring in the second minute of extra time, but hopes that this goal would see us through to the next round were dashed when Cameroon pulled one back three minutes later. At the final whistle, the score was 1–1, which meant that a penalty shoot-out would decide the outcome. This was no ordinary shoot-out, though. It became one of the longest in the history of international competitions. At 11–11, all the team, goalkeepers included, had successfully scored a penalty. Since we were the first penalty-takers, it fell to Barcelona's Samuel Eto'o and I to start off the second round of shooting.

The pressure was enormous, and it was getting to everyone, the managers included. It was difficult to stay calm and focused when all I could think about was my family, back in Ivory Coast. I knew that everyone back there – family, friends, acquaintances, people I didn't even know – would be watching. I did not want to mess it up, and as the captain I felt an added huge responsibility not to let everyone down. Should I go for the same side as I had before? Should I try something new? Unfortunately for Samuel, he obviously decided on the latter and sent his penalty sky high over the bar. My turn. I took my time and tried to stay composed. I looked down, looked at the opposition keeper one last time, ran up and sent the ball thundering safely into the opposite corner of the net from my first shot, straight past the keeper's outstretched arms. A bit close for comfort – but we were through to the semis! Psychologically, it gave us the upper hand against Cameroon for a while. Before that, we'd always felt a bit like the underdogs. They were full of experienced internationals, and they had won the competition before. But that day, everything changed for us and it gave us a lot of confidence.

In the next round we got past Nigeria – I scored the only goal – and suddenly we were into our second-ever international competition final, against the hosts, Egypt. We felt confident, but looking back, I realise we were emotionally and physically tired. The day got off to a bad start when it took our bus an hour and a half to reach the stadium as a result of chaos on the roads. Forty-five of those minutes were spent just yards from the stadium when we were held up by a group of home fans and the police did not seem able or willing to do anything about it. A mystery, but maybe they felt that it was such a big occasion that they might just try to give the home team a helping hand by not coming to the rescue of the opposition. In any event, by the time we got into the changing room, we were stressed and frustrated and our routine had been disrupted because we were later than expected.

During the game, I felt drained, lacking in energy, and for me it was a really difficult experience. We had some chances but no one scored. Egypt even missed a penalty at one stage.

So it went to a shoot-out. As the captain, I decided to go first and missed. I don't usually miss, but if I do, I have to accept that it's one of those things. It happens in life. When you take a risk, put yourself in the firing line, sometimes things don't work out. That's part of the deal, but you have to tell yourself that at least you had the courage to step up, so you should have no regrets. All the same, it could not have been a worse start. Their first penalty had already hit the spot, as did their next. Kolo Touré secured us our first point. Then they missed – 2–1 to them. If we scored on our next, we would be back to level pegging. We had hope. Unfortunately, Arouna Koné missed, and although Emmanuel Eboué gave us another point, Egypt scored two more, giving them a winning 4–2 final score.

It was a very painful loss for me, not so much because I had missed my penalty but because we had been so close – we had even beaten Egypt in our qualifying group – and we'd had so much hope that we would succeed.

The World Cup, in Germany, was a very different affair. I had dreamed of this moment for years, often thinking it was just that – a dream – and would never be a reality. I would never have dared to think of an even more extraordinary scenario – the one where I scored our country's first-ever World Cup goal against Argentina, the team in which my hero, Maradona, had played. Yet that's what happened in our first game, and although we lost it, for me it was a dream-like start to the tournament.

We were in a really tough group, including the Netherlands and Serbia as well as Argentina. Although we beat Serbia in our final game, we lost to the Dutch in our second one, so our tournament was over after two games. For us to have gone through to the knock-out stages was an achievement and it was always going to be tough but we felt we'd had a chance all the same.

The other big disappointment for me in Germany was that, after all my optimism for a good tournament because of the strength of our team, there were some difficulties within that same team that I believe affected how we played. I was the captain and had developed a profile, both at club and inter-national level. I had also become a bit of an icon in my country, largely as a result of speaking out the previous year against the political unrest there. All this meant that, whenever we went anywhere as a team, as soon as fans saw me, they would crowd around, wanting autographs or pictures of me. I never asked for this, but it didn't matter. It wasn't an easy situation for the team, and I can now see that.

I know I made mistakes during that time – who doesn't? But I will always say, hand on heart, that although I maybe mishandled certain situations, I did it with the best of intentions. In putting myself forward as a representative of the team, in speaking up, I was doing it to raise the profile of Ivory Coast, and of the great football we played. Unfortunately, I think it sometimes affected team spirit and had a knock-on effect on some of our games and therefore on our results.

Meanwhile, political tensions still existed within the country, and it remained divided in two.

It was against this background that, in early March 2007, I flew to Accra in Ghana for the ceremony to name the 2006 African Player of the Year. I had flown in accompanied by my team-mate, Michael Essien, who was also in contention for Ghana. That day was a really proud one because my mother was there to greet me backstage, and she helped to dress me in the traditional multi-coloured robes from Ivory Coast! And when my name was read out (I didn't know the result in advance), I felt so honoured and moved. I was the first Ivorian footballer to win this prestigious title. Past recipients include George Weah and Samuel Eto'o. Michael Essien was in third place, so I was in amazing company and we were all proud to represent a positive image of Africa around the world.

On 4 March, a couple of days after the ceremony, a welcome ceasefire was pronounced between the government and the rebel *Forces Nouvelles* in the north, bringing some hope of peace in the future.

Our next international game was an Africa Cup of Nations qualifier, away to Madagascar, on 24 March. On the flight back, following our 3–0 victory, I suddenly had a thought. Suppose, now that our country is no longer in a civil war, I ask the president if I could go and present my African Player of the

Year trophy in Bouaké, the rebels' stronghold, a town that no one from the southern part of the country would ever have thought of going to just a few weeks before. Then, if that was possible, why shouldn't we try to hold the return leg against Madagascar there as well? It was scheduled for 3 June, which might give the powers-that-be the time to arrange things. I was due to be received by Laurent Gbagbo at his presidential palace a couple of days later to show him the trophy, so that would be an ideal opportunity to ask.

On the flight, I asked the president of our FA, Jacques Anouma, what he thought of my crazy idea. He was actually very encouraging, so two days later, having presented my trophy to the president and a large gathering, I found myself nervously asking if my two requests might be granted.

No sooner said than done. He liked the idea, and said that I would be given safe passage there and back. Sure enough, just two days later, on 28 March, I travelled into the rebel heartland of Bouaké and I was escorted in an open-topped car by soldiers all the way along the road that led me to where I met the leader of the *Forces Nouvelles*, Guillaume Soro (who, the following month, was appointed prime minister, in a further gesture of peace).

Along the road, as I showed off this trophy that had now acquired such a big symbolic value – one of pride in our country and hope for the future – I felt strangely calm and not threatened, either by the presence of the soldiers, or by the fact that I was putting myself in possible danger just by being in that part of the country. On the contrary, the sight of thousands of men and women lining the streets, welcoming me, cheering me on, many in tears, had a huge impact on me. One elderly lady ran alongside the car for the entire journey. Others were literally throwing themselves on the bonnet, jumping in front of the car, trying to get close to me. The heat was crushing, yet all these people were determined to be there, to welcome me to their part of the country, in a longing gesture of reconciliation. Here was I, just a footballer, one from humble origins. I witnessed scenes of absolute madness and fervour, which stunned me and left me feeling very emotional.

The welcome I received from the people that day showed me that they were willing to set aside divisions, and that was a really strong sign of hope. It made people believe that we could build on that and work towards rebuilding a unified country.

On 3 June, as planned, we played our return tie against Madagascar in Bouaké.

'Why are we going there? Could it be dangerous?' some players worried beforehand.

'Guys, we have to go,' I replied. 'I went there, I saw them, they love football, they love you, they love the team, and they have always supported us, even when we were losing. So we have to go.'

The scenes before, during and after the game were as wild as those in March. The heat and humidity were unbearable, but still the queue of people trying to get into the stadium snaked round for miles. Once the actual game got under way, the cheering and the noise during our 5–0 win was incredible, and for me to score the final goal was particularly moving and perfect. It represented everything I had tried to do in bringing this game here; it showed that, despite everything that had happened, we were still one country, united behind one team.

The game itself became a symbol of an attempt to heal divisions. I saw soldiers from the army watching alongside soldiers from the rebel forces. I heard, afterwards, that people who had been forced to leave their homes and belongings and flee south when the civil war had broken out, had decided that they could now return. People were heard to say, 'If Didier has been to Bouaké, it means it's safe to return.' It was amazing to realise how much impact we as footballers could have.

Three days after the game, I visited, for the first time in about fifteen years, the two villages in the west of the country where my parents had originally come from. I don't speak the dialect they speak, so it was a bit difficult to communicate, but my parents were there, as well as relatives from my extended family, including my beloved maternal grandmother, Hélène, a tiny, beautiful, dignified lady, whose love and wisdom were visible in the way she carried herself and looked at me. I loved going back to the place where my parents had been born. It helped me to understand them better, their way of thinking and what they had wanted out of life.

The sights and smells of this scorchingly hot land hit me at once. The vast beauty of the countryside, the kindness of the people, everything made me fall in love even more with my country. The welcome I received was as crazy as everywhere else I had been that week – the car journey that took five times longer than normal because of the sea of people lining the roads, people crying tears of happiness, people reaching out for me, screaming, waving, their faces full of love. For me, this trip allowed me to rediscover my country at a deeper level and to reconnect to my roots even more strongly. I had never lost those ties, but that week strengthened them even more, and for ever. I was proud of who I was, an Ivorian at heart. I was proud of who I had become. But I was most proud of being able to give so much joy – and so much hope – to so many people.

19

BRUISING ENCOUNTERS

THE 2010 World Cup in South Africa was the first time the tournament had been held on the African continent, and for The Elephants, it was a fantastic, exciting prospect that we were really looking forward to. In addition, the 2009–10 season had finished really well for me – I'd had my best-ever season with Chelsea, during which we had won the double for the first time, and I had been chosen 2009 African Player of the Year and won the Premier League's Golden Boot, both for the second time. I had even featured on the cover of *Vanity Fair*'s June 2010 issue, which included a special feature on the World Cup. I was told at the time that the only other African who had featured on an American *Vanity Fair* cover was Nelson Mandela, so I was very aware I was in esteemed company. So to say I was up for the World Cup is an understatement. I wanted it to be something special.

In early June, the team went to Switzerland for some altitude training and to play a few friendlies before the start of the tournament. All was going perfectly. Then, in one game, against Japan, a few minutes after I had scored early in the first half, I was trying to control a ball, running at full speed, when, out of the corner of my eye, I spotted their central defender (my shot had deflected off him to open the score) flying towards me and towards a sure-fire bruising encounter. It's what they call 'clattering into someone'. I had a split second in which I instinctively raised my right forearm in an attempt to protect my chest. In retrospect, that was just as well. If he'd actually hit my chest, I hate to think what sort of damage he would have done. It was just a really clumsy tackle.

As soon as the clash occurred, I knew I was badly hurt because my forearm was in agony. Back in the dressing room, I was in tears of pain and sadness. With our first game just eleven days away, I was convinced my long-held dream of playing in an African World Cup was well and truly over.

News of the injury spread like wildfire. Straight after the game, many people contacted me to try to help. Samuel Eto'o, my Cameroonian friend and fellow striker, called and then immediately got in touch with a good surgeon he knew to see what he could do.

In the end, I was seen the next morning by a top surgeon in Berne, not too far from where we were staying. He examined the X-rays and scans – I had a bad break up towards the elbow – and said, yes, he could put a plate in the bone but I would have to wait two to three months before I could play again.

'Hold on, hold on!' I said, shaking my head in disbelief at the news. 'Let me explain something. You see that date, there, ten days away,' I said, pointing at a calendar on his desk. 'That's the World Cup; and that's the day of a game I have to play in.

I *have* to play! Is it possible?' There was a big sigh from the surgeon.

'Well,' he replied slowly, 'I've never done that before.'

'I'm not saying that,' I interrupted. 'What I'm saying is, is it *possible* to be ready, even fifty per cent possible?'

'You *can* play, yes, but with protection. And if you get hit, it's finished. You'll be out for eight, nine months or more.'

'OK, let's do it!'

Later that day, he did the surgery. He put an eight-inch metal plate along the bone, held in place by eight long metal screws, and I was fitted out with a carbon-fibre protective cast. That was quite a lot of metal in my arm – disappointingly, I never managed to set off alarms in airports – and I kept it in for five whole years, until it was finally removed in the summer of 2015. I have kept all that metal as a souvenir – a funny reminder of a not-very-funny time.

Back at the team hotel a day or two later, my phone rang.

'My son,' said a familiar voice at the other end of the line – Nelson Mandela! 'This is our World Cup,' he said, with that slow, South African delivery. 'Even if you're not playing, you have to come! We are waiting for you here.'

'I'm coming, I'm coming, I'm on my way!' I replied at once.

I had actually met Nelson Mandela the previous year at the Confederation Cup. I had been to his house, met his family and chatted to him. There was a huge sense of wisdom and peace about him, as well as immense kindness. I definitely had this feeling that I was in the presence of a unique, special human being, and I was very aware that it was a great and rare privilege to be able to spend some time with him. Since then, I'd stayed in touch with one of his daughters, Zindzi.

She had my mobile number, and so it was Zindzi who had dialled before passing the phone to her father. It was such a shock to get that call in the middle of a hotel foyer in Switzerland.

Sepp Blatter also called me to encourage me to come – a bit ironic, given everything that has happened with him and FIFA since then. 'A World Cup in Africa without you is not a World Cup,' he was gracious enough to tell me. Although it was good that he'd bothered to call, it was obviously the call from Nelson Mandela that touched me immensely, and I will never ever forget it for as long as I live.

Every day for the next week, I was praying that my arm might recover enough to allow me to take part. I was still in pain when we arrived in South Africa, but I was determined to carry on, and took part in our first training session, with my cast on, in front of all our many fans. 'I have to make it,' I kept telling myself.

After a week, I started feeling my arm again – up until then it had been worryingly numb – and I thought it felt stronger. To test it out, I tried a couple of press-ups.

'Stop! Are you mad?!' said all the coaching staff.

'No, I'm OK, I'm OK,' I replied, doing a few more for good measure. That's when I knew I would be ready for that first game. I could compete and be relied on; I hadn't come there just to cheer on the team!

Our first game was against Portugal and I came on in the sixty-sixth minute. Unfortunately, I was not 100 per cent confident of what my arm could take, and I missed an important chance right at the end. I was almost falling as the ball came to me, and in that split second, when I realised that I might fall when kicking the ball, I was scared of landing on my arm. My brain focused on that possibility rather than on controlling the ball, and I missed the shot. In the end, we drew 0–0, which was a good result for us all the same.

Our second game was against Brazil, and I started, a sign that my arm was fast recovering and the manager had confidence that I could perform for the full ninety minutes. It was not a good game for us, and we were 3–0 down after an hour. However, the one positive note was that I did manage to score – the first African ever to score against Brazil. That was a proud moment for me, even though it did not change the final outcome of the game.

In our final game, we beat North Korea 3–0, with my good friend and Chelsea team-mate, Salomon Kalou, scoring our third goal. Salomon began playing for The Elephants in 2007 and was a very big factor in our success as a team, scoring over twenty goals during the years I played with him. Despite that win, we yet again left the tournament after the group stages, which was obviously disappointing, but not surprising. Portugal and Brazil were always going to be incredibly difficult to beat and I don't think my injury changed the outcome.

For me, the positive thing that came from that World Cup was having the opportunity to play the tournament on my continent – that will always remain special. Africa was hosting these finals for the first time ever and that made me really proud, just to know that the whole world was watching and seeing what can be achieved on this amazing continent. Plus being the first African to score against the number-one iconic footballing team in the world – that felt pretty cool, I have to admit.

The 2012 Africa Cup of Nations is the one tournament that I look back on with great sadness. That was the year when we managed to put all the egos to one side and play as a team. We really felt the team had reached a maturity and a unity that meant we were at our peak. We were not scared to play, not scared to concede, we were going to push and push, and we were going to play good, positive football. This was linked to the fact that the country was finally more united than it had been in a long time. Who knows, perhaps this too played into our collective mind-set.

In any event, we got through to the final, in Gabon's biggest city, Libreville, where we were due to play Zambia. Their French manager, Hervé Renard, had instilled discipline and good spirit in the team but I felt we had our best chance of winning this tournament since I had begun to play for The Elephants.

In the final, neither team managed to score. In the second half, we were awarded a penalty, which could obviously have been a defining moment. As the captain, I stepped up to take it. For some reason, at the last minute, I sent the ball upwards. I still can't explain it because I had *never* taken a penalty like this. What happened? Who knows? As a consequence, extra time came and went and the 0–0 deadlock was not broken.

Time for another penalty shoot-out. The weather was bad – it was raining quite heavily – and, as usual in penalty shoot-outs, the tension was almost unbearable. We were the first to go. No problem, 1–0. Zambia equalised. One by one, players from each team stepped up to the spot and sent their ball into the back of the net. All were good penalties; the keepers didn't get close. This time round, I decided to go fifth, because that's often a critical time in the shoot-out, and I wanted to be sure to score this time. On we went, 5–5, 6–6, 7–7. With every penalty taken, everyone's nerves became a little more shredded.

Our next player to step up was the hugely experienced Kolo Touré. He took a really long run-up – maybe it was a bit too long and gave the keeper just that little bit longer to guess from the body language – kicked . . . and his shot was saved by the opposition keeper. The pressure was now on the Zambians. Rainford Kalaba was next to go – and he sent his ball flying over the crossbar. That was a big, big reprieve for us. Now it was Arsenal's Gervinho's turn for us. He ran up – and did the same. His shot sailed high and wide. We were in complete shock, and could hardly bear to watch as their centre back, Stoppila Sunzu, placed his ball for what could be the winning penalty, took his run-up and this time sent the ball crashing into the back of the net – 8–7 to Zambia, and we were yet again the beaten finalists.

This defeat hurt us badly. We had lost despite not conceding a single goal throughout the entire tournament, including in the final. We were the best attacking team, and I had ended the tournament joint highest scorer. How was it possible, I kept saying, that this team, with the spirit and friendship that had finally developed, with the quality of players that we had, how could we, yet again, be going home empty-handed? We had done *everything* to win, we had been incredibly united, and it had all come to nothing. All my team-mates were in tears and I sobbed with them.

The only way I can explain the result, including my missed penalty, is that it just wasn't meant to be. We could have played on for another ten hours, and still their name would have ended up on the trophy. It was a little like when Zambia won in Gabon close by where a plane had crashed nineteen years earlier, killing eighteen members of their squad and their coach. Maybe some things are just meant to be.

I returned home to England, feeling sad, crushed really. During the journey, I had some difficult family news to deal with, which made me feel even more emotional. Late that night, with my wife away in Ivory Coast, and my children safely in bed, I was on the phone to a friend, talking about the difficult last few days. Suddenly, I got this really strange feeling, as if I was being engulfed, overwhelmed by my emotions. 'I'm sorry, you know what, I've got to go,' I blurted out to him. I just knew I had to get off the phone fast. As soon as I hung up, almost without warning, I started crying and crying. I couldn't stop. All my emotions were coming through, emotions about the final, about my family, about life in general. I would never have thought it possible to cry like this, because this sort of reaction had never happened to me before. I think it was the culmination of a difficult period in my life, not helped by what was happening at Chelsea at the time.

For the next month, I was up and down emotionally. One day, my morale was good, the next day I would feel preoccupied, anxious. I'm not the sort of player who can completely ignore what is happening in my life off the pitch, so my football was not unaffected. Luckily, after a month, we had a change of manager at Chelsea. After that, I went from strength to strength and ended the season in a fantastic way. Even so, that Africa Cup of Nations final remains a game that I will always look back on with a lot of sadness.

The 2014 World Cup was my last chance to play for my country. As it was held in Brazil, the heart of football, a country where the sport is a religion and where I had always hoped to play one day, I thought that after this might be a good time to bow out of international football.

In advance of the tournament, once the English season was finished, I went to Qatar to prepare myself physically. I worked so hard that I managed to lose 3kg, or 6½lb, of which half was fat. Given that I don't exactly have much to lose in the first place, this meant that by the time I went to Brazil, I was lean and feeling in peak condition.

When we arrived, we discovered that we had a lot of Brazilian fans, because we got a fantastic, warm welcome. Although I never did get to play in the Maracana stadium – one of my lifetime ambitions – I was very happy to be playing in a country with such a passion for football.

We were the first African team to qualify three times in a row for the finals of the World Cup, and we were really proud of that achievement. If we could get through to the knock-out stages for the first time, that would make it even better. We still had Yaya and Kolo Touré, and Gervinho, and we also had good young players coming through, so we were hopeful, especially as we were in a group with Japan, Colombia and Greece.

Unfortunately, our manager did not seem to have faith in me, his captain, and left me out of the starting eleven for the first game, against Japan. I was not happy, naturally, even less so since he did not tell me until a few hours before kick-off. As ever, for me, communication is so important between a manager and his team, and I still don't understand why he couldn't just have given me a bit more warning. I came off the bench when we were losing 1–0 and completely changed the game. We ended up 2–1 winners, which, of course, was the best answer I could have given.

In the second game, the same thing happened and I was left on the bench, this time until the sixtieth minute, and we ended up losing 2–1 to Colombia. Once again, I was not happy.

It all now rested on the final game, against Greece – we had to draw to secure our qualification. This time, I was among the starters. Greece scored first, just before half-time, but we equalised on a counter-attack in the seventy-fourth minute. We were now fifteen minutes from going through. Within minutes, I was taken off, and, I don't know why, but that's when I had this gut feeling that they would score. I'd had the same feeling against Barcelona in the 2009 Champions League semi-final.

Time ticked on until ninety minutes appeared on the clock. I'd had this situation so many times before. We went into time added on. I knew it in my bones, I just knew. Sure enough, in the ninety-third minute, almost the last minute of the game, the referee gave a penalty to Greece, convinced that Samaras had been clipped from behind in the box. It was a controversial decision and still not one I agree with.

I had to watch from the bench, powerless to do anything, and I could hardly control my emotions. So I got down on my knees at the side of the pitch and prayed – it was the only thing I could do. I prayed, and I hoped. Sadly, my prayers that day were not answered, because Samaras slotted his penalty in to give Greece the win and their first qualification for the knock-out stages of the tournament – and a crushing end to our own hopes of similar progress.

What was most disappointing about that World Cup for me was the way that I had felt side-lined from the beginning, even though I was still the captain. I think the manager, Frenchman Sabri Lamouchi, felt my presence was too much for him to handle. Maybe he felt threatened by me and, as a result, he didn't really want me there. The president of our FA didn't say anything to him about how I was treated, so I decided a month after the end of the tournament that, although the manager himself had resigned by then, I too would announce my retirement from international football. I was 36 and I had just re-signed with Chelsea, so I was in a good place with my football. I decided that it would be better for me, my long-term health and my family to focus on my club football. I knew that my Ivorian fans would understand my decision, so I don't regret making it when I did.

Just six months later, in February 2015, The Elephants at long last went on to win the Africa Cup of Nations. I obviously experienced a lot of mixed emotions on the night they won. For a start, the final between Ivory Coast and Ghana went to yet another penalty shoot-out, which this time finished 9–8 in our favour but was incredibly stressful to watch. I watched it at home with friends and family, and as soon as that winning penalty went in, I started leaping about and shouting, because I was genuinely happy and relieved for my team-mates who had waited so long to win this trophy. That said, I'm only human, and have to admit that I was a bit sad not to be able to share that trophy with them. I would have loved to be there anyway, celebrating with a team that I still felt a part of, even though I had left it six months before.

For me, though, this win was about much more than my

own personal victory, or lack of it. It was about a country. With Ivory Coast now in a period of stability, we could hope that The Elephants' win would keep the momentum going for peace and unity in our land, and show people that if they could all support one team, full of different players, they could surely put divisions aside to continue to work for a common goal of national unity.

20

MY FAMILY AND OTHER PEOPLE

I HAVE not talked very much about my family – and my wife in particular – but without them I would not be the man I am and without their love and support I would never have been able to achieve what I have achieved. However, we like to keep our family life private, especially when it comes to our children. We don't do photoshoots or give interviews at home. Nonetheless, I could not tell the story of my life without including them as they are the most important part of it.

The moment I saw my future wife, Lalla Diakité, it was like a thunderbolt had hit me – *le coup de foudre*, as they say in French. I first saw her in 1995, when I was 17. I was hanging out at my Uncle Michel's shop in Vannes. After he retired from football, he opened a grocery store, and I liked to visit him during school holidays, when I had time off from football back in Levallois. I remember I had been helping him out at the shop, and was tired that day, so I was having a lie-down on his sofa in the room at the back of the shop. My cousin, Viviane, was there, too. She was the daughter of one of my aunts, who was living in Vannes by then, and her best friend was Lalla. As soon as Lalla walked in, I was immediately interested. I had never met her before, but there was something very different, very classy about her. She was also very beautiful.

She and I got chatting, and we stayed in touch over the next couple of years. I was young, but I was already very much in love. I used to write her really romantic letters, spray them with my cologne and send them off, hoping for her to reciprocate. Those were the days when people still sent love letters! Anyway, we kept the contact going for a while and I would go back to Vannes to see her whenever time and money allowed, but eventually we stopped.

Lalla is a couple of years older than I am, and I think she felt I was too young, not mature enough, living an irresponsible life – and she was right. I had moved to Le Mans by then, while she was busy with her nursing studies and bringing up her little boy, Kévin, born three years earlier. Meanwhile, I was leading the life of a young man who, for the first time, had a bit of money in his pocket. The money would come in and fly straight back out again. I would spend it on clothes, on going out, on everything other than essentials, like buying food and paying the bills. Once, I remember trying to make dinner for a group of friends, only to discover the electricity wasn't working. What was going on? Then I realised it was working in the rest of my block of flats. I just hadn't paid the bill and had ignored the reminder letters, so in the end it had simply been cut off.

I still hadn't given up hope of getting together with Lalla. One day, she came to visit me, along with Kévin and Viviane.

Something obviously clicked for her because from that day on, our relationship restarted, stronger than ever. As soon as I had a day off, I would rush to catch a train to Vannes – a 530-kilometre (330-mile) round trip – just to see her. It's amazing the energy you have when you are young and in love. I would even travel to Vannes after training in the afternoon and then catch a very early train back to be in time for training again the next morning. I knew that timetable off by heart. In fact, I was such a frequent user of the Vannes–Le Mans trains that the ticket inspectors recognised me and barely used to check my ticket.

One St Valentine's day, I pretended to Lalla that I couldn't come to Vannes to celebrate with her because I had a game the next day. As ever, she accepted the reality of my life as a footballer, and got on with her plans for the day. Suddenly, that evening, I appeared on her doorstep, ready to take her out to a nice restaurant for dinner. Not only that, but I'd bought her a present, which I handed to her at the table, in front of the whole restaurant. As Lalla is not one for grand gestures, she immediately put the little parcel in her bag, ready to open later. I insisted she got it out again, though, and open it there and then. Romantic, *moi*?

In January 2000, she moved in with me in Le Mans. I went from living like a bachelor, with friends always coming and going, and the door to my flat always open, to having completely different priorities and changing my way of life. Lalla had seen how bad I was with money, so she completely reorganised my finances, setting me a budget of what I could spend and what I had to save. She really helped me to sort myself out. And I'd known Kévin since he was a baby, so it was easy to accept him as a permanent part of my life and to raise him as if he were my son.

In March of that year, Lalla told me that she was pregnant. I could not have been happier. Everything was coming together. I had signed my first professional contract the year before, I was settled at Le Mans, and now I was settled on a personal level. Life could not have been better. For someone who had longed for a settled family life, becoming a father at 22 was perfect for me.

The day our son Isaac was born, 15 December 2000, was the best day of my life. The birth of a first child is always special, and I was overcome by the emotions of it all, not least because he was born with the umbilical cord around his neck, so there were a few dramatic moments as the doctors sought to free him and enable oxygen to reach his lungs.

Isaac's birth changed my life. What cemented my new-found responsibilities was when, a few weeks later, Isaac fell ill and I had to go to the cashpoint machine to get some money to pay for the medicines. I was still financially disorganised – better than before but still not as good as I could have been. I put my card into the slot, and it came back out – insufficient funds. I had no money left for medicines for my son and actually had to borrow some off a friend of mine. The humiliation was dreadful. 'OK, understood,' I resolved there and then. 'Never again, never again!' That day was really the day I grew up and became a responsible father.

Just over a year later, in January 2002, I was transferred to Guingamp and we moved to a lovely house near the club. We were a happy little foursome, especially as Lalla was pregnant again. On 12 March that year we welcomed our daughter,

Iman, into our life. It was the day after my birthday – what better present could I have had than an addition to the family?

Now that I had a better salary, I had been able to buy my first car, an Opel Zafira. I was very proud of it. It was comfortable and it had seven seats, so there was plenty of room for the buggies, baby chairs and the three children. I loved it.

Before long, we were on the move again, this time to Marseille. Initially, we settled in the outskirts, in a beautiful part of the city called La Treille. Soon after, though, we moved to La Ciotat, about 20 kilometres from the centre, and that was even better. It's by the sea and our house was up on the hill. We had an amazing view of the Mediterranean from our terrace, and the beach was five, ten minutes away at most. We used to have coffee on the terrace dressed in T-shirts in midwinter, while admiring the sparkling blue sea just minutes away. For the children, it wasn't a case of, 'Let's go to the seaside for our holidays.' It was more, 'Let's go to the seaside this afternoon.' When you have the sun and the sea, everything looks better, so that year, we had a fantastic quality of life and were very happy. Plus, I really thought I was staying for a long time at Marseille.

The move to Chelsea was as unexpected for my family as it was for me. It was a big upheaval. We moved to near where the new training ground would be in Cobham, and then had to find a school for Kévin, who was 12 by then. We found a good English school not far away – we did not want to send the children to an international school, because for us it was really important that they learned to speak English – and he literally started term unable to speak a word. Luckily, Kévin is smart, so within a couple of months he was gabbling away fluently. He took to it easily, unlike Lalla or me. I was ashamed to speak in front of him at first and would have to ask him regularly what things meant, so he was the one helping us adults to learn the language.

For Lalla, the move was not easy. She had friends and family in France and had to leave them behind to live in a country where she could not communicate easily. When you don't speak the language, it's hard. Although my sister was living in England at the time, and that helped, there's no doubt that it took Lalla a bit of time to adjust, not just to the language, but to the climate, and the way of doing things. France is very close to England, but it is very different in so many ways. So it was a big change of culture, and trying to settle the family, find a home and schools, was difficult.

Even Isaac, who was still only three years old, found it diffi-cult to adapt when we first arrived. The worst day was when he actually said to me, 'Dad, I want to go back to Marseille.' That was a low point. Of course, if I were to ask him now, he'd say, 'No way!' and I bet he doesn't even remember living there.

Eventually, the family did settle in, but it took time, espe-cially as, in the beginning, I wasn't feeling settled at the club. By the end of the second season, in the summer of 2006, things had improved. The children were happy in their schools and were completely bilingual.

When they are together, especially in England, they play in English, they fight and argue in English; but as soon as they're with us, as a family, we all speak French together. It makes Lalla and I laugh, because we don't have that amount of ease in both languages. Also, when the children go to France or

Ivory Coast for the holidays, they speak French together much more. They are at home in all three countries and all three cultures, which makes Lalla and me really proud and happy.

In May 2009, our son Keyran was born. We had waited until we felt really settled in England as a family before having another child, and were really delighted when he arrived.

Our youngest child, Emma, was born in December 2013. We feel incredibly lucky to have five healthy children. Iman is my first princess, and Emma is definitely my baby princess! She's incredibly smiley and sharp, so I am really looking forward to her growing into a wonderful daughter, just like her older sister.

In June 2011, Lalla and I finally got married. It surprised a lot of people that we hadn't done so before but, truthfully, we had never felt the need. Plus, for us, it didn't seem that important.

However, getting married was a way for me to say thank you to Lalla, to do something that she would remember, and that my kids and wider family would also remember. She was the mother of my children, she was my partner for life, and had been by my side from the bottom to the top. She knew me when I had nothing in my pocket, she was the one who supported me financially and emotionally in the early days when things were really tough, and she helped me with everything. She has never complained. Whatever decisions I have had to take, wherever I have had to move for my football, she has always said, 'You're the one playing, so we're with you, we'll support you.' She has always put me in a position where I have been able to live my dream. Sometimes these situations can give rise to big disagreements between a couple but that has never been the case with us, so I feel really lucky. For me, therefore, it became very important to make that commitment to her and to make her my wife.

We held our wedding at the Monte Carlo Bay hotel and basically we invited all our family and close friends for a three-day party. The middle day was the actual wedding day – the ceremony was held at the hotel followed by a lot of food and drink, music, dancing, singing and fun! We had one great big party. Obviously I'm biased but Lalla looked even more beautiful that day than usual, and our children all looked beautiful, too. We wanted the older ones, Kévin, Isaac and Iman, to be old enough to remember the day, and now, when we look at the photos, they too can say, 'Ah yes, do you remember when . . .' which, for us, is great. It was a really lovely, happy wedding – and all the better for having waited.

We try very hard to teach our children the values we think are important. Education, sharing, thinking of others and manners come high up on the list. We insist that, when they get home from school, they do their homework first before they can play or chill out. Although he is still young, even Keyran is good at that and will sit at the kitchen table with his reading book without us having to push him. For us, education is really vital in life, so we are very keen for all the children to get into good habits from an early age. I remember how tough my father was on me and how much he pushed me to continue my education until I had a qualification that meant something. I'm so glad he did that now, and I hope my children will be able to achieve the same.

They are part of a large family, and an even larger extended family, so there has never been a question of not sharing or thinking of others. As I said earlier, that is definitely where our African culture influences our way of life because that instinct to share is normal in any family. When visitors come to the house, the children always come and say hello to them, interrupting whatever they might be doing at the time. That is part of basic manners.

When it comes to material things, my children never want for anything, but we try not to buy them everything they want, even though any parent knows that nowadays it is very difficult to decide where to put the limits. Yes, when they were young, they had lots of toys. But as they grow up, we explain to them that if they want the latest pair of trainers, for example, they have to do something around the house to earn the right to have them. We have opened bank accounts for them, and explained to them how to save money, how the value increases if you leave it in for longer. Little things like that will help them to understand the value of money, I hope, even though sometimes school mates will say to them, 'Ah, why are you doing this? Your dad has loads of money!' So it's a constant, ongoing battle.

Friendships are also something we try to be very careful with. Even when Kévin was at school in Marseille, there were issues about friendships and working out who his real friends were, and who were his friends because his dad was a footballer. All my children have to be aware of this but generally they find that it's the friends they have known for longest who are usually their real ones. Sometimes, people say to them, 'Ah yes, you're the son of Didier Drogba. Why don't you . . . ?' and so on. If you're not careful or smart, you can expose your kids to situations where people can take advantage of them. We try to make them understand that when you are on top of the world, you always have people around you; then, when that's no longer the case, you look around and sometimes no one is there. That's life, but it's a tough lesson for anyone to learn.

Unfortunately, my parents now have to deal with the same problems as my kids do. In Paris, where they live, and in Ivory Coast people try to get close to them, to befriend them. At best, all these people want is to be seen with my parents, but often, they end up asking for money or special favours. 'Oh,' they will say, 'we're doing this event, and we wondered if . . .' It's very sad, but it happens to anyone who has become well known and well off – I have certainly lost money to people whom I thought would be better than that – and it happens to our extended families as well. My parents are very aware that people now treat them differently from the way they used to be treated in the past when they were 'nobody', so they're always on the look-out and try not to get duped.

I have regularly had to warn my children about one of the other potential dangers that they face in their lives – social media. I know that it can be a great thing, but it can also be incredibly harmful. 'Not everyone is your friend,' I repeat to them. 'Be careful. There are some bad people out there, and they just want to be connected to you because of the name, not to be your friend.' It's very hard, but sadly it's part of their life and they will have to be vigilant.

My children have to live with the Drogba name when it comes to football. Isaac, for example, loves playing, but sometimes he gets teased by his team-mates because he hasn't scored. 'Ha ha, guess what, Isaac, if you want to be like your dad, you've got to score!' At first, of course, he'd be upset and decide straightaway that he didn't want to go to training any more or he wanted to change position.

'Look,' I told him, 'when I play, I miss some goals. But I don't stop playing. I don't go and play defence. I come back again and I try to score. And I will miss again, but I will also score two. Or I might miss one and score two. Whatever it is, I will always try again. And you have to try. Even the best players, they miss. They miss chances, they play and they don't score, so just keep going.'

Sometimes I go to watch his games but I always try to go incognito and to avoid him seeing me, otherwise his friends all let him know. 'Hey, Isaac, your dad's here!' And the parents spend the time taking pictures of me rather than watching the game. I want the parents to watch their kids, not watch me and take photos of me. So I don't often go to watch Isaac, which is a shame, but maybe it's better for his development as a person and as a player.

Much of the way our kids are being raised, though, is down to Lalla's influence. I'm away so much that she is the one really making sure they are raised as we both want them to be. She had a tough start in life. Although she was born in Mali, she came to France with her mother when she was young. She then lost her mother and studied hard in order to support herself and Kévin, when he was little. So she had some difficult situations to deal with and has stayed very grounded when it comes to the important things in life, such as family, love, education, stability.

It might sound crazy but I knew instinctively very soon after I met her that she would be my ideal partner. Watching how she was raising Kévin, I knew that I wanted her to be the mother of my children. I was only 21 when she moved in, and 22 when Isaac was born, but I was ready to be a father. Even at that young age, I wanted a family. And even then, I was thinking, 'OK, if – God forbid – something happens to me and I'm not there any more, I know she will take care of my kids. I know she will be able to raise them.' So the love and influence that Lalla provides for our kids is the single best thing that she can give to me.

Together with my wife, we are trying to bring up our children so that they share a love for Ivory Coast and for our African roots. It's very important to both of us, because we grew up away from our countries of birth and perhaps didn't take them for granted in the way people do when they spend their entire childhood there. Once I had kids, I realised that my roots were even more significant to me than before, and I firmly believe that when you lose your ties to your homeland, you no longer have any sense of who you are and where you come from.

I was lucky growing up with my uncle – he always maintained close ties to Ivory Coast, so I had a good sense of our culture, food and music. But since spending more time there as an adult, I have gained much more knowledge and understanding of my country and this has been really enriching for me. It also means that my children have a strong sense of where I come from – and therefore their ancestry as well – and they love going back to Ivory Coast where we have a house. Plenty of friends are around, and extended family, when we go back for holidays.

At home, my preference is always to eat food that is typical of Ivory Coast. My favourite dish is one made with very ripe bananas and an aromatic sauce, and my mother's version is the best! I also love the music and use it as a great outlet for my emotions. I'm not always very demonstrative in everyday life – although, thanks to Lalla, I have certainly improved – but music has always been important to me, and I love nothing better than dancing to some of the great music that has come out of Ivory Coast.

My name is also used – unofficially – for a really strong beer in our country. 'Do you want a Drogba?' people will ask, and it is drunk in all the *maquis*, the popular small open-air restaurants that are unique to Ivory Coast. Music is played there, and people come to eat and drink, relax and have fun. The beer is supposed to be like me. They say I'm big, powerful, and you cannot beat me, and this beer is meant to be the same – bigger and stronger than normal beers, so you can't finish it, although plenty of people seem to manage! Ivorians like to have fun and to party, and, as I've said, I'm certainly like that, too. Maybe it's because many people have a really hard life, so they try to enjoy the moment, rather than worry about the future. In any event, I find that a desire to stay upbeat, not to complain, just to get on with the life you have been given is typical of my country. In many ways, that is impressive.

Although I am obviously very influenced in the way I do things by European attitudes, especially those of France and England where I have spent most of my life, I consider myself first and foremost an Ivorian and I know my great love for my homeland will continue to grow in the years to come.

21

CHARITY BEGINS AT HOME

I THINK it's my upbringing. Ever since I was a small kid, my parents always taught me to share, with those who lived in our house – uncles, aunts, cousins, brothers and sisters – and those who had less than us. Like my father, I'm the first-born in our family, and that gives me a responsibility to set the example and to protect others.

Now that I'm a bit older, I can see that this need to help others is also linked to the fact that I left my family and my country when I was very young. Although I lived apart from my parents and brothers and sisters for most of the following ten years, I did live with my extended family, and always felt very close to my parents and family back in Ivory Coast. Others are not so lucky. As well as missing my parents, I also missed out on growing up in my country of birth, and I think this, too, is a big factor in my need to reconnect with it, and give something back to a country I love so much.

My first international cap had come, somewhat to my surprise, in September 2002, when I was selected to play against South Africa. It was the first time I had gone back to

Ivory Coast in a capacity that was other than purely personal. Given the rapturous welcome the team was given as we ran out in front of a capacity crowd in the national stadium, I was shocked when, a mere ten days later, the country descended into a violent civil war. These events shook me deeply, and made me realise just how fragile the political situation had been.

After my initial appearance for the national team, I began to return regularly to Ivory Coast to play for The Elephants in our many qualifying games, both for the Africa Cup of Nations and for the World Cup finals. That's when I really started to see the country in a different way, and to learn much more about what was going on. It's fair to say that, since then, I have seen a lot of things that have really saddened and affected me, not just in Ivory Coast, but in Africa in general. By playing in other countries and visiting them for personal or humanitarian reasons, I have become involved in helping wherever I can.

Fairly soon after first playing for my national team, I began to achieve success with them, scoring regularly, and as a result, I started to acquire a certain profile both inside the team and nationally. I was made captain in 2005 and it was not long after that, when I made the appeal on live TV for my fellow people to lay down their arms, that my life in Ivory Coast changed for ever. This appeal propelled me overnight to the role of national icon – something that I had absolutely not expected. Suddenly, I had acquired a status as a national leader, and I could see people wanted me to help. I was no longer someone who simply had to lead by example within his family, but also someone who was seen as a leader among his own people. It was not because I wanted the role, it just seemed that people looked at me with hope and felt that in some small way I could help.

Even abroad, my profile changed dramatically. I would be told, 'When we say we're from Ivory Coast, people say they know nothing about the country. But when we say Didier Drogba is from there, they say, "Ah, OK! Now we know!"'

I am very aware that this sort of stamp of approval gives me a responsibility and it is one I am happy to bear. I don't see it as a burden. On the contrary, I am proud and ready to embrace it, which is why I soon realised that I needed to find a way to use my profile to try to support those in need both within my country and within my continent.

I had to start somewhere. Initially, I started visiting orphanages, hospitals, donating food, beds, clothes, anything I could do to help. I still do that, but my wife does so even more. We felt we had to. When you see those kids and families with nothing, you have to do something. We are in such a fortunate position, we cannot just walk by on the other side and pretend it's not happening. We both have a deep faith, and we know that when things are unacceptable, we have a duty to help. Our conscience simply does not allow us to do otherwise. However, two events in particular – both similar in circumstance – contributed hugely to raising to another level my commitment to help others.

The first one involved Stéphane, the young brother of one of my best friends in France. Stéphane was living in Abidjan, so for my first international game, he made a huge banner that he unfurled in the stadium for all to see: 'Fan Club Didier Drogba'. No one else knew who I was in those days, because

I'd grown up in France, so it was a really kind, uplifting gesture, and seeing that big banner every time I looked up made a huge difference for me during the game. After that, there were more and more banners at every game, and more and more fans but, as Stéphane liked to remind me every time, laughing, 'Ah, yes, but I was the first! I was the only one who knew you!'

Then, in early 2005, I got a call from his brother. Stéphane had leukaemia, and was stuck in Abidjan, with minimal access to treatment. I immediately got on the phone to anyone I could think of who might be able to help get him a visa for France so that he could be treated there, but unfortunately there were huge problems at that time between France and Ivory Coast, the political situation was terrible, and it was almost impossible for anyone to be granted a visa. I tried to call the French ambassador in Ivory Coast, but no one really knew me back then. I had just been transferred to Chelsea and did not yet have the connections I needed to speed-dial those who had the power to help this boy. By the time we finally managed to get the longed-for visa, it was too late. He was too weak to travel, and he died about two weeks later, aged 16. All his family were devastated. I regret so much that I could not do more for him, even though I did all I could. This was the first time that I had witnessed the death of someone I knew well, made all the more shocking because it was the death of a young person who should have had his whole life ahead of him, and because he was denied the chance to live by a lack of resources.

I started to realise that not only did I need to do more but I also needed to change the way I went about it. I had to improve my contacts, get to know people who mattered, those who had power and money and could bring about change more easily. I needed to know those ambassadors and presidents because I wanted to do more – and faster – and I knew that one day I would need their help. I wasn't seeking out these people in order to be happy – for me happiness comes from my family – or in order to feel important. I was seeking them out in order for them to help me to help others.

Fortunately, by then, I was becoming better and better known and people wanted to meet me too, so doors were opening for me much more easily. Initially, I was wary of seeking out these people, which was why I had tried to remain independent, to do things on my own. But eventually I realised that I could harness people's power for what I was trying to achieve, and that if I didn't do that, it would limit me too much.

That's when I decided to create my own foundation, one that would be recognised thanks to my name, but also one that I would have control over. It's great to give time and money to charitable organisations, and I was happy to do that for a while, but ultimately I wanted something that I would be responsible and accountable for, where I could decide in which direction any help should go. That was in 2007, and I made the decision to donate all my commercial earnings to the foundation, and I have continued to do so ever since.

What I really didn't want was to create a foundation that – and I've seen this happen a lot – is announced with a big fanfare and one big fund-raising event, a dinner or something. They get a load of money in, and then silence. No one knows where that money has gone. The next year, they get asked,

'How is that foundation going?' and they say, 'Ah, no, we had to stop because it didn't work out, the plans weren't viable,' or something similar. And all that goodwill, hope and money have come to nothing. I really didn't want that – not least because I do not like to fail! So until I was ready to announce something concrete, in 2010, the foundation did not officially exist, even though I was putting money into it myself and continuing the planning stage.

The second event that convinced me I had to step up my charitable and humanitarian efforts occurred in March 2009. We were playing a World Cup qualifier against Malawi in our national stadium in Abidjan, and before the game had even started a section of wall at one end of the stadium collapsed, killing nineteen people and injuring more than a hundred, including children. It may seem surprising, but the game went ahead all the same because no one on the pitch realised what had happened. We could see ambulances coming and going in the distance, but it was a very hot day and the crowd was big and noisy, so it seemed a normal scene. In these situations, quite a lot of people need medical assistance.

After the game, as soon as we heard what had happened, the whole team went to the hospital to visit the injured. While I was there, I also went to visit a little boy, Nobel, whom a French rap artist friend, Diam's, had been helping financially. She had previously contacted me because she wanted to donate money and food to orphanages and people in need, and during her visit to Ivory Coast she had met Nobel. He had leukaemia and she completely fell in love with him. On the spot, she decided to pay for his medical treatment for a year – just like that, without batting an eyelid. I was really touched by her generosity, and when the year came to an end, it was natural for me to take over from her. As this little lad was still in hospital when I went to visit the injured, I went to see how he was getting on. What awaited me was so depressing and really upset me – nine children were crammed into one small room, each suffering from the same devastating illness that is cancer. The mothers of these nine kids slept on mats on the floor, wedged between the beds. When they saw me, they all started begging me to help save their children, holding out their arms in a gesture of despair, because they knew what was happening to them, which made it even more painful to see. As a father myself, it was heart-breaking, overwhelming and deeply shocking.

That day, I resolved to do all I could to save this kid. That was also the day when I realised I had to make my foundation official, to take it up to another level altogether.

This time, thanks to my much higher profile, the visa took no time at all to come through. I'd made those connections by now! I paid for Nobel to go to Geneva and he stayed there for three months, getting the best treatment available. I went to visit him, and he became a huge Chelsea fan. 'When I'm going to come to Chelsea, I want to see Frank Lampard, I want to see Salomon Kalou, I want to say hello to everyone,' he would tell me, excited. I'd try to stay upbeat for him, but all I could reply was, 'My man, we're going to see them soon, once you're better.'

He fought and fought, but the doctors called me one day and told me that, as he had a very rare and aggressive form of leukaemia, it was not going to end well. I think I was more devastated than this child, because he did not realise what was going to happen to him. I'm not sure his parents fully took on board the reality of what the doctors were saying, either. Maybe that was just as well because they clung on to hope until the very end.

Sure enough, he started to deteriorate until one day someone from the hospital in Geneva called me to say that he had just a few days left to live. I remember that call as if it was yesterday. I remember exactly where I was sitting at home when I got the news. Afterwards, I sat there for ages, numb, in disbelief, still hoping against hope that I might be able to save him, that there was something more the doctors could do. He was a nine-year-old boy who had become a part of my life and who would now be in my heart for ever.

For the next few days, every time the phone rang, I ignored it. I dreaded the call bringing me the worst news. Finally, I answered. 'We don't understand,' the doctor said. 'This kid, he refuses to give up, he's confounded the odds and he's still alive. Somehow he is finding the strength to survive.' So I jumped on a plane and flew out to see him, one last time, which made us both really happy. Incredibly, he lived for one more month. Then I was called to be told he was nearly at the end, and the next day he died. I will never forget this little boy. I felt so bad that I was not able to save him, even though, as with Stéphane, I knew in my heart of hearts that I had done everything possible to try. All the same, this remains an incredibly painful and traumatic event for me.

The one positive thing to come out of this is that this little boy motivated me even more to get things up and running fast – but also properly. 'I *need* to build a hospital,' I announced. 'I *want* to build a hospital, so that kids who have these problems can be treated in Ivory Coast. I don't care how long it's going to take, but that's what I'm going to do.'

A key part of the project was surrounding myself with the right people, both in Ivory Coast and in England. The team I now have is made up of people I trust and who have experience of business, of moving projects forward, of raising money, and who also understand the vision I have for the future.

One of the initial obstacles was how to approach people in order to persuade them to give money. I worried that they would just say, 'You're a high-earning footballer, why don't you just go off and do all this yourself?' In fact, from 2007, whenever I signed commercial endorsement deals with companies such as Pepsi, Nike and Samsung, I decided to donate the money I received to the foundation, and I have continued to do so ever since. I was leading by example, and people would realise that I was personally committing to the project. Some of the brands I work with, such as Pepsi and Turkish Airlines, have gone even further and supported foundation events through additional sponsorship.

The purpose of the foundation is health and education because I believe if you can give people these two things, then they stand a better chance in life. Our focus on health has been on kids and mothers. With education, it can be as simple as providing books for schools. One thing at a time, though. No point in running before we could walk. It soon became clear that we couldn't do everything all at once.

The initial plan was to build a clinic specifically for children, where their mothers could also be looked after in better conditions than the ones I had witnessed when visiting Nobel. It was clear that on top of trying to treat kids for major illnesses, such as cancer, we also needed to provide basic medicines. They were just as likely to die from diabetes because there was no insulin available. We also wanted to have another clinic attached to the children's one, where adults could receive basic healthcare and a chance just to stay alive.

Finally, and this is in the future, I would like to build a school to provide access to education for those who do not have it. For me, this is fundamental and the only way forward for Ivory Coast and for Africa as a whole. Education is the only way for such countries to get themselves out of these situations, because the more you educate people, the more they can have an opinion; the more they have an opinion, the less they will fight, because they will have more information, and they can then say, 'OK, let's stop fighting, let's sit down, let's debate, let's do things differently.' Also, if you can't read or write, you are unduly influenced by those around you, your neighbour, your family, your local leader. Whereas if you are literate, you can say, 'Hang on, I don't agree with this, there may be another way.' Crucially, you also have the possibility of changing your life, of having control over your destiny, in a way that you don't if you are illiterate.

Ivory Coast had been in a civil war since 2002, which was a situation that nobody wanted. People were dying senselessly. When I went round the country and saw what was happening, and when I travelled to other African countries or read about countries, such as Rwanda, that had suffered terrible human-itarian disasters, I was trying to understand how these things could happen, and I kept coming back to the fact that the percentage of illiteracy in all these countries was far too high. It was unacceptable. Education is therefore of vital importance in the fight against poverty and for democracy. Otherwise, what hope do people have?

When we started talking to people about our plans, the vast majority were incredibly positive. They still are, which is great. People want to help. The mayor of the part of Abidjan where we wanted to build the clinic helped us to get the land to build it, and Mr Abramovich made a large personal donation to my foundation, without being asked, which was really moving, because he did not have to do that. This is why, when people think that I respect the club because of the results, and that I respect the owner because of what he has brought to the club financially, they are wrong. It's more than respect, and you have to be on the inside to understand why I say that, for me, Chelsea is much more than a football club; it's like a family.

Eventually, I realised that building one large hospital is not the way forward, because it's all very well building it, but how were we going to maintain it, where was the money going to come from? After all, it's very expensive to run a large hospital. I did think of building several small clinics in different parts of the country, but realised that people would not be able to travel to these to get the help they needed. Would the people there have the experience required to run these clinics? I wasn't so sure.

In London, I spoke to a friend who is a cardiac surgeon. He has built some mobile clinics and taken them to countries such as Haiti and Niger in order to treat and operate on people. He explained that this approach was a much better way of reaching the right people. You could take the bus to one region, stay a month or two, then go elsewhere, and so on. In addition, it was a cheaper and more efficient way of doing things because the doctors and medical staff came from abroad only when required, so the overheads were much lower.

So that's now the plan. The clinic in Abidjan is finished, and is of a sustainable size and we hope to open soon, once the equipment is installed and the staff have been hired. That's a fantastic, exciting prospect. Beyond that, we will set up the mobile clinics that can be sent to treat people farther afield. I am so proud of what we have achieved with the help of so many wonderful, committed people, and it motivates me to keep going in what we are doing.

When it comes to the education element, we have for some time now been delivering several thousand school kits to schools around the country. We supply different schools every year, so that more and more children are able to access the basic tools needed to get an education. The kits contain essentials that every kid in the developed world takes for granted – pencils, paper and books. Again, we don't want to be over-ambitious for the moment, but prefer to be consistently helpful on a smaller scale.

We have also provided funds in recent years for other projects in Africa, including helping victims of flash floods in Senegal and Burkina Faso. So we don't only look at what is happening in Ivory Coast.

Back in 2007, I thought it would be easy to build and run a hospital. I thought we'd be up and running in a year, all sorted. Luckily, I didn't realise how much harder and longer it would be. If I had, maybe I would have been discouraged. The political unrest and civil war that continued, off and on, for almost ten years undoubtedly slowed us down and compli- cated things. In addition, I soon understood how much more complex it is to keep an organisation going smoothly – not least financially – once the initial aim has been achieved. As well as the money I personally donate, we regularly hold big events to raise money, such as fund-raising balls. To date, we have hosted four charity events in London which have helped contribute a lot of money to the foundation and have helped us to realise these projects. The last one, held in London in April 2015, raised a considerable amount of money in one evening, but an enormous amount of work went into organising it. These events have been organised by me, my PR manager Caroline and her team at Sports PR. It's a huge amount of work, so not something that can be done every year, but we had amazing support from music artists, sponsors, my team-mates such as JT, Frank, Michael Essien, Florent Malouda, Salomon Kalou, Ramires, Branislav Ivanovic and Gary Cahill who were there that night. Players like Thierry Henry, and Djibril Cissé were also there, with Djibril doing some DJing. Many people donated auction prizes and I was overwhelmed by the generosity of everyone that was there that night. It was nothing short of incredible.

My long-term aim is for the clinic to be run by a specialist organisation that knows how to run medical centres of this sort. My speciality is football, not medicine or running a clinic. I will always stay involved, but not on a day-to-day basis, because that's impossible.

In the future, I would also like the foundation to be associated with a big humanitarian organisation or NGO. That way, it can have a higher profile and a bigger reach, and it won't rely so much on individual funding. So that's my long-term aim, and as I don't give up easily, believe me, I'm working on it!

22

ONE WORLD UNI

I N 2006, I was asked by the United Nations if I would consider becoming one of their Goodwill Ambassadors. They had already appointed Zinedine Zidane for Europe and Ronaldo for South America, and they wanted me to represent Africa. Both Zidane and Ronaldo were footballing icons of mine, so to be alongside them was an honour but, more than that, if they thought I could help with the UN's work of fighting poverty, disease and other problems, then there was no question I wanted to help. My only fear was that I might disappoint the people who had put so much faith in me.

I was also worried about how much time I would be able to give to the role, because my Chelsea commitments, together with those of the national team, plus my existing charity work, left me little time to go travelling to different parts of the African continent. But I was quickly reassured that this would not be a problem. So since January 2007 I have been part of a group of sports people who help the United Nations Development Programme (UNDP) to convey messages they feel should have a global reach.

: of our role as ambassadors is to champion the cause f the eight Millennium Development Goals (MDGs), which range from eradicating extreme poverty and hunger, and combatting HIV/AIDS, to reducing child mortality. For me, for example, there is a different campaign each year, the aim of which is to raise awareness of one of the many particular challenges facing Africa. I really believe in what the UNDP tries to do around the world, and I think their work can make a positive difference to people's lives, so I'm proud to be associated with the organisation and to give my time.

The first campaign I was involved with, in 2008, had me on the jury for the UNDP Red Ribbon Awards, which are given to NGOs throughout the world for their work on HIV/AIDS issues. This was certainly an important introduction to what the UNDP does.

On a similar theme, though separate from my work with the UNDP, in November 2009 I teamed up with Bono to help launch an initiative with Nike on the eve of World AIDS Day. Nike announced a partnership between Bono's 'Red' fund and the Global Fund to fight AIDS, tuberculosis and malaria, and the idea was to sell special red laces under the banner 'Lace Up. Save Lives.' All proceeds would be split between the two funds, and for me to help launch this programme was a big honour. It was particularly important for me because AIDS and HIV have really destroyed so many lives on my continent.

The UN campaigns below all relate to one of the Millennium Development goals and are those that I have been proud to be involved in, including sometimes having to travel to the places affected by the problems. The campaigns include:

- mobilising people to eradicate the use of cluster bombs/ munitions
- highlighting the impact that armed violence has on economic development, health and education in Africa
- fighting to beat the spread of malaria
- helping the Ebola recovery efforts

Often, the campaigns cover issues that I am personally aware of or feel a connection to. The malaria one, for example, felt close to home because, surprisingly perhaps, I have twice had the illness – once when I was a teenager, and once, in 2010, when I was already playing for Chelsea. Both times I caught the illness because I was tired and run down, my immune system made me more vulnerable, and so after being bitten by the mosquito carrying the malaria parasite, I was not able to fight back.

However, I was young, strong, fit, and had easy access to the right medical care, and I realised I was lucky. I knew how often that was not the case in Africa. I have seen first-hand the devastating effects that malaria can have on individuals and families when treatment is too little and too late. It's vital that we continue trying to provide the tools to prevent, diagnose and treat this terrible illness, not least because the economic impact of this disease in countries that are already in difficulty is enormous. Worryingly, in 2014, in those countries in West Africa affected by Ebola, the rate of malaria infection started rising again because people either avoided getting treated or were turned away from clinics that were too busy trying to contain the Ebola epidemic.

Now that I've retired from international football, I will have more time to travel to places affected by some of the issues I'm involved with.

In 2010, I had a call from my PR, Caroline, to say that *Time* magazine in America wanted to interview me and organise a photoshoot, as I had been named on their annual list of 'The 100 most influential people in the world'. More than that, I was to feature on the cover of the magazine along with Lady Gaga and Bill Clinton! This was a proud moment for me, as I am always wanting people around the world to see Africa in a positive way and to see all the positive work we are doing there, promoting peace, education and health.

In December of 2011, I was given the Beyond Sport 'Humanitarian in Sport Award' for my work in Ivory Coast, trying to bring about better healthcare and peace. The war in Ivory Coast had been devastating, and the problems with health were enormous, so as a neutral sportsman, my message and my actions could really be of help and the award was a great way of highlighting it for a bigger audience.

In May 2012, I became involved with the Zenani Mandela Campaign for road safety, which I thought was a great campaign. Its aim is to improve road safety for children, particularly in developing countries. More children die in Africa on the roads than are killed by HIV/AIDS or malaria. That's a terrifying number. The campaign was named after Nelson Mandela's great-granddaughter, Zenani, who was killed in 2010, aged just 13, by a drunk driver. The whole family was devastated and as I was still in touch with them, it felt natural to try to help them in any way I could.

In October 2014, I was really honoured to be asked to speak at the opening ceremony of the World Investment Forum, which takes place every year within the United Nations Conference on Trade and Development (UNCTAD). I was invited as a result of the work I was doing for my foundation, which made me so proud because it was an acknowledgement that it was starting to be recognised as a force for good.

The forum itself was a huge event, held in Geneva, to coincide with UNCTAD's fiftieth anniversary. On the podium were not only the President of Switzerland and the President of UNCTAD, but also the Secretary General of the United Nations, Ban Ki-moon. I felt very humbled to be part of such an impressive gathering of people, and to have an audience of close on 400 delegates, all listening to me intently while I delivered my seven-minute speech.

I wrote the speech myself, then sent it to a friend, who made a few changes, additions and amendments. In essence, though, it was me who decided on the content, which was not difficult because I care so much and I believed in what I was talking about. When that's the case, you just want to spread the message. I talked firstly about how entrepreneurship and investment were needed for sustainable development in Africa. Then, speaking specifically about my own country, I talked about how big the potential was in terms of agriculture, industry, services and mining, how we had a young population, with 50 per cent under the age of 20. I also outlined the foundation's plans for healthcare and education, and how we were also trying to boost the earning potential for women in rural parts of the country by developing specific agricultural schemes that would enable them to earn some money of their own. As ever, it's a small beginning, and there is so much to be done, but we have to start somewhere.

I was very nervous but I believe I got our message across. I hope to be able to continue this sort of awareness-raising public speaking in years to come. I enjoy it, and I'm actually quite used to doing it now, after years of captaining our national team. In Africa, quite a lot of protocol is attached to that role, which includes making speeches. We would often have a minister come for lunch with us, for example, and the president of our FA would speak, then I would have to say a few words. Although at first I used to find this an ordeal and would be absolutely terrified, by the end I was used to it and I'm now much more comfortable speaking in front of others.

More recently, I was amazed to be honoured for my charity work in Africa with the Barclays Spirit of the Game Award. It aims to recognise and reward people who champion the true spirit of the game, so I was really moved to be chosen. But my work in Africa is all about trying to help people, especially kids, to give them a chance to dream, and since it's easier to dream when you are in good health, that's what my foundation is working towards, and the various UN and other campaigns I get involved in.

As ever, these experiences have taught me that my voice can be used as a force for change and that I can serve as a positive example for others. I take the ambassadorial role very seriously and am comfortable with it, and I hope to be given further opportunities in the future to speak publicly about the issues relating to my country and my continent, which are so close to my heart.

23

WHERE TO NOW?

I AM still surprised at the way my life has turned out. Yes, I always wanted to be a footballer, but I never expected to reach the stage where I am recognised on the street wherever I go. I'm a simple man, and I don't think I have changed as a person, I have just adapted to certain situations. Some people have told me I have changed but sometimes it is the way others view you that changes. There is an expection sometimes on the part of others of how I should behave that can be hard to live up to.

In Ivory Coast, my profile is at a level that is difficult for people to understand unless they see it for themselves. As an example, I get women coming up to me saying, 'I've just had a son, and I called him Drogba.' Not Didier, but Drogba. That's crazy, but I now understand and accept how much impact I have had just by scoring goals.

Sometimes I stop and think, 'Why me? Why has all this happened to me?' But I believe in destiny, and I strongly believe in God. I genuinely think that he put me on this earth and, in effect, said, 'You have to give back, you have to contribute something.' Football has given me so much, but now I understand that it has given me a higher purpose. It has given me the power to help others through the profile that I have. This guides my life – my sport has been a way for me to help others and in future I will continue to use it for this purpose.

Although I no longer play for Chelsea, I very much hope that one day I will come back in a different role. A few days before the last game of the 2014–15 season, I had a meeting with the manager and other representatives from the club, and they said, 'You have to stay connected with the club, you cannot go and disappear. You are part of the history of the club. We respect your desire to keep playing, to enjoy more football, but as soon as you decide to stop playing, come back here.' For me, it would be perfect if Frank and I ended up representing Chelsea together in the future. It would be a logical conclusion of our on-pitch partnership.

Over the years, I have got to know Mr Abramovich better and he always impresses me. He is still a very simple, shy man, who loves and knows his football. I have had lunch with him many times, and he likes to know what his players are feeling, how his team is doing. He is a very private person, so I have deliberately not talked much about him because it would not feel right to do so, but we understand each other and for me, he is a man of honour, and I feel very privileged to have such a good relationship with him.

Also, José Mourinho and I have a special relationship and a special understanding, as I have already said. He brought me to the club, he brought me back to it a second time, not for old time's sake but because he told me I could contribute to the club, and each time he gave me belief in myself. That's because he is different from other coaches. The majority of coaches, when they arrive at a new club, they will say, 'I'll try to win but it will be difficult.' José says, 'I'm here to win.' That rubs off on his players who soon start to share his mentality. That's what happened with me, and I'll always be grateful to him for what he has given me as a player.

I know it was the right decision – to have one more adventure before I hang up my boots – because I just wanted to enjoy playing football while I still could.

Similarly, I have always enjoyed wherever it is that I have lived, whether it was England, France, Africa, China, Turkey or now Montreal, which I am really appreciating. I am relishing the new challenge of Major League Soccer because I am still ambitious in football and excited to discover what is in store for me, wherever it is I go on to live.

I therefore hope to return to Chelsea as soon as my playing days are over, but for now, I'm doing what I wanted to do, which was to enjoy my last few years of playing football. I was really happy to join MLS team Montreal Impact in the summer of 2015 and even happier to score a perfect hat-trick on my first start. After ten matches I have scored nine goals, a level that will be hard to maintain. I'm realistic, though. I know I am not the same player I was five years ago, but I read the game better than a 21 year old.

Ideally, therefore, I see my future in England, associated with Chelsea, but I also very much want to develop my foundation into something bigger. Actually, what I would really like would be for it to become smaller and smaller eventually, because that would mean that we were living in a better world where there was no need for it. But I'm a realist, and until that happens, I want my foundation to be there to help others.

I'm not perfect, and I'm well aware of it, but I try to keep my feet on the ground and to remember where I came from. I started with minus nothing, so everything I now have is a big plus. I know how fragile life can be, how fast things can change, so whatever status I might have in the eyes of others, whatever fame or money I might have acquired, what is important to me now is how I make use of them and the privileged position I am in to give back, to contribute in this life and to try to make a mark on the world.

I think I have left my mark in football. That is something that cannot be taken away from me. However, I hope in the future people will say, 'He was a good football player, but he also had a brain, and he was able to use it for other things.' Normally, I don't like to speak about what I am doing but I am at a stage in my life where I realise I have to because I feel it can make a difference.

My wife and I are bringing up our children so that they, too, will want to be involved with my foundation and will want to help others. That is our hope. They are very lucky, they have everything they will ever want, so they, too, have a responsibility to give something back. For me, that is how you create a legacy, the best legacy ever, in fact.

One day, I will leave this earth. And if, that day, my family is continuing my work, the work I started, I think I will die a happy man.

APPENDIX I

MY TOP CHOICES

This isn't my top 4–3–3, it's my top 5–5–3. It's a list of the best players and moments in my career, mainly with Chelsea. Like all lists, it's very difficult to arrive at a final choice, and I could have compiled each one very differently, but here are some of the most memorable, at least for me:

My top five Chelsea 'players':

1. Roman Abramovich, as without him, we would never have achieved what we did.
2. José, because if it hadn't been for him, I might never have been a Chelsea player. He also changed the life of my family.
3. JT, Frank Lampard and Petr Čech. It's not so much that they are equal, more that they should be considered as 'one'.
4. Claude Makélélé, a fantastic friend from the moment I arrived and an equally fantastic team player.
5. The fans – they are, quite simply, essential.

My top five non-Chelsea 'players':

1. Carles Puyol, a tough defender but a gentleman, a real gentleman.
2. Aruna Dindane, the Ivory Coast striker, who fed me so many balls. Together, we had such a great partnership.
3. Lionel Messi, because there is only one.
4. Rio Ferdinand and Nemanja Vidić, as a unit, because they were tough to play against. For me to score against them, I had to wake up very early!
5. The entire Bayern Munich team of 2012, because that year they really were *very* good.

My top three moments with Chelsea (very difficult to choose!):

1. Well, obviously, winning the Champions League in 2012.
2. Winning the Premier League in 2010.
3. All the goals I ever scored at Wembley – that's quite a few!

APPENDIX II

CAREER MILESTONES

CLUB FOOTBALL

Current: Montreal Impact (2015–)

Previous: Levallois (1993-97), Le Mans (1997–2002), Guingamp (2002–2003), Marseille (2003–2004), Chelsea (2004–2012), Shanghai Shenhua (2012–2013), Galatasaray (2013–2014), Chelsea (2014–2015)

INTERNATIONAL FOOTBALL

Ivory Coast: 106 appearances, 66 goals
Ivory Coast all-time top scorer
Africa Cup of Nations Team of the Tournament: 2006, 2008, 2012

HONOURS & ACHIEVEMENTS

Chelsea
Champions League (1): 2011-12
Premier League (4): 2004-05, 2005-06, 2009-10, 2014-15
FA Cup (4): 2006-07, 2008-09, 2009-10, 2011-12
League Cup (3): 2004-05, 2006-07, 2014-15.
FA Community Shield (2): 2005, 2009.

Galatasaray
Süper Lig (1): 2012-13
TFF Süper Kupa (1): 2012-13
Türkiye Kupası (1): 2013-14

Appearances in major finals: 22

Individual awards

African Footballer of the Year: 2006, 2009
BBC African Footballer of the Year: 2009
PFA Team of the Year: 2006–07, 2009–10
UNFP Player of the Year (France): 2004
Turkish Footballer of the Year: 2013
Ivory Coast Player of the Year: 2006, 2007, 2012
Chelsea Players' Player of the Year: 2007
ESM Team of the Year: 2006–07
UEFA Team of the Year: 2007
FIFA/FIFPro World XI: 2007
Onze d'Or: 2004
Africa Cup top scorer: 2012
UEFA Cup top scorer: 2003–04
Ligue 1 Goal of the Year: 2003–04
Ligue 1 Team of the Year: 2003–04
Ligue 1 Player of the Year: 2003–04
Premier League Golden Boot: 2007, 2010
Golden Boot Landmark Award 10: 2006–07
Golden Boot Landmark Award 20: 2006–07
Golden Foot: 2013
IFFHS World Goal-getter of the 21st century
UEFA Champions League Final Man of the Match: 2012
Time Top 100: 2010

Beyond Sport Humanitarian in Sport Award: 2011
British GQ Sportsman of the Year: 2012
GQ Turkey Man of the Year: 2013
Football Writers' Association Tribute Award 2015

FACT FILE

- Chelsea have never won the Premier League without Didier Drogba
- Named Premier League's best-ever African player by Opta in 2015
- First African player to win the Premier League Golden Boot
- First African to score 100 Premier League goals
- First African to score 50 goals in European competitions
- Captain of first Ivory Coast team to reach the World Cup finals; scored their first goal in the competition
- Scored 15 times in 15 games against Arsenal – played 1,175 minutes, scoring on average one goal every 78 minutes and 20 seconds
- Scored 9 goals in finals for Chelsea – 4 x FA Cup, 4 x League Cup, 1 Champions League
- Only man ever to score in four separate FA Cup finals (all of which Chelsea won). Including semi–finals, Drogba has scored 8 goals in 8 Wembley cup ties
- Scored 10 goals in major finals and won 15 trophies
- Voted Chelsea's greatest player of all time, by their fans, in 2012
- Chelsea's fourth highest goal scorer of all time
- Named the world's top goalscorer in the 21st century by the International Federation of Football History & Statistics

(IFFHS) in 2012. Drogba's 92 goals in international and continental club matches between 2001 and 2012 make him the best among his peers

APPENDIX III

CLUB CAREER RECORD

Club	League	Goals	Coup de France	Goals
Le Mans				
1998-99	2	0	0	0
1999-00	30	7	0	0
2000-01	11	0	3	1
2001-02	21	5	1	1
Total	**64**	**12**	**4**	**2**
Guingamp				
2001-02	11	3	0	0
2002-03	34	17	3	4
Total	**45**	**20**	**3**	**4**
Marseille				
2003-04	35	19	2	1
Total	**35**	**19**	**2**	**1**

Club	League	Goals	FA Cup	Goals
Chelsea				
2004-05	26	10	2	0
2005-06	29	12	3	1
2006-07	36	20	6	3
2007-08	19	8	1	0
2008-09	24	5	6	3
2009-10	32	29	4	3
2010-11	36	11	2	0
2011-12	24	5	3	2
2014-15	28	4	2	0
Total	**254**	**104**	**29**	**12**

Club	Chinese Super League	Goals	Chinese Cup	Goals
Shanghai Shenhua				
2012	11	8	0	0
Total	**11**	**8**	**0**	**0**
Galatasaray				
2012-13	13	5	0	0
2013-14	24	10	3	1
Total	**37**	**15**	**3**	**1**

Club	MLS	Goals	Canadian League	Goals
Montreal Impact				
2016	6	3		
2015-16	14	12	0	0
Total	**20**	**9**	**0**	**0**
Overall totals	**466**	**193**	**41**	**20**

upe de la Ligue	Goals	Europe	Goals	Other	Goals	Total	Goals
0	0	0	0	0	0	2	0
2	0	0	0	0	0	32	7
0	0	0	0	0	0	14	1
2	1	0	0	0	0	24	7
4	**1**	**0**	**0**	**0**	**0**	**72**	**15**
0	0	0	0	0	0	11	3
2	0	0	0	0	0	39	21
2	**0**	**0**	**0**	**0**	**0**	**50**	**24**
2	1	16	11	0	0	55	32
2	**1**	**16**	**11**	**0**	**0**	**55**	**32**
League Cup	**Goals**	**Europe**	**Goals**	**Other**	**Goals**	**Total**	**Goals**
4	1	9	5	0	0	41	16
1	0	7	1	1	2	41	16
5	4	12	6	1	0	60	33
1	1	11	6	0	0	32	15
2	1	10	5	0	0	42	14
2	2	5	3	1	0	44	37
0	0	7	2	1	0	46	13
0	0	8	6	0	0	35	13
5	1	5	2	0	0	40	7
20	**10**	**74**	**36**	**4**	**2**	**381**	**164**
	Goals	**Continental**	**Goals**	**Other**	**Goals**	**Total**	**Goals**
		0	0	0	0	11	8
		0	**0**	**0**	**0**	**11**	**8**
		4	1	0	0	17	6
		8	2	1	1	36	14
		12	**3**	**1**	**1**	**53**	**20**
	Goals	**Continental**	**Goals**	**Other**	**Goals**	**Total**	**Goals**
		0	0	0	0	9	9
		0	**0**	**0**	**0**	**9**	**9**
28	**12**	**102**	**50**	**5**	**3**	**631**	**273**

PHOTOGRAPHIC ACKNOWLEDGEMENTS

The author and publisher would like to thank the following for permission to reproduce photographs:

Pierre Andrieu/AFP/Getty Images, Marc Atkins/Offside, Yaw Bibini/ Reuters/Corbis, Hamish Blair/Getty Images, Chelsea FC/PA Images, Condé Nast New York, Adam Davy/Empics Sport/PA Images, Delorme/ L'Equipe/Offside, Adrian Dennis/AFP/Getty Images, L'Equipe/ Offside, Sebastien Feval/AFP/Getty Images, Franck Fife/AFP/Getty Images, Francotte/L'Equipe/Offside, Laurence Griffiths/Getty Images, Lionel Hahn/L'Equipe/Offside, Mike Hewitt/Getty Images, Boris Horvat/AFP/Getty Images, Owen Humphreys/PA Images, Gerard Julien/AFP/Getty Images, Kampbel /AFP/Getty Images, Toshifumi Kitamura/AFP/Getty Images, Andres Kudacki/AP/PA Images, Niklas Larsson/AFP/Getty Images, Annie Leibovitz/Contact Press Images, Alex Livesey/Getty Images, Alain Mounic/L'Equipe/Offside, Osman Orsal/Reuters/Action Images, Mark Pain/REX Shutterstock, Peter Parks/AFP/Getty Images, Joern Pollex/Bongarts/Getty Images, Sergey Ponomarev/AP/PA Images, Anne-Christine Poujoulat/AFP/Getty Images, Ben Radford/Getty Images, Michael Regan/Getty Images, Michael Regan/Livepic/Action Images, Matt Roberts/REX Shutterstock, Suhaib Salem/Reuters/Action Images, Kambou Sia/AFP/Getty Images, Javier Soriano/AFP/Getty Images, Pete Souza/White House/Reuters/

INDEX